COWLES FOUNDATION
FOR RESEARCH IN ECONOMICS
AT YALE UNIVERSITY

MONOGRAPH 24

COWLES FOUNDATION

For Research in Economics at Yale University

The Cowles Foundation for Research in Economics at Yale University, established as an activity of the Department of Economics in 1955, has as its purpose the conduct and encouragement of research in economics and related social sciences with particular emphasis on the development and application of logical, mathematical, and statistical methods of analysis. The professional research staff have, as a rule, a departmental appointment and some teaching responsibility.

The Cowles Foundation continues the work of the Cowles Commission for Research in Economics founded in 1932 by Alfred Cowles at Colorado Springs, Colorado. The Commission moved to Chicago in 1939 and was affiliated with the University of Chicago until 1955. In 1955 the professional research staff of the Commission accepted appointments at Yale and, along with other members of the Yale Department of Economics, formed the research staff of the newly established Cowles Foundation.

A list of Cowles Foundation Monographs appears at the end of this volume.

The Computation of Economic Equilibria

by Herbert Scarf

with the collaboration of Terje Hansen

New Haven and London, Yale University Press

1973

Published with assistance from the foundation
established in memory of Philip Hamilton McMillan
of the Class of 1894, Yale College.

Designed by Sally Sullivan
and set in Times Roman type.
Printed in the United States of America by
The Murray Printing Co., Forge Village, Massachusetts.

Published in Great Britain, Europe, and Africa by
Yale University Press, Ltd., London.
Distributed in Latin America by Kaiman & Polon,
Inc., New York City; in Australasia and Southeast
Asia by John Wiley & Sons Australasia Pty. Ltd.,
Sydney; in India by UBS Publishers' Distributors Pvt.,
Ltd., Delhi; in Japan by John Weatherhill, Inc., Tokyo.

To the memory of my father
Louis H. Scarf

Contents

Preface

One of the major triumphs of mathematical economics during the past quarter of a century has been the proof of the existence of a solution for the neoclassical model of economic equilibrium. This demonstration has provided one of the rare instances in which abstract mathematical techniques are indispensable in order to solve a problem of central importance to economic theory.

When cast in a mathematical form the general equilibrium model becomes a complex system of simultaneous equations and inequalities for the determination of all prices and output levels in the economy. Aside from an occasional special case, however, the system is so complex that the existence of a solution can be guaranteed only by an appeal to fixed point theorems rather than by more elementary and constructively oriented techniques. As a consequence, general equilibrium analysis has remained at a level of abstraction and mathematical theorizing far removed from its ultimate purpose as a method for the evaluation of economic policy.

The present monograph attempts to remedy this difficulty by providing a general method for the explicit numerical solution of the neoclassical model. The method should be of interest not only to economists concerned with the techniques of economic planning, but to applied mathematicians in a variety of fields whose work requires the solution of highly nonlinear systems of equations.

An elaborate history of my own involvement and that of others in the development of this method is given in chapter 1. It is appropriate, however, to emphasize the important contributions of my friend and collaborator Terje Hansen. Many of the ideas presented here were first suggested by Professor Hansen; and the entire monograph benefited substantially from our close association during the past six years.

I would like, also, to express my gratitude to Rolf Mantel, Marcus Miller, Donald Richter, John Shoven, John Spencer, and John Whalley, all of whom have been students of economics at Yale during the last ten years. In distinct ways they have participated in the elaboration and application of the methods of this volume.

The Cowles Foundation, with which I have been associated since 1963, has provided an exceptional atmosphere for the development of this work. My colleagues, including Tjalling Koopmans, Martin Shubik, Alvin Klevorick, and Robert Aumann (who visited the Cowles Foundation in 1965), have supplied me with advice and continuing intellectual support. Gerard Debreu, who was for many years on the staff of the Cowles Foundation, has remained my good friend and valued advisor on all aspects of mathematical economics. The standards of mathematical rigor and clarity of thought which prevail at Cowles are well known to the economics profession. But perhaps more important is the persistent though subtle suggestion that the highest aim of even the most theoretical work in economics is an ultimate practical applicability.

Outside of the Cowles Foundation, the two professional colleagues with whom I have collaborated most closely on the development of fixed point methods are Harold Kuhn and Curtis Eaves. Their independent discoveries have been a source of stimulation and occasional drama. Both Kuhn and Gerard Debreu were kind enough to read the manuscript with unusual care and to provide many suggestions that have been incorporated into the text.

I should also like to offer thanks to the staff of the Cowles Foundation, including Althea Strauss, Laura Harrison, and the inspired typist of the manuscript, Glena Ames. To the Yale University Press I am grateful for the fine editorial assistance provided.

I am indebted to the National Science Foundation and the Ford Foundation for their generous support over a period of many years. The book was written during my tenure as an Overseas Fellow at Churchill College, Cambridge University, in 1969–70. At Churchill, I found a stimulating environment and the leisure necessary in order for me to complete this work.

H. S.

New Haven
May 1973

CHAPTER 1

The Problem of Computing Equilibrium Prices

1.1. THE SETTING OF THE PROBLEM

One of the major themes of economic theory is that the behavior of a complex economic system can be viewed as an equilibrium arising from the interaction of a number of economic units with different motivations.

This point of view has considerable generality and does not necessarily require that economic decisions be formulated exclusively in terms of highly developed markets. Even an economy in which production and distribution decisions are rigidly centralized cannot have adequate information available to its planning agencies to eliminate all areas of individual choice and initiative. The vast majority of detailed economic decisions must be delegated to subordinate units, whose behavior is elicited rather than controlled. A mature economic system, engaged in the production of a large variety of consumer goods and industrial products, must provide a series of political, administrative, and institutional arrangements that reward and motivate its members and guide them toward the selection of mutually consistent economic decisions.

The model of competitive equilibrium elaborated by Walras (1874) and other members of the neoclassical school is perhaps the most fully articulated formulation of this theme. Its primary abstraction is the exclusive reliance on prices generated by perfectly functioning markets to transmit information concerning relative scarcities and to constrain the otherwise independent choices of producers and consumers. The behavior of producing units is characterized in a severe and consciously simplified fashion. Provided with a complete knowledge of relative prices at the present moment and those expected to prevail in the future, individual units select their production and investment plans from the menu furnished by the current state of technology. They are motivated exclusively by a desire to maximize the present value of the stream of profits generated by their decisions. Any tendency toward monopolistic behavior based upon the technological superiority of large-scale production is explicitly avoided

1

by the assumption of constant returns to scale in production, or possibly decreasing returns deriving from the ownership of factors peculiar to certain firms.

The consuming units—households or government agencies—are assumed to respond with equal passivity to market prices. Each agent's wealth, calculated by the presumptive sale of his privately owned assets, is allocated freely among consumer goods, leisure, and savings in order to maximize some indicator of preferences. Prices, wealth, and the budget constraint place the only restrictions on private economic choice and on the determination of market demand.

For prices to play their correct role as indicators of relative scarcity the resulting production and consumption decisions must be mutually consistent: in each market total consumer demand must be equal to the aggregate supply provided by producers. Not only must current markets for consumer goods, labor, and capital services be cleared, but there must also be a sufficient flexibility of futures markets to produce some degree of coincidence of expectations. Of course supply and demand will not be equal in all markets if the individual agents base their decisions on an arbitrary system of prices. A specific commodity whose price is sufficiently low may have a demand considerably larger than the amount supplied by the producing units, with compensating imbalances for other commodities. The requirement of consistency places severe restrictions on the price vector and resultant production and consumption plans; in many instances the conditions are sufficiently restrictive to yield a unique vector of equilibrium prices.

Walras seems to have satisfied himself about the existence of an equilibrium price vector by observing that the requirements of market clearing —when placed in an appropriate mathematical form—involved a system with as many equations as unknowns. Barone (1908), one of the earliest advocates of the competitive model for planning purposes, was also content with this argument for consistency. But although the observation that a system of *n* equations in *n* unknowns generally has a solution is fairly credible when the equations are linear, it is misleading for nonlinear equations of the type arising in the competitive model. Such a system may easily have no solutions at all, or only those which are meaningless from an economic point of view.

A precise mathematical argument that the equations and inequalities of the general equilibrium model do have a meaningful solution may be unnecessary if the primary function of this construction is to provide economists with a sense of ease and security about the functioning of a market economy. One may be perfectly content with economic intuition as a substitute for mathematical logic for this purpose. But a formal argument for the existence of equilibrium prices may be of considerable importance if the general equilibrium model is to be taken seriously as a basis for the evaluation of economic policy. In order to determine the distributional effects of a change in tariffs—to take an example from the area of international trade—we should ideally be able to compare relative prices and production plans before and after the proposed change. This may be done either by a traditional geometric analysis or by the use of high-speed computers if the number of sectors is sufficiently large. But it is difficult to imagine a numerical procedure for determining equilibrium prices in the absence of any compelling argument that these prices do indeed exist.

The modern study of existence theorems for the competitive model was first taken up by Wald in 1935. He introduced, in order to facilitate his analysis, a restriction on the individual demand functions that has subsequently played a major role in the study of stability of the competitive equilibrium. Wald assumed that an individual's demand for any specific commodity would rise if the price of any other commodity were to increase. This assumption, which we now know to be quite superfluous in the study of existence, rules out the possibility of any serious complementarity of different goods in the preferences of individual consumers. Under this assumption, and others on the production side, Wald was able to demonstrate not only the existence of a vector of prices that would clear all markets, but its uniqueness as well.

During the 1940s an important methodological shift took place in the working techniques available to mathematical economists. Spurred largely by the development of game theory, the activity analysis model of production and of linear programming, economists slowly replaced the methods of differential calculus, which had been successfully used for many decades, by considerations of convexity. This development was fruitful in at least two respects. First the description of production possibilities as a discrete list of feasible activities was more closely suited to the requirements of the modern digital computer than earlier descriptions in terms of production functions with continuously variable input ratios. And secondly the techniques of convexity made it possible to discuss a variety of problems in mathematical economics from a global, rather than a local, point of view. The Kuhn-Tucker treatment of the maximization of a nonlinear function subject to a series of nonlinear constraints is an excellent example of the role played by convexity in describing necessary and sufficient conditions for a global maximum.

The stage was set, by the late 1940s, for a reexamination of the existence problem for the competitive model based on the availability of this new methodology. Only one ingredient was lacking. Useful as these geometric concepts had been for problems arising on the production side of the economy, they could not hope to be adequate for the analysis of a problem involving a number of interacting units. The reason is one which is perhaps not fully understood without an intimate knowledge of this area, but it is nevertheless quite simple to state. The determination of prices that simultaneously clear all markets cannot, in general, be formulated as a maximization problem in a useful way. Rather than being a single maximization problem, the competitive model involves the interaction and mutual consistency of a number of maximization problems separately pursued by a variety of economic agents. The problem involves, in a fundamental way, the reconciliation of distinct objectives and not the maximization of a single indicator of social preference.

Consider, for example, a model in which a number of consumers are engaged in the exchange of commodities which they initially own and in which production is explicitly ignored. For every vector of non-negative prices $x = (x_1, x_2, \ldots, x_n)$ the typical consumer will calculate his demand for each of the n commodities by maximizing his utility subject to the customary budget constraint. His excess demand, as a function of the price vector, will be positive for those commodities whose stock he wishes to increase by exchange and negative for the remaining items. The market excess demand functions

$$g_1(x_1, \ldots, x_n), g_2(x_1, \ldots, x_n), \ldots, g_n(x_1, \ldots, x_n)$$

are obtained by summing the individual excess demand functions over all potential participants in the exchange.

If there are no income transfers among the members of the economy, the individual excess demand functions will satisfy the condition that the value of excess demand at the price vector x is identically zero. This is merely a restatement of the assumption that an individual's purchases are financed entirely from the sale of his assets in the determination of his demand functions. When individual excess demands are aggregated to form the set of market excess demand functions, we obtain the identity

$$x_1 g_1(x) + x_2 g_2(x) + \ldots + x_n g_n(x) \equiv 0$$

known as the Walras law, which holds for all price vectors x.

An equilibrium price vector $\hat{x}$ is one for which all of the market excess demands are less than or equal to zero:

$$g_1(\hat{x}_1, \ldots, \hat{x}_n) \leq 0$$
$$g_2(\hat{x}_1, \ldots, \hat{x}_n) \leq 0$$
$$\vdots$$
$$g_n(\hat{x}_1, \ldots, \hat{x}_n) \leq 0,$$

with a zero price for any commodity whose demand is strictly less than its supply. If production is introduced into the model, the equilibrium conditions may be somewhat more complex, but even in this relatively simple case there is no meaningful maximization problem whose solution is equivalent to the determination of an equilibrium price vector. Of course an artificial problem such as

$$\text{minimizing} \quad g_1^2(x) + g_2^2(x) + \ldots + g_n^2(x)$$

will produce an appropriate price system if the sum of squares can be reduced to zero. But it is important to remark that this latter problem is a nonconvex programming problem, which possesses no suitable technique for the determination of a global, rather than a local, minimum. A stationary point in which the sum of squares differs from zero will provide no information whatsoever about the existence of solutions to the system of equations.

In order to study the solution of systems of equations as general as those arising in the competitive model it has been found necessary to import from combinatorial topology a series of sophisticated concepts and theorems having to do with fixed points of a continuous mapping. The first of these theorems was stated and demonstrated by Brouwer early in this century (1910). To indicate the content of Brouwer's theorem, let us consider the set of points in n-dimensional space whose coordinates are non-negative and sum to unity. By a continuous mapping of this set into itself we mean a systematic procedure for associating with each point x of the set an image x' also in the set which depends in a continuous fashion on x (fig. 1.1.1). Such a mapping is a generalization of the ordinary notion of a continuous function of a single variable; both the independent and dependent variables are now arbitrary points in the set, rather than restricted to being real numbers.

Brouwer's theorem states that any such mapping must have at least one fixed point—a point that is transformed into itself by the mapping. The

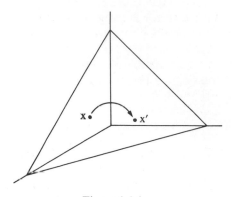

Figure 1.1.1

theorem has a remarkable generality and simplicity of statement, particularly when it is contrasted to the substantial difficulties in its proof. It has been applied in many fields, primarily to demonstrate the existence of solutions to systems of equations; in economics the first use was quite possibly made by von Neumann in the proof of the minimax theorem (1928) and subsequently in his analysis of an expanding economy (1937). But it was not until the early 1950s that a number of authors—Arrow and Debreu (1954), Gale (1955), Kuhn (1956), McKenzie (1954, 1959), Nash (1950), and Nikaido (1956)—realized more or less simultaneously the intimate connection between Brouwer's theorem and the existence problem for the competitive model.

By a suitable definition of the mappings involved in Brouwer's theorem and its generalizations, the consistency of the Walrasian model was finally established. Under assumptions of great generality, essentially convexity of the production set and of the individual preferences, we now know that there will exist at least one vector of prices which equilibrates the independent decisions of the producing and consuming units in the economy. Even after the shortcomings of the Walrasian model are admitted—and there are many ways in which it deviates seriously from economic reality —the solution of the existence problem undoubtedly represents one of the most impressive uses of mathematical techniques in economic theory.

But the price paid for the conclusion was quite high. The mathematical sophistication required for some degree of fluency with this methodology tended to make these arguments inaccessible to the large majority of economists whose preparations for a professional career did not include the study of combinatorial topology. Important as the conclusions in this area may be, few members of the profession were interested in following long chains of arguments that were simultaneously mathematically intricate and devoid of economic intuition.

This difficulty, which is partly pedagogical, may be alleviated by a general rise in mathematical literacy among economists and by simplifications and refinements in our methods of exposition. But there is a far more serious difficulty which may be seen by contrasting the study of economic equilibria with the large body of work in mathematical programming during the last two decades. Research in linear programming, to take only one example, has been conducted both on a theoretical level and with an enthusiasm for serious practical applications. The duality theorem for linear programs has been of great theoretical importance in its suggestions for the use of efficiency prices in providing decentralized signals on the production side of the economy. And the techniques of decomposition have also figured as an interesting parable of a possible relationship between a central planning agency and its subordinate sectors (Dantzig 1963). Nevertheless, the impact of linear programming would have been considerably less were it not for its success in solving specific numerical problems of practical importance.

The simplex method, variants of which were independently invented by Kantorovitch (1939) and Dantzig (1951), is an exceptionally efficient algorithm for the solution of linear programming problems. Aided by the simultaneous development of high-speed computers, this method can solve problems involving thousands of constraints and even larger numbers of variables without excessive difficulty. A substantial number of concrete applications have been made during the last two decades, primarily—in the United States—at the level of the firm. These methods have become as common and accessible as classical techniques for solving systems of linear equations and flourish in every large industrial firm with a staff oriented toward operations analysis.

As one moves away from the United States to those countries more sympathetic to national economic planning, linear programming techniques are used in the determination of investment policies, the construction of economic plans, and the coordination of economic activities carried out by a variety of subordinate agencies. There have even been suggestions that large-scale and highly detailed planning in the socialist countries of Eastern Europe be done by the solution of linear programming problems at a national level.

There are, of course, difficulties in the way of implementing such an ambitious conception. The problem of collecting reliable data on the technological processes that are currently available is enormous, to say nothing of the difficulty of inventing appropriate input-output coefficients for productive techniques that remain to be discovered. But the drawback to which this monograph is addressed is of a different sort: the inability to incorporate a flexible treatment of consumer demands into the conventional linear programming formulation. The demands of the consuming sectors are an important ingredient of national economic planning which cannot easily be controlled. Unless the system is prepared to tolerate strict rationing, consumers will respond not only to the availability of items, but also to their price. Without the benefits of market-determined prices for consumer goods, the most ambitious central plan may provide a host of items whose demands are inadequate to remove them from the shelves—and may produce insufficient quantities of other highly valued items. This is even more seriously felt if the foreign trade sector is large and the ultimate consumer a citizen of some other country. The objective function for a linear programming formulation of national planning must be sensitive not only to the planner's preferences—which may themselves represent a compromise between a number of planning agencies—but also to those of the eventual user.

The proper way of introducing consumer demands formed part of the fascinating discussion in the 1930s about the organization of production in a socialist economy. The suggestion put forward by Lange (1936, 1937) was to allow markets for both consumer and producer goods out of which prices, providing the correct evaluation of relative scarcity, would emerge. The major distinction between Lange's proposal and the Walrasian picture of competitive equilibrium was in the state ownership of the capital stock and, as a consequence, its first claim on an appropriate return to capital. Even here Lange attempted to mimic the Walrasian model by his concept of a social dividend, in which each consumer would be treated as a shareholder in the state productive enterprise. Individual income would be augmented by a part of capital's return, with the remainder ploughed back to finance investment plans.

At this point Lange's plan was not in the nature of an institutional reform that would permit the emergence of a large market sector free from government intervention. It was put forward rather as a response to earlier critics of the possibility of rational allocation of resources under socialism. Lange's target was twofold: first the contention of von Mises (1920) that efficiency prices are a peculiar attribute of a system in which all resources are privately owned. Lange's rebuttal might be paraphrased by saying that while the Walrasian model does require a complete description of income generation arising from the participation of factors in production, it does not require the private ownership of all capital goods. The returns to capital flowing to the government sector may contribute to the formation of market demand, in addition to that arising from the private sector. But the use of markets to determine relative prices was primarily oriented toward a second line of attack. Granted that under socialism prices could also play the role of decentralized signals capable of eliciting correct production decisions, how were they to be determined in an environment suspicious of unrestrained market forces?

The possibility that the parameters of the Walrasian model could be estimated statistically and the equilibrium prices be obtained by an explicit mathematical calculation had been discussed and rejected several years earlier by Barone, who concluded that the computational difficulties were insurmountable. If the activities to be used at equilibrium were known in advance, then relative prices could be determined by solving the system of linear equations expressing the conditions that each of these activities make a profit of zero. This point is, strictly speaking, not necessarily correct, since the system may involve a smaller number of equations than unknowns; but Barone's argument, reinforced by Hayek (1940) and Robbins (1934), was rather that no computational procedure existed for solving the vast number of nonlinear equations—and inequalities—required to select the correct set of activities. And given the computational techniques available at that time, the argument was surely valid.

For Lange, explicit mathematical procedures were to be replaced by the use of markets as an analogue computer to determine the equilibrium prices. A central planning board would issue to households and producing units a comprehensive list of prices for consumer goods, intermediary products, and primary inputs into production. Each productive unit would be required or induced to select that plan which maximizes profit, under the explicit instruction that their actions would have no influence on relative prices. Income would be generated by wage payments and the distribution of the social dividend, at which point the consuming units would express their demands for the entire range of consumer goods. A disequilibrium would be indicated either by a discrepancy between supply and demand—in the form of large inventories or explicit shortages—or by a large positive profit in any sector, after deducting a charge for capital. These signals would then set off a systematic revision of the list of prices, with an increase for those products in excess demand and a decrease for the remainder. The process—virtually identical with the Walrasian "tâtonnement"—would continue with the expectation of eventual convergence to equilibrium.

This discussion took place more than thirty years ago when the modern electronic computer, capable of performing a million additions per second, was completely unknown. Numerical calculations that once were prohibitively time-consuming can now be done in a fraction of a second, and perhaps earlier objections to the feasibility of calculating equilibrium prices, which led Lange to the use of markets as an analogue device, are no longer valid. Lange seems to have believed something similar to this himself. In an article written shortly before his death, Lange (1967) returned to the debate and asked how his earlier position would have been modified had today's computer technology been available in the 1930s. At one point he writes, "Were I to rewrite my essay today, my task would be much simpler. My answer to Hayek and Robbins would be: so what's the trouble? Let us put the simultaneous equations on an electronic computer, and we shall obtain the solution in less than a second. The market process with its cumbersome *tâtonnements* appears old-fashioned. Indeed it may be considered as a computing device of the pre-electronic age."

Unfortunately, even the large electronic computer has not made the problem of computing equilibrium prices as effortless as this quotation would indicate. Certain special cases can indeed be solved using linear or nonlinear programming techniques. But prior to the last several years no procedure had ever been suggested that could determine the solution of a general Walrasian model of even modest size with a reasonable amount of computing time.

The intrinsic difficulty of the problem may be illustrated by considering a relatively small model of exchange involving, say, twelve commodities. One suggestion for determining a price vector $x = (x_1, x_2, \ldots, x_{12})$ satisfying

$$g_1(x_1, \ldots, x_{12}) \leq 0$$
$$\vdots$$
$$g_{12}(x_1, \ldots, x_{12}) \leq 0$$

is to take a large number of vectors evenly distributed on the simplex, arrange them in an arbitrary order, and systematically evaluate the excess demand functions until a price vector is reached for which the excess demands are small. The excess demand functions will be homogeneous of degree zero in the prices, and this permits us to impose an arbitrary restriction such as $x_1 + x_2 + \ldots + x_{12} = 1$ on the prices to be examined.

For a search procedure of this sort to be successful the grid of price vectors must be fairly dense; let us therefore examine all price vectors whose coordinates, in addition to summing to unity, are non-negative fractions with a denominator of 200. The possible price for each commodity will range therefore between zero and one in increments of .005.

It is a simple enough matter to calculate that the number of distinct price vectors being examined under this scheme is of the order of 10^{18}. If we assume that for each price vector the evaluation of excess demand requires 10^{-6} seconds—which is far too small—and that only one one-thousandth of the entire list is examined before an equilibrium price vector is obtained, the total time of computation will be 10^9 seconds or more than 10,000 days. However crude these estimates may be, they surely indicate that an unstructured search cannot hope to be successful in determining an equilibrium vector of prices even for a problem of modest size.

A more attractive procedure may be to mimic the Walrasian tâtonnement on the computer: begin with an arbitrary price vector x and calculate the market excess demands $g_1(x), g_2(x), \ldots, g_n(x)$. Then adjust upward the price of those commodities whose excess demand is positive and decrease the price of the remaining commodities to determine a new price vector x'. For example, x' may be defined by

$$x'_1 = x_1 + \delta_1 g_1(x)$$
$$\vdots$$
$$x'_n = x_n + \delta_n g_n(x),$$

with $\delta_1, \ldots, \delta_n$ the non-negative weights describing the speed of adjustment of the price of each commodity. Of course nothing is being claimed about the economic realism of this particular adjustment mechanism—or, for that matter, any other; from our point of view the only relevant consideration is whether the sequence of prices obtained by iteration eventually converges.

This problem, in both its discrete and continuous versions, was intensively studied by a number of authors in the 1950s. It is an elementary mathematical observation that convergence cannot be guaranteed for an arbitrary set of market excess demand functions satisfying the Walras law. The presumption of this line of analysis was that severe restrictions would be placed on the class of market demand functions by insisting that they arise from the summation of individual demand functions derived from utility maximization. Unfortunately this is not the case: a number of examples have been constructed—satisfying all of the requirements of the Walrasian model—for which the tâtonnement is globally unstable (Scarf 1960). Beginning with an arbitrary price vector not in equilibrium, the sequence of prices may continually oscillate and never converge. In fact, Sonnenschein (1973) has recently been able to construct market demand functions whose second partial derivatives are arbitrary—aside from the constraint imposed by the Walras law at equilibrium. The range of possible counterexamples is therefore substantially increased since local stability is controlled entirely by the matrix of second partial derivatives.

The major positive conclusion, obtained by Arrow and Hurwicz (1958) and by Arrow, Block, and Hurwicz (1959), is that the price adjustment mechanism will be globally stable if the market excess demand functions are assumed to display gross substitutability between all commodities. It is curious that this restrictive assumption corresponds so closely to that used by Wald in his demonstration of the existence of an equilibrium price vector.

If no structural assumption other than the Walras law is placed on the market demand functions—and Sonnenschein's work would suggest that no additional requirement is plausible—then the existence of an equilibrium price vector for an exchange economy is fully equivalent to Brouwer's fixed point theorem. (This argument may be found in Uzawa 1962.) Any adjustment mechanism that is guaranteed to converge from an arbitrary initial price vector will serve therefore as a demonstration of Brouwer's theorem itself. As profound as economists may be, it is unlikely that they would have demonstrated one of the more sophisticated mathematical theorems of the twentieth century as a casual by-product of their concern with the general equilibrium model.

The central problem of this monograph is the description of an efficient computational procedure for the approximation of a fixed point of a continuous mapping. Of course Brouwer's original demonstration in 1910 was not concerned with effective computational procedures, and Brouwer himself eventually rejected the theorem because of its "non constructive" aspects. During the subsequent years the proof of the theorem was substantially simplified and it can now be presented with no reference at all to combinatorial topology (for example, Burger 1963). But in spite of its widespread use as a mathematical tool, even in fields that are not contemptuous of numerical analysis, it is only recently that any serious attempt has been made to place Brouwer's theorem in a computational setting.

The algorithms to be discussed in this monograph are all instances of a single combinatorial theorem (theorem 4.2.3) whose proof involves an iterative computational procedure which can easily be implemented on a computer. The theorem itself does not seem to have appeared previously in the literature of combinatorial topology, but the specialization that yields an algorithm for the approximation of a fixed point does have a similarity to Sperner's lemma—a combinatorial result that has been used for many years in the proof of Brouwer's theorem. Theorem 4.2.3 may be specialized in a variety of other directions as well. It can be used to provide an effective computational procedure to approximate a fixed point of an upper semicontinuous point-to-set mapping—the generalization of Brouwer's theorem due to von Neumann (1937) and Kakutani (1941). It can also be used to solve nonlinear programming problems of the conventional sort and to determine equilibrium prices and production levels in a Walrasian model in which production is described by a finite list of activities. A final application is given in chapter 8 to the determination of a vector in the core of a balanced n-person game.

Theorem 4.2.3 is itself a blend of two quite distinct ideas. One of them derives from Lemke and Howson (1964) and Lemke (1965), who provided a finite computational procedure for the determination of a Nash equilibrium point for an arbitrary two-person non-zero-sum game with a finite number of pure strategies for each player. This was a problem which had never before been examined from an effective computational point of view and whose solution had previously been guaranteed only by the use of Brouwer's theorem or Kakutani's theorem. In common with several earlier authors (Kuhn 1961, Mangasarian 1964) Lemke recognized that the problem could be placed in the following form: given a square matrix

$$A = \begin{bmatrix} a_{11} & a_{12} & \cdots & a_{1n} \\ \vdots & \vdots & & \vdots \\ a_{n1} & a_{n2} & \cdots & a_{nn} \end{bmatrix}$$

and a vector $b = (b_1, b_2, \ldots, b_n)'$, find a non-negative vector $x = (x_1, \ldots, x_n)$ such that

$$a_{11}x_1 + a_{12}x_2 + \ldots + a_{1n}x_n \leq b_1$$
$$\vdots$$
$$a_{n1}x_1 + a_{n2}x_2 + \ldots + a_{nn}x_n \leq b_n,$$

with the additional proviso that $x_i = 0$ if the ith inequality is strict.

Systems of linear inequalities with the additional complementary slackness condition had previously appeared in the study of quadratic programming, and a number of effective algorithms for their solution had been proposed (see, for example, Wolfe 1959). But these algorithms all used, in the proof that termination would occur in a finite number of iterations, the monotonically increasing character of the quadratic objective function. And this line of argument was not available for the two-person non-zero-sum game, which could not be cast in the form of a constrained maximization problem. The remarkable insight of Lemke and Howson was that an entirely different finiteness argument (to be described in chapter 2) could accommodate the complementary slackness conditions in the absence of an objective function.

Lemke's argument has been pursued by a number of authors   including Cottle and Dantzig (1968)—in the study of the above system of linear inequalities. Our own concerns, however, are quite different. The inequalities involved in Brouwer's theorem and in the determination of equilibrium prices are invariably of a highly nonlinear character. This has made it necessary to replace the sequence of linear programming pivot steps used by Lemke by an alternative construction suitable to the nonlinearities of the problem. For the finiteness argument to remain applicable, this new construction of "primitive sets" must share many of the standard properties of a feasible basis for a system of linear inequalities. It must be capable—as is the concept of a feasible basis—of distinguishing certain collections of columns selected from a matrix and of admitting an operation analogous to a pivot step.

Primitive sets do have these appropriate properties and form one of the basic ingredients of our series of algorithms. The concept first appeared, under a different name, in an article written in 1965 by Scarf (1967a). This paper made use of Lemke's argument and provided a proof of theorem 4.2.3. The orientation was, however, not toward the determination of equilibrium prices or the approximation of fixed points of a continuous mapping. Instead the paper described a set of conditions that were sufficient for the core of an n-person game to be nonempty and a computational procedure that would approximate a vector in the core should the conditions be satisfied. The relationship between the core and the competitive equilibrium, previously shown by Scarf (1962) and Debreu and Scarf (1963), suggested an eventual applicability of these methods to the determination of equilibrium prices. This possibility was, however, not explored.

In a doctoral thesis written in 1966 Mantel (1968) gave an ingenious demonstration of the existence of equilibrium prices for a Walrasian model based on theorem 4.2.3 which made no use of conventional fixed point theorems. Mantel's approach did not seem at that time to be computationally efficient, for it involved a complex limiting operation at one point. His ideas undoubtedly warrant reexamination in light of our present knowledge of computational techniques. They did serve, nevertheless, to indicate a strong relationship between the Walrasian model—and therefore fixed point theorems—and the method developed for determining a vector in the core of an n-person game.

This relationship was made explicit in two papers by Scarf which appeared in 1967 (1967b, 1967c). The first of these developed a combinatorial lemma, which was a particular specialization of theorem 4.2.3 and which could be used to approximate a fixed point implied by Brouwer's theorem. In the second paper the algorithm underlying this theorem was shown to be directly applicable to the approximation of equilibrium prices and production levels in the Walrasian model. It became clear as a consequence of the latter paper that the game-theoretic problem originally motivating theorem 4.2.3 was at best a circuitous approach to a numerical solution of the general equilibrium model.

In June 1967 Hansen, then a graduate student at Yale, discovered a class of matrices that could be used instead of primitive sets in these two applications. Hansen's discovery not only was attractive theoretically, but also offered substantial reductions in the computer storage required to carry out the computations (1968). The formal similarity between this class of matrices and primitive sets suggested that Hansen's construction might be a special case of the earlier methods, a conjecture whose verification forms the subject of chapter 6.

At this point I was entirely unaware of any geometrical interpretation of Hansen's work. In the spring of 1968 Kuhn suggested that primitive sets could be replaced—in the algorithm for Brouwer's theorem—by a concept of long familiarity in combinatorial topology: simplicial subdivisions of the simplex. He drew upon an earlier paper of his (1960), which provided an explicit description of a particular simplicial subdivision of the simplex. He then constructed a computational procedure that was as spare in its storage requirements as that proposed by Hansen. The two methods—independently discovered by Hansen and Kuhn—turned out, astonishingly, to be identical when implemented on the computer. This topic will be discussed in chapter 7.

Kuhn's observation that primitive sets and simplicial subdivisions have similar formal properties is of considerable importance. For example, Eaves (1970) has shown that theorem 4.2.3 itself has an analogous formulation in terms of simplicial subdivisions. This formal similarity raised the question as to which of these two constructions to stress initially in the current monograph. The argument for focusing on simplicial subdivisions relies primarily on their long use in combinatorial topology. But they are a more difficult concept than primitive sets to present to the uninitiated reader whose primary concern is with numerical calculations. The arguments involved in providing an explicit and useful simplicial decomposition of the simplex are surprisingly intricate. On the other hand, primitive sets also have an intimate connection with the familiar concept of feasible bases for a system of linear inequalities (theorem 2.8.4), and in at least one particular instance—the application to n-person game theory—they have an additional interpretation of considerable usefulness. I have therefore decided to begin with the newer concept and subsequently to discuss the relationships between the two at some length.

The fact that a numerical procedure will terminate with the correct answer in a finite number of iterations is no guarantee that it will be of any use in practice. The simplex method derives its importance from the observation that for most problems it will terminate in a far smaller number of iterations than the theoretical upper bound. A similar observation seems to obtain in each of the several hundred applications of the present series of algorithms that have been tried. The computational procedure will invariably examine a minute fraction of all possible price vectors: in virtually all cases no more than two or three times the minimum number that could conceivably be examined in proceeding along the shortest path from the initial price vector to the final answer. The techniques are admittedly slower—by perhaps a factor of 10 to 100—than the simplex method for problems of a corresponding size, since they proceed by means of small changes in the tentative solution. But of course the simplex method is not available for this class of problems.

Actual computational experience of Hansen and myself will be discussed in an appendix, and some evidence will be available to the reader from examples scattered throughout the text. At this point it may be appropriate merely to say that a problem involving ten unknown prices will typically require 2 minutes or less of computation time on an IBM 7094. The number of iterations varies roughly as the square of the number of sectors (the time of computation may involve a somewhat higher power) so that a problem involving 20 prices may require 8–10 minutes on this computer. This is a large amount of time but the 7094 is a relatively slow computer and we are only beginning to experiment with a variety of shortcuts which take advantage of the special structure of certain problems and can be expected to reduce the computation time substantially. There is no doubt that problems involving 30 or 40 sectors will eventually be feasible if the cost is justified by the intrinsic interest of the problem and the reliability of the data.

The potential applications of this methodology are not only to the determination of equilibrium prices and production levels in a centrally planned economy. Aside from its obvious pedagogical usefulness in expositing the essential aspects of the Walrasian model, the algorithms should be capable of contributing to areas of economic theory such as the study of international trade and taxation policy. The effects of changes in tariffs and taxes can be studied in a far more disaggregated fashion than that permitted by two-dimensional diagrams and with no assumption that the tariff changes be sufficiently small to justify a local analysis (Miller and Spencer 1971, Shoven and Whalley 1972).

The economics profession is in the process of adjusting itself to a renewed interest in policy questions at a microeconomic level. Instead of a primary preoccupation with macroeconomics and growth, we now see a concern with the problems of pollution and disposal, with housing markets, with taxation and with the general problems of income maintenance. The distribution of economic output, rather than efficiency considerations alone, has become an essential ingredient in the evaluation of economic proposals. If the profession's analytical stance is to be maintained, the implications of policy suggestions in these areas can be examined only in terms of some theoretical formulations that are attentive to the motivations of a variety of interdependent economic units. The Walrasian model of competition, even though it is sufficiently flexible to incorporate a number of formal modifications, is far from being the exclusive analytical framework for the study of microeconomic problems. But it is an important method of analysis and one whose usefulness, we hope, will be enhanced by the ability to obtain specific numerical solutions.

1.2. THE NEOCLASSICAL MODEL OF EXCHANGE

In the previous section I have alluded to the intimate relationship between fixed point theorems and the proof that there exist prices which clear all markets in an equilibrium model of exchange. It is appropriate, at this point, to describe the exchange model in greater mathematical detail. Brouwer's theorem will be taken up in the next chapter; the reader whose interest is in the application of fixed point theorems to problems other than the general equilibrium model may prefer to go directly to chapter 2.

Let the number of commodities available for exchange be n; a typical vector of commodities will be denoted by $x = (x_1, x_2, \ldots, x_n)$, with x_i a non-negative number describing the quantity of the ith good. Each participant in the exchange economy is assumed to have a set of preferences that rank arbitrary commodity vectors. For the somewhat restrictive purposes of the present monograph it will typically be adequate to describe each individual's preferences by a utility function $u(x_1, x_2, \ldots, x_n)$, rather than by a more formal analysis of the underlying preference ordering. Whenever it is convenient, we shall assume that each consumer's utility function is defined and continuous on the entire non-negative orthant in n-dimensional space and is monotonically increasing in each commodity separately. Convexity of the preference relationship will be insured by requiring that each utility function be quasi-concave, i.e.,

$$(1.2.1) \qquad u[\alpha x + (1 - \alpha)x'] \geq \min[u(x), u(x')]$$

for any pair of commodity bundles x and x' and for any α between zero and one. Whenever we wish to refer to the preferences of a specific consumer, say, the ith, we shall add a subscript—$u_i(x)$—to his utility function.

In the model of exchange each consuming unit is endowed with an initial vector of assets

$$w^i = (w_1^i, w_2^i, \ldots, w_n^i)$$

reflecting his ownership of commodities prior to trade. At an arbitrary vector of prices $\pi = (\pi_1, \pi_2, \ldots, \pi_n)$ the ith consumer's income, obtained under the assumption that he can dispose of his entire stock of assets at these prices, is

$$I^i = \sum_{j=1}^{n} \pi_j w_j^i.$$

Given his income and the list of prices, each consumer will determine his demand for commodities in the conventional way: by maximizing utility subject to the constraint that expenditure shall not exceed income. This will typically result in a vector of demands

$$d_1^i(\pi), d_2^i(\pi), \ldots, d_n^i(\pi)$$

each of which is a function of relative prices alone, because income is itself a linear function of prices.

If the preferred sets are not strictly convex, the demand functions need not be uniquely defined at all prices; the consumer may be indifferent to an entire interval of commodity bundles. A variation of our computational technique is quite adequate to deal with this difficulty, but it would seem appropriate to avoid it initially and to require that each individual's demand be a single-valued function of relative prices.

The demand functions will, by their definition, be homogeneous of degree zero: if all prices are multiplied by the same positive factor, demand will be unchanged. This permits us to impose an arbitrary normalization on the price vector to be examined. It is most useful for our purposes to require that the price vector satisfy

$$\pi_1 + \pi_2 + \ldots + \pi_n = 1,$$

in addition to having its coordinates non-negative. In geometric terms the price vector will lie on the unit simplex in n-dimensional space.

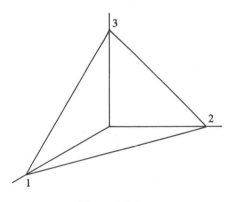

Figure 1.2.1

The conditions that we have already imposed are sufficient to demonstrate that each consumer's demand is a continuous function of prices in the interior of the simplex. Continuity need not hold on the boundary of the simplex, however, since the demand for a particular commodity may become unbounded as the price of that commodity tends to zero. For example, the utility function

$$u(x_1, x_2, \ldots, x_n) = x_1^{a_1} x_2^{a_2} \ldots x_n^{a_n},$$

with $a_j \geq 0$, $\Sigma_1^n a_j = 1$, will generate a vector of demands given by

$$\frac{a_1 I}{\pi_1}, \frac{a_2 I}{\pi_2}, \ldots, \frac{a_n I}{\pi_n},$$

with income I given in terms of the vector of initial assets $(w_1, w_2, \ldots, w_n)$ by

$$I = \sum_1^n \pi_j w_j.$$

In this example demands need not be continuous as one of the prices tends to zero.

It is difficult to imagine that this technical problem has much economic content; consumers would not be expected to demand arbitrarily large quantities of any particular commodity even if its price were quite small. In the study of the existence of equilibrium prices this difficulty has been successfully overcome, but at the cost of a somewhat more elaborate analysis than I would care to present here. Given our primary concern with computational techniques, we shall find it convenient to require that the demand functions be continuous on the entire unit simplex and not only in the interior. We shall make this assumption in our discussion of computational procedures even though many of our numerical examples will employ utility functions—such as the Cobb-Douglas function described above—for which the assumption is not valid. The reader should have no difficulty in adjusting to this slight ambiguity.

The market demand functions $d_1(\pi)$, $d_2(\pi)$, $\ldots$, $d_n(\pi)$ are obtained by the summation of individual demand functions. Given our assumptions they will be defined and continuous on the entire price simplex. They will, in addition, satisfy one important structural condition known as the Walras law—derived from the summation of individual budget constraints. The ith consumer's demands satisfy the identity

$$\pi_1 d_1^i(\pi) + \ldots + \pi_n d_n^i(\pi) \equiv \pi_1 w_1^i + \ldots + \pi_n w_n^i,$$

which expresses the fact that expenditure is equal to the income generated by the sale of his assets. If these identities are added over the set of consuming units and if the vector $w = (w_1, w_2, \ldots, w_n)$ represents the sum of the individual asset vectors, we obtain the identity known as the Walras law in the following form:

(1.2.2) $\pi_1 d_1(\pi) + \ldots + \pi_n d_n(\pi) \equiv \pi_1 w_1 + \ldots + \pi_n w_n.$

The Walras law may be written in a more convenient fashion if we introduce the notion of excess demand. For each commodity let us define

$$g_j(\pi) = d_j(\pi) - w_j,$$

a quantity which measures the increase in total assets—either positive or negative—that is desired at a particular vector of prices. The Walras law may then be written in the form

(1.2.3) $$\pi_1 g_1(\pi) + \ldots + \pi_n g_n(\pi) \equiv 0$$

for all price vectors, whether they be in equilibrium or not.

An equilibrium price vector $\hat{\pi}$ is one for which all excess demands are less than or equal to zero:

$$g_1(\hat{\pi}) \le 0$$

(1.2.4) $$\vdots$$

$$g_n(\hat{\pi}) \le 0.$$

At this vector of prices the total market demand can be satisfied by the stock of assets that are available prior to trade. It is a simple consequence of the Walras law that a commodity whose excess demand is strictly negative at equilibrium will have a price of zero associated with it.

There are a number of relatively special cases in which the existence of an equilibrium price vector, as well as its determination, can be treated in an elementary fashion. For example, assume that all consumers have an identical utility function $u(x)$ which, in addition, is assumed to be concave and homogeneous of degree one:

$$u[\alpha x + (1 - \alpha)x'] \ge \alpha u(x) + (1 - \alpha)u(x') \quad \text{for} \quad 0 \le \alpha \le 1,$$

and

$$u(\lambda x) = \lambda u(x) \quad \text{for} \quad \lambda \ge 0.$$

Using our previous notation let w^i represent consumer i's vector of assets, and

$$w = \sum_i w^i$$

the total stock of assets prior to trade.

The separating hyperplane theorem assures us of the existence of a price vector $\hat{\pi} = (\hat{\pi}_1, \ldots, \hat{\pi}_n)$ such that $\hat{\pi} \cdot w = u(w)$ and $\hat{\pi} \cdot x \ge u(x)$ for all non-negative x. In particular, if the common utility function is differentiable, this price vector may be taken to be the vector of partial derivatives of u, at the point of total supply.

We shall verify that $\hat{\pi}$ is an equilibrium price vector. Notice first that

$$d^i(\hat{\pi}) = \left(\frac{\hat{\pi} \cdot w^i}{\hat{\pi} \cdot w} \right) w,$$

since for any commodity vector x satisfying $\hat{\pi} \cdot x \leq \hat{\pi} \cdot w^i$ we must have

$$u(x) \leq \hat{\pi} \cdot x \leq \hat{\pi} \cdot w^i = \frac{\hat{\pi} \cdot w^i}{\hat{\pi} \cdot w} u(w) = u\left(\frac{\hat{\pi} \cdot w^i}{\hat{\pi} \cdot w} \cdot w\right).$$

Moreover, because

$$\sum_i d^i(\hat{\pi}) = w \sum_i \frac{\hat{\pi} \cdot w^i}{\hat{\pi} \cdot w} = w,$$

the market demands at prices $\hat{\pi}$ are in equilibrium with the supply of stocks.

The assumption of identical preferences is, of course, highly restrictive. Another example that can also be treated in an elementary fashion arises when each consumer has a Cobb-Douglas utility function

$$u_i(x) = x_1^{a_1^i} x_2^{a_2^i} \ldots x_n^{a_n^i},$$

with weights a_j^i which are positive and satisfy $\sum_{j=1}^n a_j^i = 1$, but which may differ among the consumers.

At prices π, the ith consumer's demand vector is

$$\frac{a_1^i \sum_j \pi_j w_j^i}{\pi_1}, \frac{a_2^i \sum_j \pi_j w_j^i}{\pi_2}, \ldots, \frac{a_n^i \sum_j \pi_j w_j^i}{\pi_n}.$$

The market demand functions will then be given by

$$\frac{\sum_j \pi_j \sum_i a_1^i w_j^i}{\pi_1}, \ldots, \frac{\sum_j \pi_j \sum_i a_n^i w_j^i}{\pi_n}$$

or, in an alternative notation, by

$$\frac{\sum_j \pi_j b_{1j}}{\pi_1}, \ldots, \frac{\sum_j \pi_j b_{nj}}{\pi_n},$$

where

$$b_{kj} = \sum_i a_k^i w_j^i.$$

We notice that the sum of the elements in the jth column of the square matrix (b_{kj}) is

$$\sum_k b_{kj} = \sum_i w_j^i \sum_k a_k^i = \sum_i w_j^i = w_j.$$

A price vector $\hat{\pi}$ will be in equilibrium if demand is equal to supply in all markets or

$$\frac{\sum_j \hat{\pi}_j b_{kj}}{\hat{\pi}_k} = w_k,$$

which may be put in the form

$$\begin{bmatrix} b_{11} - w_1 & b_{12} & & b_{1n} \\ b_{21} & b_{22} - w_2 & \cdots & b_{2n} \\ \vdots & & & \\ b_{n1} & b_{n2} & \cdots & b_{nn} - w_n \end{bmatrix} \begin{bmatrix} \hat{\pi}_1 \\ \hat{\pi}_2 \\ \vdots \\ \hat{\pi}_n \end{bmatrix} = 0.$$

Since the off-diagonal entries in this matrix are positive and the column sums are zero, the existence of a nontrivial, semipositive vector satisfying this system of linear equations may be obtained from a standard theorem in the theory of positive matrices (see, for example, Karlin 1959).

In both of these examples the equilibrium price vector may be determined by elementary techniques which exploit some special characteristic of the problem. Simplifications of this sort are unfortunately not available to us in the more general problem in which the market excess demand functions $g_j(\pi)$ are essentially arbitrary, subject only to the requirements of continuity on the unit simplex and the Walras law. Brouwer's theorem or one of its variants is required to demonstrate the existence of a price vector for which all markets are cleared. And an effective computational procedure for the numerical determination of equilibrium prices must be based on an algorithm of the type described in the following chapters.

CHAPTER 2

The Determination of an Approximate Fixed Point of a Continuous Mapping

2.1. CONTINUOUS MAPPINGS AND BROUWER'S THEOREM

A mapping is a generalization of the ordinary notion of a function of a single variable. Both the independent and the dependent variables are permitted to lie in arbitrary sets rather than being restricted to an interval on the line. In order to define a mapping we merely require a systematic rule that associates a unique value of the dependent variable y to each choice of the independent variable x in some specific set.

The word mapping has a geometric connotation and a specific mapping may very well derive from some underlying geometric construction. For example, the surface of a sphere in three dimensions is mapped into itself by rotating each point around an axis through the north and south poles by a fixed angular amount (fig. 2.1.1). But geometric considerations may be completely absent, as in the mapping which associates with an arbitrary price vector on the unit simplex that unique vector of consumer demands which maximizes some strictly concave utility indicator.

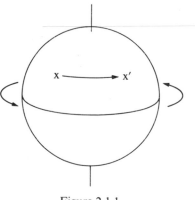

Figure 2.1.1

Our primary concern will be with mappings that carry a specific set S into itself. For each x in S the image of x under the mapping $y = f(x)$ will also belong to the set S (fig. 2.1.2). There is no requirement that every point

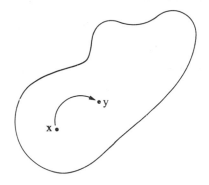

Figure 2.1.2

of S be an image for some value of x; it is quite conceivable that the mapping carries the set S into a small subset of itself. For example, the unit square in two dimensions is mapped into itself by associating with each point in the square its projection onto the main diagonal (fig. 2.1.3). In this case

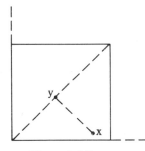

Figure 2.1.3

if the coordinates of x are (x_1, x_2), then the coordinates of the image will be

$$y_1 = \frac{x_1 + x_2}{2},$$

$$y_2 = \frac{x_1 + x_2}{2}.$$

Fixed point theorems may be stated for a large variety of sets S. For most of the applications of our computational techniques it will be sufficient, however, to restrict our attention to the simplex in n-dimensional space, defined to be the set of all vectors $x = (x_1, x_2, \ldots, x_n)$ with

$$x_i \geq 0, \quad \text{and}$$

(2.1.1)

$$x_1 + x_2 + \ldots + x_n = 1.$$

A mapping is then described by a rule that associates with each x on the simplex an image $y = f(x)$ which is itself on the simplex (fig. 2.1.4).

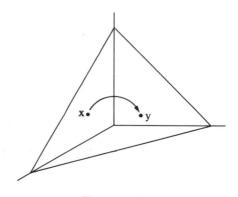

Figure 2.1.4

Each coordinate of y is a function of the independent variable x, and the mapping may be defined by an explicit presentation of these n functions:

$$y_1 = f_1(x_1, \ldots, x_n)$$
$$\vdots$$
$$y_n = f_n(x_1, \ldots, x_n).$$

The functional relationships are completely arbitrary aside from the requirement that the image be itself on the simplex, which can be stated in mathematical form by the following two conditions:

$$f_i(x_1, \ldots, x_n) \geq 0 \qquad \text{for} \quad i = 1, \ldots, n, \quad \text{and}$$

(2.1.2)

$$\sum_{i=1}^{n} f_i(x_1, \ldots, x_n) \equiv 1 \qquad \text{for} \quad x \text{ on the simplex } S.$$

The mapping will be *continuous* if small changes in the independent variable are associated with images that are close to each other. This is equivalent to saying that each of the n functions $f_1(x), \ldots, f_n(x)$ is a continuous function in the customary sense of the word. Our concern will be exclusively with mappings of the simplex into itself that satisfy this additional requirement of continuity. Let us consider a few examples.

EXAMPLE I. Let us associate with each x in S the point y that is the midpoint of the line segment connecting x with the center of the simplex $(1/n, \ldots, 1/n)$ (fig. 2.1.5). Here $y_i = (x_i + 1/n)/2$ and the mapping is certainly continuous. If this example were modified by assuming that the vector $(1/n, \ldots, 1/n)$ is mapped into, say, the vertex $(1, 0, \ldots, 0)$ without changing the mapping elsewhere, the new mapping would be discontinuous.

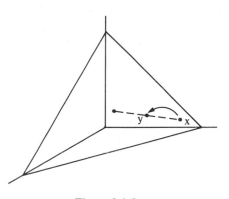

Figure 2.1.5

EXAMPLE II. Let A be a non-negative $n \times n$ matrix whose column sums are all equal to unity. The mapping $y = Ax$ will then be continuous, and it is easy to verify that it maps the simplex into itself. If the matrix has some negative entries or if the column sums differ from unity, the mapping is still continuous, since it is linear, but the image of x will not necessarily lie in the simplex. If the matrix A is strictly positive and the column sums are unrestricted, the modified mapping given by

$$y_i = \sum_j a_{ij}x_j \Big/ \sum_l \sum_m a_{lm}x_m$$

will be a continuous mapping of the simplex into itself.

EXAMPLE III. A class of mappings of great importance in mathematical economics arises from a particular formulation of the adjustment of prices to excess demands in a model of exchange. Let the components of the vector $x = (x_1, \ldots, x_n)$ represent the prices for commodities $1, \ldots, n$, and let the excess demands at this vector of prices be represented by the continuous functions $g_1(x), \ldots, g_n(x)$. The excess demands are assumed to satisfy the identity

$$\sum_1^n x_i g_i(x) \equiv 0,$$

which is known as the Walras law and was justified in the previous chapter.

A vector $\hat{x}$ is an equilibrium price vector if all of the excess demands are less than or equal to zero at this system of prices, i.e., $g_i(\hat{x}) \le 0$. One procedure for determining such a price vector, of great intuitive appeal in economics, is to start with an arbitrary price vector x and to modify it by raising the prices of those commodities whose excess demands are positive and lowering the price of any commodity whose excess demand is negative. A specific version of such an adjustment mechanism would be to define the new price vector by $y = x + g(x)$.

This association does produce a continuous mapping defined for all x in S, but the mapping is not necessarily into S, for the coordinates of y may be negative and need not sum to unity. The following, somewhat artificial modification does provide a continuous mapping of the simplex into itself,

$$y_i = \frac{x_i + \max[0, g_i(x)]}{1 + \sum_l \max[0, g_l(x)]},$$

since the components of y are clearly non-negative and the mapping has been constructed so that the coordinates of y sum to unity.

Many other examples of continuous mappings of the simplex into itself appear in a variety of arguments in mathematical economics and related topics, all motivated by the possibility of applying the major theorem concerning continuous mappings.

Let $y = f(x)$ be a continuous mapping of the simplex into itself. Then there exists a fixed point of the mapping, i.e., a vector $\hat{x}$ such that $\hat{x} = f(\hat{x})$.

This very powerful and important theorem was first demonstrated by Brouwer in 1910. His original motivation was of course geometric; the existence of a fixed point of an arbitrary continuous mapping was an important topological property of the simplex not necessarily shared by other geometrical figures. For example, the continuous mapping of the circumference of a circle in which each point is rotated clockwise by 45°

does not have a fixed point, and this displays an important topological distinction between the boundary of a circle and the simplex.

But the users of Brouwer's fixed point theorem rarely have the same geometrical motivation. For them Brouwer's theorem is a technique of great generality and facility for demonstrating that a system of equations —in this case $x - f(x) = 0$—does indeed have a solution. And if the system of equations is sufficiently complex and nonlinear, this may be virtually the only procedure available for demonstrating the existence of a solution. The transformation of an analytical question concerning the solution of equations into a geometrical statement about continuous mappings of the simplex is in many instances quite artificial, but it may be necessary for the application of this powerful technique.

Let us see what Brouwer's theorem says in the examples we have already discussed. Each of these examples is a continuous mapping of the simplex into itself and Brouwer's theorem may be applied.

EXAMPLE I. In this example the mapping is given by $y_i = (x_i + 1/n)/2$, and it is easy enough to verify that the unique fixed point of the mapping is given by the center of the simplex $\hat{x} = (1/n, \ldots, 1/n)$. Every other vector on the simplex is carried by the mapping into a point different from itself.

Under the modified mapping, which is no longer continuous and in which the center $(1/n, \ldots, 1/n)$ is mapped into $(1, 0, \ldots, 0)$, there will be no fixed points. Of course a discontinuous mapping *may* have fixed points— more or less by accident—but they are not guaranteed by Brouwer's theorem.

EXAMPLE II. In this example the mapping is given by $y = Ax$, with A a non-negative square matrix whose column sums are equal to unity. Brouwer's theorem states the existence of a vector $\hat{x}$ on the simplex with $\hat{x} = A\hat{x}$. In other words, such a matrix has a characteristic root of unity, which is associated with a non-negative characteristic vector, a well-known result obtainable by far simpler techniques.

In the generalized mapping

$$y_i = \sum_j a_{ij} x_j / \sum_l \sum_m a_{lm} x_m,$$

in which the column sums are no longer unity but the matrix A is, for simplicity, strictly positive, Brouwer's theorem asserts the existence of a vector $\hat{x}$ such that

$$\lambda \hat{x}_i = \sum_j a_{ij} \hat{x}_j,$$

where

$$\lambda = \sum_l \sum_m a_{lm} \hat{x}_m.$$

λ is therefore a strictly positive characteristic root, associated with a non-negative characteristic vector of A.

EXAMPLE III. In this example the mapping is given by

$$y_i = \frac{x_i + \max[0, g_i(x)]}{1 + \sum_l \max[0, g_l(x)]},$$

with $g_i(x)$, the excess demand functions, assumed to be continuous and to satisfy the identity $\Sigma_l x_l g_l(x) \equiv 0$. A fixed point of the mapping $\hat{x}$ is of considerable economic significance since, as we shall see, it represents an equilibrium price vector in which all of the excess demands $g_i(\hat{x})$ are less than or equal to zero.

To see this let us begin by rewriting the condition $\hat{x} = f(\hat{x})$ in the form

$$c\hat{x}_i = \hat{x}_i + \max[0, g_i(\hat{x})],$$

with $c = 1 + \Sigma_l \max[0, g_l(\hat{x})]$. If c is in fact greater than one, then the condition $\hat{x}_i(c - 1) = \max[0, g_i(\hat{x})]$ implies that $g_i(\hat{x}) > 0$ for every i with $\hat{x}_i > 0$. Since all $\hat{x}_i \geq 0$ and some are strictly positive, this violates the Walras law $\Sigma \hat{x}_i g_i(\hat{x}) = 0$. We conclude that $c = 1$, and therefore $g_i(\hat{x}) \leq 0$ for all i. The Walras law then implies that $\hat{x}_i = 0$ if $g_i(\hat{x}) < 0$ and if the conditions for an equilibrium price vector are met.

The example is interesting in the following respect. The particular mapping is a modification of the fundamental price adjustment mechanism in which prices are revised in proportion to excess demand—the discrepancy between demand and supply. If the mapping is iterated, we obtain a sequence of price vectors, each one responsive to the excess demand evaluated at the previous price vector. While economic intuition might suggest that this sequence of price vectors converges to an equilibrium price vector, this need not be the case. Unless some restrictive assumptions are placed on the excess demand functions, the price sequence may oscillate and approach no limit at all. On the other hand, the fixed point implied by Brouwer's theorem does indeed serve as an equilibrium price vector. The example illustrates quite well the role that Brouwer's theorem has played in providing existence proofs, rather than a constructive and computationally oriented procedure for obtaining an equilibrium price vector.

Before proceeding in the next section of this chapter to a discussion of our computational procedure for Brouwer's theorem, let us examine a specialization of the third example, which is of some interest in itself. Let A be an $n \times n$ matrix with only positive entries, and b a positive vector of size n. Consider the functions

$$g_i(x) = b_i - \lambda(x) \sum_j a_{ij} x_j,$$

with

$$\lambda(x) = \sum_l b_l x_l \Big/ \sum_l \sum_m x_l a_{lm} x_m.$$

While these functions are not excess demand functions arising from any familiar economic model, the identity $\Sigma_i x_i g_i(x) \equiv 0$ is satisfied, and the method of example III can be applied. We obtain, therefore, a vector $\hat{x}$ such that $g_i(\hat{x}) \leq 0$ and $\hat{x}_i = 0$ if the inequality is strict. If $\xi = \lambda(\hat{x})\hat{x}$, then ξ is a non-negative vector with

$$\sum_j a_{ij} \xi_j \geq b_i \qquad \text{for} \quad i = 1, \ldots, n$$

and such that $\xi_i = 0$ if the ith inequality is strict.

The existence of a vector with these peculiar properties is an instance of a larger class of problems involving linear inequalities to which I have alluded in the previous chapter. The more general theorems in this area —essentially obtained by weakening the conditions on the matrix A— may be shown to include a simplex method for certain quadratic programming problems, the minimax theorem for two-person zero-sum games (and therefore the duality theorem for linear programming), and, more impressively, the existence of Nash equilibrium points for an arbitrary two-person non-zero-sum game with a finite number of pure strategies of each player.

More importantly, however, one of the ingenious innovations made in this area of study will also serve as a fundamental argument in our algorithms for Brouwer's theorem and related problems. In a very definite sense this particular problem is concerned with what might be called the linear analogue of Brouwer's theorem.

2.2. Preliminary Concepts for the Algorithm

In this section I introduce some of the preliminary concepts of our computational procedure for approximating a fixed point of a continuous mapping of the simplex S into itself. The algorithm will be concerned with subsets of S that are themselves simplices, i.e., the convex hull of n points lying on S. It will be useful for us to distinguish certain of these subsimplices according to the following definition.

2.2.1. [DEFINITION] *A subsimplex of S will be said to have the same orientation as S if it is defined by a system of inequalities of the form*

$$x_1 \geq a_1$$
$$x_2 \geq a_2$$
$$\vdots$$
$$x_n \geq a_n$$

for some non-negative $a_1, \ldots, a_n$, with $\Sigma_1^n a_i < 1$.

In figure 2.2.1 only subsimplex A has the same orientation as S.

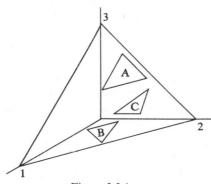

Figure 2.2.1

Now let us select a very large list of vectors $x^{n+1}, \ldots, x^k$ located arbitrarily on the simplex S. The first vector in the list has been designated by x^{n+1} rather than x^1 purely for reasons of notational convenience, which will become clear in the sequel. The larger the number of vectors in the list, the better the degree to which the algorithm approximates a fixed point, and in some numerical applications the number of vectors has been as large as 10^{30}. So large a list of vectors would be impossible to store in a computer, but there is no difficulty in circumventing this requirement in practice. (See fig. 2.2.2.)

The only restriction on this list of vectors will be the following, which corresponds in a formal way to nondegeneracy assumptions typically made in linear programming.

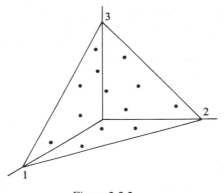

Figure 2.2.2

2.2.2. [ASSUMPTION] *No vector in the list has a zero component, and no two vectors in the list have identical ith components for any i.*

Let us select an arbitrary subset of n of these vectors and ask whether it is possible to draw a subsimplex with the same orientation as the large simplex S and with each side passing through one and only one of the n vectors. Given n such vectors $x^{j_1}, x^{j_2}, \ldots, x^{j_n}$, there is a simple way to tell whether a subsimplex with these properties can be found by examining the $n \times n$ matrix whose columns are the components of the respective vectors:

$$X = \begin{bmatrix} x_1^{j_1} & x_1^{j_2} & \ldots & x_1^{j_n} \\ x_2^{j_1} & x_2^{j_2} & \ldots & x_2^{j_n} \\ \vdots & & & \\ x_n^{j_1} & x_n^{j_2} & \ldots & x_n^{j_n} \end{bmatrix}.$$

2.2.3. [LEMMA] *A necessary and sufficient condition for there to be a subsimplex with the same orientation as S and with each side passing through precisely one of the n vectors is that in the matrix X the smallest element in the various rows shall appear in different columns.*

Before describing the proof of this lemma, which is quite simple, let us examine several examples. If the three columns of

$$\begin{bmatrix} \underline{.4} & .5 & .7 \\ .5 & .2 & \underline{.1} \\ \underline{.1} & .3 & .2 \end{bmatrix}$$

are the coordinates of three vectors on the simplex, then—assuming the validity of the lemma—no such subsimplex can be drawn through them since the minima of the first, second, and third rows appear in the first, third, and first columns, respectively. On the other hand, the row-minima of the matrix

$$\begin{bmatrix} .4 & .5 & \underline{.2} \\ .5 & \underline{.2} & .6 \\ \underline{.1} & .3 & .2 \end{bmatrix}$$

are located in the third, second, and first columns and the lemma implies that such a triangle can be found. It is in fact the subsimplex defined by $x_1 \geq .2, x_2 \geq .2, x_3 \geq .1$.

In general, a subsimplex with the same orientation as S will be given by $x_1 \geq a_1, \ldots, x_n \geq a_n$ for some choice of $a_1, \ldots, a_n$. For each coordinate i, one of the n vectors must lie on the side $x_i = a_i$, and if this vector is denoted by x^{j_i}, then $x_i^{j_i} = a_i$. But each of the remaining $n - 1$ vectors x^j must be in the subsimplex and satisfy $x_i^j > a_i$. This implies that $x_i^{j_i}$ is the smallest member of its row in the matrix X. Since the vectors lying on the ith side are assumed to be different for different i, the row-minima of X must therefore lie in different columns.

The remaining part of the lemma, demonstrating that the condition is sufficient to construct the required subsimplex, is easy because the subsimplex is then given by the set of $x = (x_1, \ldots, x_n)$ with $\Sigma_1^n x_i = 1$ and

$$x_1 \geq \min[x_1^{j_1}, \ldots, x_1^{j_n}]$$
$$\vdots$$
$$x_n \geq \min[x_n^{j_1}, \ldots, x_n^{j_n}].$$

The particular geometric property described in lemma 2.2.3 depends merely on the subset of n vectors that have been selected and not on the remaining vectors in the list. Our algorithm for approximating a fixed point of Brouwer's theorem will be concerned with a set of n vectors that have not only this property, but an additional one that depends on all of the vectors $x^{n+1}, \ldots, x^k$ in the entire list.

2.2.4. [DEFINITION] (Scarf 1967b) *The n vectors $x^{j_1}, \ldots, x^{j_n}$ are defined to be a primitive set of vectors if:*

a. *a subsimplex satisfying the conditions of lemma 2.2.3 can be drawn; and*

b. *no vector in the list $x^{n+1}, \ldots, x^k$ is interior to this subsimplex.*

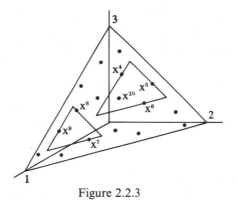

Figure 2.2.3

This definition is of considerable importance to us and will be illustrated both geometrically and with a numerical example. In figure 2.2.3 two triples of vectors (x^4, x^5, x^6) and (x^7, x^8, x^9) are considered. In both of these cases the first requirement for being a primitive set is successfully passed, since the appropriate subsimplex can be drawn through the three vectors in the set. The first triple is, however, not a primitive set because the vector x^{10} is *interior* to its subsimplex, whereas the second triple is indeed a primitive set.

As a second example, assume that there are seven vectors $x^5, \ldots, x^{11}$ in the list whose components are given by the columns of the following matrix:

(2.2.5)

$$
\begin{bmatrix}
.7 & .6 & .2 & .1 & .21 & .5 & .3 \\
.1 & .2 & .4 & .3 & .39 & .01 & .15 \\
.1 & .09 & .2 & .41 & .31 & .19 & .15 \\
.1 & .11 & .2 & .19 & .09 & .3 & .4
\end{bmatrix}.
$$

$$x^5 \quad x^6 \quad x^7 \quad x^8 \quad x^9 \quad x^{10} \quad x^{11}$$

Consider the vectors x^6, x^7, x^9, x^{11}, whose associated matrix is given by

$$
\begin{bmatrix}
.6 & \underline{.2} & .21 & .3 \\
.2 & .4 & .39 & \underline{.15} \\
\underline{.09} & .2 & .31 & .15 \\
.11 & .2 & \underline{.09} & .4
\end{bmatrix},
$$

$$x^6 \quad x^7 \quad x^9 \quad x^{11}$$

with the minimum element in each row underlined. These vectors form a primitive set since the requisite subsimplex is given by $x_1 \geq .2$, $x_2 \geq .15$, $x_3 \geq .09$, $x_4 \geq .09$, and, as the reader may verify, no column in the matrix represents a vector strictly interior to this simplex for no column has all of its four coordinates strictly larger than these four numbers.

The reader should, at this moment, attempt to determine other groups of four columns that also represent primitive sets. For example, if the column x^{11} is eliminated from the primitive set (x^6, x^7, x^9, x^{11}) is there a replacement x^j (with $j \neq 11$) such that (x^6, x^7, x^9, x^j) also forms a primitive set? The computer will be constantly asking a similar question at each iteration of our algorithm.

Before turning to this question—of replacing a vector in order to move to an "adjacent" primitive set—let us turn to one slight extension of the definition of a primitive set which is crucial for the algorithm.

We have been concerned exclusively with primitive sets whose associated subsimplices are strictly interior to the large simplex; remember that part of the nondegeneracy assumption 2.2.2 which requires that no vector in the list $x^{n+1}, \ldots, x^k$ have a zero component. But it will be necessary to extend this definition to include subsimplices some of whose sides are sides of the original simplex S.

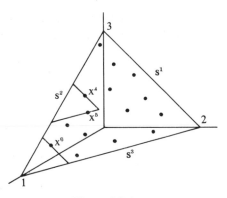

Figure 2.2.4

In figure 2.2.4 the pair of vectors x^4 and x^5 cannot form a primitive set by themselves; in the extended definition x^4, x^5, and the side s^2, on which the second coordinate is equal to zero, will be defined as a primitive set. As another example, the triple consisting of the vector x^6 and the two sides s^2 and s^3 will also be taken as a primitive set.

In the extended definition a primitive set will be defined by $n - m$ vectors from the list $x^{n+1}, \ldots, x^k$ in conjunction with m sides of the large simplex S. The subsimplex with the same orientation as S, which is defined by these n objects, will have a face lying on the side $x_i = 0$ if the side s^i is among the members of the primitive set.

2.2.6. [EXTENDED DEFINITION] *The $n - m$ vectors $x^{j_1}, \ldots, x^{j_{n-m}}$, along with the m sides $s^{i_1}, \ldots, s^{i_m}$, form a primitive set if no vector $x^{n+1}, \ldots, x^k$ is interior to the simplex defined by $x_{i_1} \geq 0, \ldots, x_{i_m} \geq 0$ and*

$$x_i \geq \min[x_i^{j_1}, \ldots, x_i^{j_{n-m}}] \quad for \quad i \neq i_1, \ldots i_m.$$

In the list given by the matrix 2.2.5 the two vectors x^5, x^6 and the sides s^3, s^4 form a primitive set since there are no vectors in the list interior to the subsimplex of S given by $x_1 \geq .6$, $x \geq .1$, $x_3 \geq 0$, $x_4 \geq 0$. Again the reader may find it useful to ask what replacement—either side or vector—can be made if s^3 is removed from this collection of four objects to obtain a new primitive set.

The definition of a primitive set may be put in a form that is somewhat more convenient for computation, though less visual geometrically, if we adopt the convention that the side s^1 be represented by the vector $x^1 = (0, M_1, \ldots, M_1)$, s^2 by $x^2 = (M_2, 0, \ldots, M_2)$, etc., with $M_1, M_2, \ldots, M_n$ greater than unity and different from each other, in order to preserve nondegeneracy. With this convention the vectors $x^{j_1}, \ldots, x^{j_n}$—some of which may represent sides of the simplex S—form a primitive set if and only if there are no vectors in the list $x^{n+1}, \ldots x^k$ interior to the subsimplex defined by

$$x_1 \geq \min[x_1^{j_1}, \ldots, x_1^{j_n}]$$
$$\vdots$$
$$x_n \geq \min[x_n^{j_1}, \ldots, x_n^{j_n}].$$

The vectors $x^1, \ldots, x^n$ will occasionally be referred to as *slack vectors*, to suggest an analogy with the corresponding concept in linear programming.

2.3. THE REPLACEMENT OPERATION

If k is large and the vectors in the list $x^{n+1}, \ldots, x^k$ are more or less uniformly distributed on the simplex, then the n vectors of a primitive set will be quite close to each other and have their ith coordinates close to zero if the side s^i is a member of the primitive set. This is one aspect of the definition of a primitive set that is of considerable use in the algorithm for Brouwer's theorem.

The concept has one additional property, analogous to a pivot step in linear programming—more precisely one should say a dual pivot step—that is of even greater importance in the algorithm. If a primitive set $x^{j_1}, \ldots, x^{j_n}$ is given and a specific member of this set is eliminated, then in general there will be a unique replacement such that the new collection of n vectors forms a primitive set. The replacement operation has a very simple geometrical interpretation, as figure 2.3.1 illustrates.

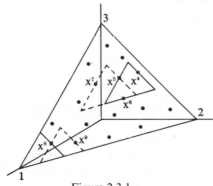

Figure 2.3.1

Consider the primitive set formed by the three vectors x^4, x^5, x^6, and suppose that x^4 is to be eliminated from this set. We take the side of the subsimplex on which x^4 lies and move it parallel to itself into the simplex until we first reach another member of the primitive set—in this case the vector x^5. (The nondegeneracy assumption implies that only one such vector will be reached.) In the original primitive set the vector x^4 lay on the face of the subsimplex on which the first coordinate was constant; in the new primitive set this role will be taken by the vector x^5. We then search in the cone defined by $x_1 \geq x_1^5, x_3 \geq x_3^6$ for that vector in the list $x^4, \ldots, x^k$ with the largest second coordinate. This is the vector x^7, and the triple (x^5, x^6, x^7) forms a new primitive set. If there were no vectors in this cone, the side s^2 (or, in our notation, the vector x^2) would replace x^4 in forming a new primitive set.

Another example of a primitive set is given by the vectors x^2, x^3, x^8. If x^2 is eliminated from this primitive set, the geometrical construction leads to the vector x^9 and the new primitive set (x^3, x^8, x^9). The first of these primitive sets also illustrates the one replacement operation that cannot be carried out. The geometrical rule is inoperative if we attempt to remove x^8 from the primitive set (x^2, x^3, x^8), and no replacement is then possible. This exemplifies the general proposition that the replacement is both possible and unique except for the special case in which the primitive set consists of $n - 1$ sides and one additional vector that we are attempting to remove.

In the general case, let the components of the vectors $x^{j_1}, \ldots, x^{j_n}$, which form a primitive set, be represented by the columns of the $n \times n$ matrix

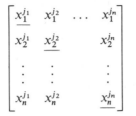

$$
\begin{bmatrix}
\underline{x_1^{j_1}} & x_1^{j_2} & \cdots & x_1^{j_n} \\
x_2^{j_1} & \underline{x_2^{j_2}} & & x_2^{j_n} \\
\vdots & \vdots & & \vdots \\
x_n^{j_1} & x_n^{j_2} & & \underline{x_n^{j_n}}
\end{bmatrix}
$$

and let us suppose, for the sake of simplicity, that the columns have been relabelled so that the smallest element in row i appears in the ith column, for $i = 1, \ldots, n$. This is equivalent to saying that the vector x^{j_i} lies on the side of the subsimplex whose ith coordinate is constant.

Assume, for definiteness, that the first vector x^{j_1} is to be eliminated from this primitive set. This vector lies on the face where the first coordinate is constant. The geometry of the replacement step suggests that we move this face parallel to itself into the subsimplex until we first encounter another vector that is not a side in the primitive set. This vector will always exist—unless the remaining $n - 1$ vectors in the primitive set are all sides—and will be that vector in the primitive set with the second smallest first coordinate, say, x^{j_α} (fig. 2.3.2).

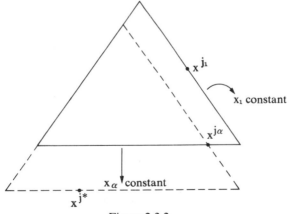

Figure 2.3.2

In the new simplex x^{j_α} will lie on the face whose first coordinate is constant. We must therefore find a replacement to lie on that face of the new subsimplex whose αth coordinate is constant. To do this we merely move the face on which x^{j_α} lay, parallel to itself and away from the subsimplex, until we first encounter a vector in the list. This vector, or the side s^α if no such vector is encountered, is the replacement for x^{j_1}.

We have therefore demonstrated the following theorem.

2.3.1. [THEOREM] *Let* $x^{j_1}, \ldots, x^{j_n}$ *be a primitive set. If a vector is removed, there is always a replacement producing a new primitive set, except in the case in which the remaining $n - 1$ vectors are all sides of the large simplex S.*

It will be a matter of some importance for us to demonstrate that the replacement operation is unique, that only a single replacement is possible if a given vector is eliminated from a primitive set. This is by no means difficult, but let us examine a numerical example before proceeding. Consider the matrix of the preceding section, which we have now augmented by four additional columns to represent the sides of the simplex S. (The nonzero entries in the first four columns are somewhat arbitrary.)

$$
\begin{bmatrix}
0 & 19 & 18 & 17 & .7 & .6 & .2 & .1 & .21 & .5 & .3 \\
20 & 0 & 18 & 17 & .1 & .2 & .4 & .3 & .39 & .01 & .15 \\
20 & 19 & 0 & 17 & .1 & .09 & .2 & .41 & .31 & .19 & .15 \\
20 & 19 & 18 & 0 & .1 & .11 & .2 & .19 & .09 & .3 & .4
\end{bmatrix}.
$$
$$
\quad x^1 \quad x^2 \quad x^3 \quad x^4 \quad x^5 \quad x^6 \quad x^7 \quad x^8 \quad x^9 \quad x^{10} \quad x^{11}
$$

The vectors x^2, x^3, x^4, x^5 form a primitive set since there are no vectors in the list $x^5, \ldots, x^{11}$ interior to the subsimplex $x_1 \geq .7$, $x_2 \geq 0$, $x_3 \geq 0$, $x_4 \geq 0$. The coordinates of these vectors are represented by the columns of the matrix

$$
\begin{bmatrix}
19 & 18 & 17 & \underline{.7} \\
\underline{0} & 18 & 17 & \mathbf{.1} \\
19 & \underline{0} & 17 & .1 \\
19 & 18 & \underline{0} & .1
\end{bmatrix},
$$
$$
\quad x^2 \quad x^3 \quad x^4 \quad x^5
$$

in which the minimum element in each row has been underlined.

In order to remove the vector x^2 from the primitive set we begin by finding that row whose underlined element appears in the column associated with x^2—in this case the second row. We then look for the second smallest element in this row, the entry .1, set in boldface type. In the sub-simplex representing the new primitive set the vector x^3 will lie on the face whose third coordinate is constant, x^4 on the face whose fourth coordinate is constant, and x^5 on the face whose second coordinate is constant. In order to determine the replacement for x^2 we examine all vectors in the list $x^1, \ldots, x^{11}$, with $x_2 > .1$, $x_3 > 0$, $x_4 > 0$, and select the one with the largest first coordinate—in this case x^6. The new primitive set is therefore given by x^3, x^4, x^5, x^6.

Let us attempt to remove the vector x^3 from this new primitive set, whose associated matrix is given by

$$\begin{bmatrix} 18 & 17 & .7 & \mathit{.6} \\ 18 & 17 & \mathit{.1} & .2 \\ \underline{0} & 17 & .1 & \mathbf{.09} \\ 18 & 0 & .1 & .11 \end{bmatrix}.$$
$$\quad x^3 \quad x^4 \quad x^5 \quad x^6$$

The underlined element in the column associated with x^3 appears in the third row, and we therefore examine this row to determine the second smallest element, which is .09. Among all the vectors in the list satisfying the inequalities $x_2 > .1$, $x_3 > .09$, $x_4 > 0$, x^{11} has the largest first co-ordinate, so the new primitive set consists of x^4, x^5, x^6, x^{11}.

Let us attempt one additional replacement by removing x^4 from this primitive set. In the matrix

$$\begin{bmatrix} 17 & .7 & .6 & \mathit{.3} \\ 17 & \mathit{.1} & .2 & .15 \\ 17 & .1 & \mathit{.09} & .15 \\ \underline{0} & \mathbf{.1} & .11 & .4 \end{bmatrix}$$
$$\quad x^4 \quad x^5 \quad x^6 \quad x^{11}$$

the second smallest element in row 4 is set in boldface type. It may be seen that x^{10} has the largest second component of all vectors in the list $x^5, \ldots, x^{11}$, with $x^1 > .3$, $x_3 > .09$, $x_4 > .1$. The vector x^{10} replaces x^4 and the new primitive set is given by x^5, x^6, x^{10}, x^{11}.

The reader may find it useful to continue with these calculations and convince himself that the following quadruples of vectors do represent primitive sets, each obtained from the previous one by a replacement operation:

$$(x^2, x^3, \ x^4, \ x^5)$$

$$(x^6, x^3, \ x^4, \ x^5)$$

$$(x^6, x^{11}, x^4, \ x^5)$$

$$(x^6, x^{11}, x^{10}, x^5)$$

$$(x^6, x^{11}, x^{10}, x^3)$$

$$(x^6, x^2, \ x^{10}, x^3)$$

$$(x^6, x^2, \ x^{10}, x^5)$$

$$(x^4, x^2, \ x^{10}, x^5)$$

$$(x^4, x^{11}, x^{10}, x^5)$$

As these examples indicate, the replacement operation involves the examination of all vectors in the list $x^{n+1}, \ldots, x^k$ that satisfy strict inequalities on $n - 1$ of the coordinates to determine the vector whose remaining coordinate is maximal. The particular coordinate to be maximized, and the inequalities themselves depend on the original primitive set and the vector chosen to be removed. The replacement operation may be summarized by the following rule.

2.3.2. [REPLACEMENT RULE] *Let $x^{j_1}, \ldots, x^{j_n}$ be a primitive set with the associated subsimplex*

$$x_1 \geq a_1 = \min[x_1^{j_1}, \ldots, x_1^{j_n}]$$
$$\vdots$$
$$x_n \geq a_n = \min[x_n^{j_1}, \ldots, x_n^{j_n}].$$

To remove a given vector, find the face of the subsimplex containing this vector, say, the one on which coordinate i^* is constant. Then find the vector x^{j_α} with the second smallest i^*th coordinate. If x^{j_α} originally lay on the face on which coordinate $\bar{i}$ was constant, the replacement satisfies the inequalities

$$x_i > a_i \quad for \quad i \neq i^*, \bar{i}, \quad and$$

$$x_{i^*} > x_{i^*}^{j_\alpha}.$$

The replacement vector has the largest $\bar{i}$th coordinate among all those members of $x^1, \ldots, x^k$ satisfying these inequalities.

The replacement operation, simple as it is to carry out on examples of moderate size, does seem to require an examination of all of the vectors $x^{n+1}, \ldots, x^k$, and this will surely be prohibitive in any specific problem in which k is very large. But the difficulty is more apparent than real. If the vectors in the lists are selected with sufficient regularity, the search operation may be converted into a simple arithmetic computation with minimal storage requirements and great speed. There are many ways to do this, depending, for example, on the region of the simplex to be emphasized and on the particular tie-breaking rules selected should the grid violate the nondegeneracy assumption 2.3.1. In one variation, to be explored at length in chapter 6, the speed with which the replacement step can be carried out depends only on the dimension n and is entirely independent of the number of vectors in the list. In the application of the series of algorithms based on the concept of primitive sets, the constraints that prohibit the solution of large problems derive not from the difficulties of the replacement step, but rather from the evaluation of complex functions that determine the vectors to be eliminated from the sequence of primitive sets.

2.4. UNIQUENESS OF THE REPLACEMENT STEP

In this section I demonstrate the fact—intuitively clear from a geometric point of view—that no vector other than that described by rule 2.3.2 will generate a new primitive set. The reader whose geometric intuition has already convinced him of this may prefer to go on to the next section.

Let the columns of

$$ X = \begin{bmatrix} x_1^{j_1} & \mathbf{x}_1^{j_2} & \cdots & x_1^{j_n} \\ x_2^{j_1} & x_2^{j_2} & & x_2^{j_n} \\ \vdots & & & \\ x_n^{j_1} & x_n^{j_2} & & x_n^{j_n} \end{bmatrix} $$

represent the coordinates of n vectors in a primitive set. We assume that the minimum element in row i appears in column i, so that the subsimplex is given by

$$ x_1 \geq a_1 = x_1^{j_1}, x_2 \geq a_2 = x_2^{j_2}, \ldots, x_n \geq a_n = x_n^{j_n}. $$

Let x^{j_1} be the column to be removed, and let us assume, to be specific, that the next smallest element in the first row appears in the second column.

If the vector x^{j^*} replaces x^{j_1}, the new primitive set will be described by the matrix

$$
X^* = \begin{bmatrix}
x_1^{j^*} & x_1^{j_2} & \cdots & x_1^{j_n} \\
x_2^{j^*} & x_2^{j_2} & & x_2^{j_n} \\
\vdots & & & \\
x_n^{j^*} & x_n^{j_2} & & x_n^{j_n}
\end{bmatrix}.
$$

Since these vectors represent a primitive set, each column of X^* must contain one and only one row-minimum. If $x_3^{j^*} < x_3^{j_3}$, then column 3 would contain no row-minima, so that we must have $x_3^{j^*} > x_3^{j_3} = a_3$ and, similarly, $x_4^{j^*} > x_4^{j_4} = a_4, \ldots, x_n^{j^*} > x_n^{j_n} = a_n$. This indicates that $n - 2$ of the inequalities that are proposed for x^{j^*} must be satisfied.

Two possibilities remain for the location of the row-minima for rows 1 and 2. Either $x_1^{j^*}$ is the minimum in row 1 and $x_2^{j_2}$ in row 2, or the reverse. Consider the first of these cases, in which the new subsimplex would be given by $x_1 \geq x_1^{j^*}, x_2 \geq a_2, \ldots, x_n \geq a_n$. Because this represents a primitive set, x^{j_1} cannot be interior to this subsimplex. But $x_2^{j_1} > a_2, \ldots, x_n^{j_1} > a_n$, so that we must have $x_1^{j_1} \leq x_1^{j^*}$. On the other hand, since x^{j^*} is not interior to the original subsimplex, we must have, by essentially the same argument, $x_1^{j^*} \leq x_1^{j_1}$. The two vectors x^{j^*} and x^{j_1} then have an identical first coordinate and by the nondegeneracy assumption they are the same vector. The other way of locating the row-minima in the first two rows must therefore be correct.

This tells us that in addition to the inequalities $x_i^{j^*} > a_i$ for $i = 3, \ldots, n$, we must also have $x_1^{j^*} > x_1^{j_2}$. Consequently, all $n - 1$ inequalities referred to in rule 2.3.2 must be satisfied, and the new subsimplex is given by

$$
x_1 \geq x_1^{j_2}, \; x_2 \geq x_2^{j^*}, \; x_3 \geq a_3, \ldots, x_n \geq a_n.
$$

Clearly x^{j^*} must have the largest second coordinate of all of those vectors satisfying the $n - 1$ inequalities. This demonstrates the following theorem.

2.4.1. [THEOREM] *The only replacement for a given vector resulting in a new primitive set is that described by rule 2.3.2.*

2.5. A COMBINATORIAL LEMMA

Now that the concept of a primitive set has been described and we have become familiar with the replacement operation, we are ready to demonstrate a simple combinatorial lemma on which the algorithm for approximating a fixed point of a continuous mapping is based. Consider an arbitrary selection of vectors $x^1, \ldots, x^{n+1}, \ldots, x^k$ lying on the simplex S —aside from the first n which, according to our convention, represent the sides of S—and satisfying the nondegeneracy assumption.

Let us also assume that each of these vectors has associated with it a specific label, an integer selected from the set $\{1, 2, \ldots, n\}$. For the moment these labels will be completely arbitrary, except for the proviso that $x^1, x^2, \ldots, x^n$ are labelled $1, 2, \ldots, n$, respectively. In each of our applications, however, the mode of associating a specific integer with the vector x^j will depend upon the characteristics of the problem. For example, in the approximation of a fixed point of a continuous mapping the specific label given to the point x^j will depend on the signs of $f_i(x) - x_i$ (evaluated at the point x^j); in the competitive model of exchange the label will depend on which of the commodities have a non-negative excess demand at the prices x^j.

2.5.1. [THEOREM] (Scarf 1967b) *Let each vector in the list* $x^1, \ldots, x^{n+1}$, $\ldots, x^k$ *be labelled with one of the first n integers. Let* x^i *(for i = 1, \ldots, n)* *be given the label i. Then there exists a primitive set each of whose vectors has a different label.*

The theorem is demonstrated by constructing a specific sequence of primitive sets, each of which is obtained from the previous one by replacing a single vector. The sequence begins with one of the n primitive sets containing $n - 1$ vectors representing the sides of S and can terminate only when a primitive set is obtained, all of whose labels are distinct. The argument that the sequence cannot cycle and must therefore terminate in a finite number of iterations is exceptionally ingenious and was first introduced by Lemke and Howson in their algorithm which calculates a Nash equilibrium point in a two-person non-zero-sum game.

Let us begin with the primitive set consisting of $x^2, \ldots, x^n$ and one additional vector x^j (as illustrated in figure 2.5.1 for $n = 3$). As we have seen, x^j must be that vector in the list $x^{n+1}, \ldots, x^k$ with the largest first coordinate. If x^j has the label 1 associated with it, the problem is over since the vectors $x^2, \ldots, x^n$ are labelled $2, \ldots, n$. In general, this will not be the case and the label associated with x^j will be one of the integers $2, \ldots, n$.

The next step in the algorithm is to remove the other vector in the primitive set that has the same label as that associated with x^j and to bring in a new vector $x^{j'}$. (In figure 2.5.1 it has been assumed that x^j bears the label 2.) If $x^{j'}$ has the label 1, then again the problem will be over since this second primitive set will have all of its vectors associated with distinct labels. If $x^{j'}$ has a label different from 1, precisely one other vector in the primitive set will have the same label, and the next replacement step is to remove this vector from the primitive set.

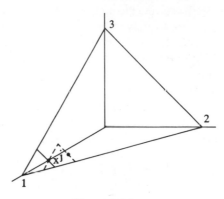

Figure 2.5.1

In general, the algorithm will be faced at each iteration with a primitive set $x^{j_1}, \ldots, x^{j_n}$ whose associated labels have the following properties:

1. None of the vectors will be associated with the label 1;
2. all of the vectors will have distinct labels, except for a single pair whose labels are identical; and
3. one member of the pair of vectors with identical labels will have just been brought into the primitive set.

The algorithm proceeds by eliminating from the primitive set that vector in the pair with identical labels which has *not* just been brought into the primitive set and by finding its unique replacement. If the new vector has the label 1, the algorithm terminates; otherwise we are in an identical situation having properties 1, 2, and 3, and the algorithm continues.

This sequence of replacement operations can terminate only with a primitive set of the required type. Since there are a finite number of possible primitive sets that can be composed from the list $x^1, \ldots, x^k$, the algorithm will terminate in a finite number of steps if it can be demonstrated, first, that it never returns to the same position and, secondly, that every required replacement can in fact be carried out.

Lemke's argument that the algorithm does not cycle is quite distinct from any previously used in mathematical programming, which typically assume that each position has associated with it an objective function that is strictly increasing as the algorithm proceeds. In our problem there is no objective function being maximized, nor can anything be demonstrated to be strictly increasing from one primitive set to the next. Lemke's argument instead exploits the observation that at each position there are precisely *two* vectors with identical labels. One of these vectors has just been introduced into the primitive set, and the algorithm calls for the other to be eliminated.

If the positions of the algorithm are described schematically by a graph (fig. 2.5.2), then cycling would be indicated by the first return of the path

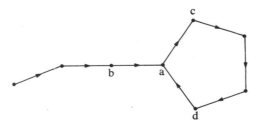

Figure 2.5.2

to a position, say, a, which was previously visited. Suppose that the label which appears twice in position a is l_a, in position b, l_b, etc. In the move from position d to position a, one of the vectors with label l_d is removed; it must therefore be replaced by a vector with label l_a. But if this replacement operation is reversed and the new vector with label l_a is removed from position a, only two possible adjacent primitive sets can be reached, either position b or position c, and *neither one of them* corresponds to position d. This demonstrates that if the algorithm cycles, the first revisited primitive set must be the initial one which contains the vectors $x^2, \ldots, x^n$ and some other vector x^j (fig. 2.5.3).

Figure 2.5.3

But this is, again, impossible for in the initial position only one of the two vectors with the common label (the vector other than x^j) can be removed, and there is only one adjacent primitive set. The algorithm therefore cannot cycle.

Lemke's argument may be displayed somewhat more vividly in the following way. Let us imagine a house consisting of a finite number of rooms, each of which has precisely two doors. Assume that one of the rooms has a door leading to the outside of the house. Then there must be at least one other door leading to the outside! And that other door may be found by this simple rule: Begin with the known outside door and proceed from room to room, never departing from a room by the door used in entering it. One can never return to a room previously entered.

Theorem 2.5.1 has therefore been demonstrated, subject only to verifying that every required replacement step can indeed be carried out. But the replacement operation will fail only if we are at a primitive set consisting of $n - 1$ sides and are asked to remove the remaining vector. Since this primitive set cannot be the one at which the algorithm began, it must contain the side x^1 which has the label 1. But the algorithm will already have terminated at the first position in which one of the vectors in the primitive set has the label 1. This demonstrates theorem 2.5.1.

The reader may wish to try his hand with an example based on the eleven vectors $x^1 \ldots, x^{11}$ of section 2.3. Let us select the labels in the following fashion:

Vector	Label
x^1	1
x^2	2
x^3	3
x^4	4
x^5	2
x^6	3
x^7	2
x^8	4
x^9	1
x^{10}	2
x^{11}	4

The algorithm begins with the primitive set (x^2, x^3, x^4, x^5), whose labels are 2, 3, 4, 2, respectively, and proceeds through the following steps, the last of which represents a primitive set all of whose labels are distinct.

$$x^2, x^3, \quad x^4, \quad x^5$$
$$2 \quad 3 \quad 4 \quad 2$$

$$x^6, x^3, \quad x^4, \quad x^5$$
$$3 \quad 3 \quad 4 \quad 2$$

$$x^6, x^{11}, x^4, \quad x^5$$
$$3 \quad 4 \quad 4 \quad 2$$

$$x^6, x^{11}, x^{10}, x^5$$
$$3 \quad 4 \quad 2 \quad 2$$

$$x^6, x^{11}, x^{10}, x^3$$
$$3 \quad 4 \quad 2 \quad 3$$

$$x^2, x^{11}, x^{10}, x^3$$
$$2 \quad 4 \quad 2 \quad 3$$

$$x^2, x^{11}, x^1, \quad x^3$$
$$2 \quad 4 \quad 1 \quad 3 \quad ,$$

The example is also useful in illustrating the fact that there may be primitive sets with distinct labels other than the one reached by starting from a specific corner of the simplex S. The vectors x^6, x^7, x^9, x^{11} also form a primitive set with distinct labels—a primitive set that differs from the one obtained above.

The algorithm may then be initiated at this latter primitive set by removing the vector x^9 that is associated with the label 1 and replacing it by some other vector x^j. If x^j has the label 1, another primitive set with distinct labels will have been found. Otherwise the new primitive set (x^6, x^7, x^j, x^{11}) will have properties 1, 2, and 3, so that the algorithm may be continued. As before, the algorithm will never return to the same position and must therefore either terminate with a new primitive set or reach a position from which the required replacement step cannot be carried out. For the latter of these two possibilities to occur, the indicated position would be that containing all sides of the simplex S other than the first. This is clearly impossible because reversing this path has led us to the primitive set (x^2, x^{11}, x^1, x^3), rather than (x^6, x^7, x^9, x^{11}). In other words, the algorithm must terminate with a new primitive set all of whose labels are distinct. The situation may be portrayed by a graph (figure 2.5.4) in which the first chain begins with the primitive set containing $x^2, \ldots, x^n$ and in which all of the remaining initial and terminal positions represent primitive sets with distinct labels. This argument may be used to demonstrate a generalization of theorem 2.5.1, which was stated first by Kuhn (1968) and in a somewhat different form by Eaves (1970).

2.5.2. [THEOREM] *There are an odd number of primitive sets with distinct labels.*

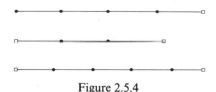

Figure 2.5.4

The label 1 is missing at every vertex of figure 2.5.4 other than those with a complete set of distinct labels. A quite different graph would be drawn if our computational procedure had focussed on those vertices for which the label 2 was the only missing label. The odd number of vertices with a complete set of labels would, of course, also appear in this new graph, but none of the intermediary vertices would coincide with those shown above. And primitive sets that belong to the same component of one of these graphs might very well not be connected in the other.

2.6. BROUWER'S THEOREM

We are now in a position to apply our method to the approximation of a fixed point of a continuous mapping of the simplex S into itself. Let the coordinates of the mapping be given by

$$y_1 = f_1(x_1, \ldots, x_n)$$
$$\vdots$$
$$y_n = f_n(x_1, \ldots, x_n),$$

with $f_i(x)$ defined and continuous on the simplex and satisfying $f_i(x) \geq 0$ and $\Sigma_1^n f_i(x) \equiv 1$.

Let us select an arbitrary list of vectors $x^{n+1}, \ldots, x^k$ lying on the simplex S and augment the list by the vectors $x^1, \ldots, x^n$ representing the sides of S. To determine the label to be associated with a vector x^j, we examine the coordinates of $f(x^j) - x^j$:

$$f_1(x^j) - x_1^j, f_2(x^j) - x_2^j, \ldots, f_n(x^j) - x_n^j.$$

Since the sum of these numbers equals zero, at least one of them, say, the ith, must be non-negative. We associate the label i with the vector x^j. If several of the coordinates are non-negative, it makes no difference which of the possible labels are associated with x^j, but it is necessary to have the same label associated with this vector whenever it turns up in the algorithm. This can be done, for example, by selecting the smallest index i for which $f_i(x^j) - x_i^j$ is non-negative, and in other ways as well. The vectors $x^1, \ldots, x^n$ will, as usual, receive the labels $1, \ldots, n$, respectively.

If theorem 2.5.1 is applied, we obtain a primitive set all of whose vectors are differently labelled (fig. 2.6.1). The geometric subsimplex

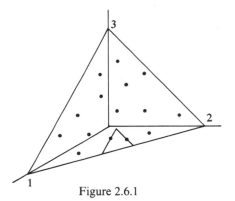

Figure 2.6.1

associated with this primitive set has the property that for every coordinate i (for $i = 1, \ldots, n$) there is at least one vector x in the subsimplex with $f_i(x) - x_i \geq 0$. If the vector x^i is in the primitive set, the subsimplex contains the side $x_i = 0$, and any vector in the subsimplex that is on.this side will do. On the other hand, if x^i is not in the primitive set, there must be some vector x^j in the primitive set with the label i, and this vector will satisfy $f_i(x) \geq x_i$.

Let us demonstrate Brouwer's theorem by taking a finer and finer collection of vectors which, in the limit, become everywhere dense on the simplex. Each such collection will determine a geometric subsimplex with the above property. As the vectors are increasingly refined, a convergent subsequence of subsimplices may be found, which tend in the limit to a single vector x^*. From the continuity of the mapping the vector x^* must have the property that $f_i(x^*) \geq x_i^*$ for all i. But since $\Sigma_1^n f_i(x^*) = \Sigma_1^n x_i^*$, we see that $f_i(x^*) = x_i^*$ for all i, and x^* is indeed a fixed point of the mapping. We have therefore demonstrated:

2.6.1. [BROUWER'S THEOREM] *A continuous mapping of the simplex S into itself has at least one fixed point.*

In applying the algorithm it is, in general, impossible to select an ever finer sequence of grids and a convergent sequence of subsimplices. An algorithm for a digital computer must be basically finite and cannot involve an infinite sequence of successive refinements. Moreover, and this is an important point, there is no theoretical argument that prevents these subsimplices from being located at quite different regions of S as the grid is refined. The passage to the limit is the nonconstructive aspect of Brouwer's theorem, and we have no assurance that the subsimplex determined by a fine grid of vectors on S contains or is even close to a true fixed point of the mapping.

However, in all of the applications of Brouwer's theorem with which we are familiar, there is never any necessity to determine a vector that is close to a true fixed point. We are invariably concerned instead with the determination of a vector that is almost a fixed point, in the sense of being quite close to its own image. As the following argument indicates, if the grid is sufficiently fine, any vector in the subsimplex with distinct labels will have this property.

Since the mapping is continuous (and the simplex is a closed and bounded set) for any $\varepsilon > 0$, there will be a $\delta > 0$ such that $|f(x') - f(x)| \leq \varepsilon$ whenever $|x' - x| \leq \delta$. Here the norm $|y|$ is taken, to be specific, as $\max(|y_1|, \ldots, |y_n|)$. Let the grid be so fine that for any two points x and x' in the same primitive set we have $|x' - x| \leq \delta$. But then for any x in the subsimplex we must have $f_i(x) - x_i \geq -(\varepsilon + \delta)$, since for any coordinate i there is an x' in the subsimplex with $f_i(x') - x_i' \geq 0$, and therefore

$$f_i(x) - x_i = [f_i(x) - f_i(x')] + [x_i' - x_i] + [f_i(x') - x_i']$$
$$\geq -\varepsilon - \delta.$$

Moreover, we also have

$$f_i(x) - x_i = -\sum_{j \neq i} [f_j(x) - x_j]$$
$$\leq (n - 1)(\varepsilon + \delta),$$

and therefore $|f(x) - x| \leq (n - 1)(\varepsilon + \delta)$.

In practice this bound is quite weak, and the difference between a vector in the subsimplex and its image under the mapping is substantially smaller. The degree of approximation can be improved substantially by using standard techniques of numerical analysis, such as Newton's method or one of its variants.

The material of the next two sections of this chapter is primarily of theoretical interest and has no particular bearing on the implementation of our numerical techniques. The reader whose interest is specifically in computational procedures for approximating fixed points may prefer to move directly to chapter 3.

2.7. A GENERALIZATION OF PRIMITIVE SETS*

As the reader may have noticed, neither the concept of a primitive set nor the replacement operation requires the vectors $x^{n+1}, \ldots, x^k$ to lie on the simplex S. The definition may be extended in the following fashion.

2.7.1. [DEFINITION] *Let $x^1, \ldots, x^{n+1}, \ldots, x^k$ be an arbitrary list of vectors in Euclidean n-space no two of which have the same ith component for any i. A subset of n of these vectors, $x^{j_1}, \ldots, x^{j_n}$, is defined to be a primitive set if there is no vector x^j in the list with*

$$x_1^j > \min[x_1^{j_1}, \ldots, x_1^{j_n}]$$
$$\vdots$$
$$x_n^j > \min[x_n^{j_1}, \ldots, x_n^{j_n}].$$

Consider, for example, the following matrix whose twelve columns represent the vectors $x^1, x^2, \ldots, x^{12}$:

$$
\begin{array}{cccccccccccc}
1 & 2 & 3 & 4 & 5 & 6 & 7 & 8 & 9 & 10 & 11 & 12
\end{array}
$$
$$
\begin{bmatrix}
0 & 49 & 48 & 12 & 3 & 2 & 9 & 5 & 4 & 41 & 40 & 39 \\
50 & 0 & 48 & 6 & 7 & 9 & 44 & 43 & 42 & 5 & 2 & 8 \\
50 & 49 & 0 & 47 & 46 & 45 & 3 & 8 & 10 & 6 & 9 & 4
\end{bmatrix}.
$$

The three vectors x^7, x^8, x^{12} are associated with the submatrix

$$
\begin{bmatrix}
9 & \underline{5} & 39 \\
44 & 43 & \underline{8} \\
\underline{3} & 8 & 4
\end{bmatrix}
$$

in which the minimum element in each row is underlined; since there is no vector in the list strictly larger than $(5, 8, 3)$ in all coordinates, these three vectors form a primitive set.

Of course, the geometric interpretation of a primitive set in terms of a subsimplex with sides parallel to the coordinate hyperplanes is no longer

---

* Sections marked by asterisks may be skipped in reading without disturbing the continuity of the argument.

available to us in this more general formulation. And the replacement step cannot be visualized by a parallel movement of one face of a simplex. But the replacement operation can be carried out by precisely the same algebraic calculations as those of section 2.3. For example, consider the list given above, and let us attempt to remove the vector $(9, 44, 3)'$ from the primitive set given by the columns of

$$\begin{bmatrix} 9 & \underline{5} & 39 \\ 44 & 43 & \underline{8} \\ \underline{3} & 8 & \mathbf{4} \end{bmatrix}.$$

The underlined element in the first column appears in the third row; we therefore examine this row to determine the second smallest element, the entry 4 set in boldface type. To determine the replacement for the first column we examine all vectors x^j in the list with $x_1^j > 5$, $x_3^j > 4$ and select the one with the highest second coordinate. This is $(12, 6, 47)'$, so the new primitive set is

$$\begin{bmatrix} 12 & \underline{5} & 39 \\ \underline{6} & 43 & 8 \\ 47 & \mathbf{8} & \underline{4} \end{bmatrix};$$

the reader may verify that there is no vector in the list with all of its coordinates strictly larger than $(5, 6, 4)'$.

As an additional example let us remove the third column from this primitive set; the second smallest entry in the third row is 8, set in boldface type. We therefore examine all vectors x^j in the list with $x_2^j > 6$ $x_3^j > 8$ and select the one with the largest first coordinate, namely, $(4, 42, 10)'$. The new primitive set is given by

$$\begin{bmatrix} 12 & 5 & \underline{4} \\ \underline{6} & 43 & 42 \\ 47 & \underline{8} & 10 \end{bmatrix}.$$

Now let us consider the general case in which the coordinates of the vectors $x^1, \ldots, x^k$ are given by the columns of

(2.7.2) $$X = \begin{bmatrix} x_1^1 & \cdots & x_1^n & \cdots & x_1^j & \cdots & x_1^k \\ \vdots & & & & & & \\ x_n^1 & & x_n^n & & x_n^j & & x_n^k \end{bmatrix}.$$

Let $x^{j_1}, \ldots, x^{j_n}$ be a primitive set according to our generalized definition. Then it is very easy to argue that a replacement for a specific vector in the primitive set—if the replacement exists—is unique and must be given by the rules of section 2.3. To see this we merely notice that the argument of 2.4 never uses, at any point, the previous assumption that the vectors x^j actually lie on the simplex S. The argument applies without any change to this more general case.

On the other hand, theorem 2.3.1—that a replacement step does exist in all cases except when the remaining $n - 1$ vectors of the primitive set are sides of S—does seem to involve the structure of the simplex in a crucial way. In order to obtain a corresponding statement for the more general case, some additional conditions must be placed on the first n vectors.

2.7.3. [DEFINITION] *The vectors* $x^1, \ldots, x^{n+1}, \ldots, x^k$ *will be said to be in standard form if:*

a. $x_i^i = \min[x_i^1, x_i^2, \ldots, x_i^k]$ *for* $i = 1, \ldots, n$; *and*
b. $x_i^j > \max[x_i^{n+1}, \ldots, x_i^k]$ *for* $i, j = 1, \ldots, n$ *and* $i \neq j$.

In other words, the entries in columns $n + 1, \ldots, k$ of X are all bounded by the entries in the first n columns of X, from below by the diagonal elements and from above by the nondiagonal elements. (The numerical example of this section is therefore in standard form.) The reader should have no difficulty in verifying the following generalization of our earlier results.

2.7.4. [THEOREM] *Let the vectors* $x^1, \ldots, x^{n+1}, \ldots, x^k$ *be in standard form. Then the replacement for a given vector in a primitive set will always exist—unless the remaining* $n - 1$ *vectors in the primitive set are among the first* n *vectors in the list—and be given by rule 2.3.2.*

In virtually all of the applications of our class of algorithms, it will be sufficient to consider vectors $x^{n+1}, \ldots, x^k$ that do lie on the unit simplex. The only example known at present that is treated more naturally by the extended definition of the present section is a game-theoretic problem described in chapter 8. For this particular application we shall need the analogue of theorem 2.5.1—in which the vectors $x^1, \ldots, x^k$ are given a label from one of the first n integers—and also the analogues of some extensions of this theorem, which are developed in subsequent chapters.

2.7.5. [THEOREM] *Let the vectors* $x^1, \ldots, x^k$ *be in standard form and assume that each vector is given a label selected from the first* n *integers. Let* x^i *have the label* i *for* $i = 1, \ldots, n$. *Then there exists a primitive set* $(x^{j_1}, \ldots, x^{j_n})$ *all of whose labels are distinct.*

The argument for this theorem is virtually identical with that of section 2.5. We begin with the primitive set consisting of the vectors $x^2, \ldots, x^n$ and that vector x^j from the remainder of the list with the largest first coordinate. If x^j has the label 1, the problem has terminated; if not, then precisely one of the vectors $x^2, \ldots, x^n$ will have a label identical with that of x^j. We remove this vector from the primitive set and continue the process until a primitive set with distinct labels—whose existence again depends on the fact that we cannot cycle—is reached.

2.8. The Relationship between Primitive Sets and Systems of Linear Inequalities*

It may be instructive at this point to indicate the intimate relationship between primitive sets and the familiar notion of a dual feasible basis in linear programming. Let A be a matrix with n rows and k columns:

$$(2.8.1) \qquad A = \begin{bmatrix} a_{11} & \cdots & a_{1n} & \cdots & a_{1j} & \cdots & a_{1k} \\ \vdots & & & & & & \\ a_{n1} & \cdots & a_{nn} & \cdots & a_{nj} & \cdots & a_{nk} \end{bmatrix}.$$

A set of n linearly independent columns $j_1, j_2, \ldots, j_n$ of this matrix is said to form a dual feasible basis for the system of inequalities

$$(2.8.2) \qquad \sum_{i=1}^{n} y_i a_{ij} \geq 1 \qquad \text{for} \quad j = 1, \ldots, k$$

if there is a non-negative solution with equality in 2.8.2 for $j = j_1, j_2, \ldots, j_n$.

In some abstract sense dual feasible bases and primitive sets are quite similar concepts. Each of them distinguishes certain collections of n elements selected from a larger set of size k. And, more importantly, there is a replacement operation that is valid for both. A given member of a primitive set may be eliminated and there is typically a unique replacement for it. In much the same way, a column of a dual feasible basis may be eliminated and a dual pivot step will, under conditions of non-degeneracy, find a unique replacement.

But the relationship between the two concepts is, in fact, even closer than that suggested by the similarity of their properties. Let $(x^1, \ldots, x^{n+1}, \ldots, x^k)$ be an arbitrary set of vectors no two of which have the same ith coordinate for any i and which we take—without any loss of generality —to have strictly positive components. Let λ be a positive parameter that will subsequently tend to infinity. For each such λ define a matrix $A(\lambda)$ with n rows and k columns, with the entry in row i and column j given by

(2.8.3) $$a_{ij}(\lambda) = (x_i^j)^{-\lambda}.$$

We have the following theorem.

2.8.4. [THEOREM] *Make the nondegeneracy assumption that no two vectors in the list $x^1, \ldots, x^k$ have the same ith coordinate for any i. Then the vectors $x^{j_1}, \ldots, x^{j_n}$ form a primitive set if and only if, for all sufficiently large λ, columns $j_1, \ldots, j_n$ of $A(\lambda)$ form a dual feasible basis for*

$$\sum_{i=1}^{n} y_i a_{ij}(\lambda) \geq 1.$$

To demonstrate this theorem let us begin by assuming that the columns $j_1, \ldots, j_n$ form a dual feasible basis for all sufficiently large λ. There will then exist non-negative $y_1(\lambda), \ldots, y_n(\lambda)$ such that

(2.8.5) $$\sum_{i=1}^{n} y_i(\lambda)(x_i^j)^{-\lambda} \geq 1$$

for $j = 1, \ldots, k$, with *equality* for $j = j_1, \ldots, j_n$. From 2.8.5 it follows that for every j there is at least one index i with

$$y_i(\lambda)(x_i^j)^{-\lambda} \geq \frac{1}{n},$$

and therefore

(2.8.6) $$n^{1/\lambda} y_i(\lambda)^{1/\lambda} \geq x_i^j.$$

But, on the other hand, the *equality* described by 2.8.5 for $j = j_1, \ldots, j_n$ permits us to say that $y_i(\lambda)(x_i^j)^{-\lambda} \leq 1$ for any one of these js. In other words,

(2.8.7) $$x_i^j \geq y_i(\lambda)^{1/\lambda}$$

for $j = j_1, \ldots, j_n$ and $i = 1, \ldots, n$. This implies that

$$\min[x_i^{j_1}, \ldots, x_i^{j_n}] \geq y_i(\lambda)^{1/\lambda}$$

for $i = 1, \ldots, n$. Combining this series of inequalities with 2.8.6 tells us that for every column j there exists at least one index i with

$$x_i^j \leq n^{1/\lambda} \min[x_i^{j_1}, \ldots, x_i^{j_n}],$$

and since this is true for all sufficiently large λ, there must be at least one index i with

$$x_i^j \leq \min[x_i^{j_1}, \ldots, x_i^{j_n}].$$

The vectors $x^{j_1}, \ldots, x^{j_n}$ therefore form a primitive set.

To demonstrate the converse let us now assume that the vectors $x^1, \ldots, x^n$ form a primitive set (there is no loss in generality in taking these to be the first n vectors for we are not assuming the vectors to be in standard form) and attempt to show that columns $1, \ldots, n$ of $A(\lambda)$ are a dual feasible basis for all sufficiently large λ. Rearrange the vectors so that the row-minima lie along the main diagonal of the matrix

$$\begin{bmatrix} \underline{x_1^1} & \cdots & x_1^n \\ \vdots & & \\ x_n^1 & \cdots & \underline{x_n^n} \end{bmatrix}$$

and let us then solve the equations

$$\sum_{i=1}^n y_i(\lambda)(x_i^j)^{-\lambda} = 1, \qquad j = 1, \ldots, n.$$

As the first step in our argument we wish to show that

$$y_i(\lambda) \sim (x_i^i)^\lambda \qquad \text{as } \lambda \to \infty,$$

in the sense that the ratio $y_i(\lambda)/(x_i^i)^\lambda$ tends to unity. To see this we express —for example—$y_1(\lambda)$ as the ratio of two determinants:

$$(2.8.8) \qquad y_1(\lambda) = \frac{\begin{bmatrix} 1 & 1 & \cdots & 1 \\ (x_2^1)^{-\lambda} & (x_2^2)^{-\lambda} & \cdots & (x_2^n)^{-\lambda} \\ \vdots & & & \\ (x_n^1)^{-\lambda} & (x_n^2)^{-\lambda} & \cdots & (x_n^n)^{-\lambda} \end{bmatrix}}{\begin{bmatrix} (x_1^1)^{-\lambda} & (x_1^2)^{-\lambda} & \cdots & (x_1^n)^{-\lambda} \\ (x_2^1)^{-\lambda} & (x_2^2)^{-\lambda} & \cdots & (x_2^n)^{-\lambda} \\ \vdots & & & \\ (x_n^1)^{-\lambda} & (x_n^2)^{-\lambda} & \cdots & (x_n^n)^{-\lambda} \end{bmatrix}}.$$

Consider the denominator first. It can be written as the sum of $n!$ terms, each of the form

$$(\pm 1)(x_1^{j_1}\, x_2^{j_2} \dots x_n^{j_n})^{-\lambda},$$

with $(j_1, j_2, \dots, j_n)$ a permutation of the first n integers. But aside from the permutation $(1, 2, \dots, n)$ we have

$$(x_1^{j_1}\, x_2^{j_2} \dots x_n^{j_n}) > (x_1^1\, x_2^2 \dots x_n^n).$$

The denominator is therefore equal to $(x_1^1\, x_2^2 \dots x_n^n)^{-\lambda}$ plus terms of lower order as $\lambda \to \infty$. Similarly the numerator equals $(x_2^2 \dots x_n^n)^{-\lambda}$ plus terms of lower order, and we see that $y_1(\lambda) \sim (x_1^1)^{\lambda}$.

In order to conclude that the first n columns of $A(\lambda)$ form a dual feasible basis for sufficiently large λ, we must show that

$$\sum_{i=1}^{n} y_i(\lambda)(x_i^j)^{-\lambda} \geq 1 \qquad \text{as } \lambda \to \infty$$

for $j = n + 1, \dots, k$. But if this is not so, then there is a sequence of λs and some j for which

$$\sum_{i=1}^{n} y_i(\lambda)(x_i^j)^{-\lambda} < 1,$$

and therefore

$$\sum_{i=1}^{n} \left(\frac{x_i^i}{x_i^j} \right)^{\lambda} \leq 1.$$

It follows that $x_i^j \geq x_i^i$ for all i. Since $j > n$, we conclude from the nondegeneracy assumption that $x_i^j > x_i^i = \min[x_i^1, \dots, x_i^n]$ for $i = 1, \dots, n$. This contradicts the assumption that $\{x^1, \dots, x^n\}$ forms a primitive set and concludes the proof of theorem 2.8.4.

I shall make no particular use of the contents of this theorem in the remainder of this book other than to point out that virtually all of our subsequent results have a valid analogue when the concept of a primitive set is replaced by that of a dual feasible basis. It may also be of some historical interest to note that it was precisely this theorem that led to the original definition of primitive sets.

CHAPTER 3

Some Numerical Applications of Brouwer's Theorem

3.1. PRELIMINARY REMARKS

In the previous chapter I have discussed a computational procedure that determines, in a finite number of iterations, a vector which lies within a preassigned distance from its image under a continuous mapping. General arguments of this sort, however, give very little indication of whether the algorithm will be useful in any specific numerical problem. For example, the simplex method for linear programming derives its importance as a practical computational device not from any theoretical bounds on the maximum number of possible pivot steps required to solve a problem of given size, but rather from the empirical observation that the method generally terminates in a surprisingly small number of iterations.

When our algorithm is applied to examples of moderate size, the number of vectors $x^{n+1}, \ldots, x^k$ on the simplex is typically quite large—in some instances as many as 10^{30} or 10^{40} such points—and the number of possible primitive sets is exceptionally high. If even a modest proportion of these primitive sets were to be encountered in the course of the algorithm, the computational burden would be prohibitive.

The algorithm has already been applied to several hundred examples ranging up to $n = 20$, and our computational experience is sufficiently rich to permit some general observations. An indication of this experience will be provided by numerical examples in the text, but at this point it may be sufficient to say that the algorithm has performed remarkably well. In virtually all of our examples the number of iterations seems not to exceed the minimum number of iterations that might conceivably be taken with hindsight by more than a factor of two or three. Typically the algorithm will examine a sequence of primitive sets that lie more or less on a straight line connecting the initial vertex with the terminal primitive set. And these examples include many in which simpler algorithms, such as the gradient method, fail to converge. There is no doubt that the method is efficient and that problems involving as many as 30 or 40 variables will eventually be within the range of the algorithm.

There is one technical problem that must be resolved before the numerical examples of the present chapter can be displayed. At each iteration of the algorithm the new vector to be introduced into the primitive set is obtained by examining all vectors x^j in the grid that satisfy $n - 1$ inequalities of the form $x_i^j > a_i$, and selecting that vector whose remaining coordinate is maximal. This would seem to require keeping a record of all of the vectors $x^{n+1}, \ldots, x^k$ and making a systematic search through this list at every iteration. But this large a number of vectors cannot be stored in a computer, and even if it were possible, a search of this size would be prohibitively expensive in terms of computer time.

Both of these problems can be solved if the grid $x^{n+1}, \ldots, x^k$ is selected in a regular fashion. For example, let the grid consist of all of the vectors $(m_1/D, m_2/D, \ldots, m_n/D)$, with m_i representing positive integers whose sum is D. In this case the list of vectors need not be stored since they are available in simple, analytical form. Moreover it is an easy matter to determine a vector that maximizes a specific coordinate, subject to inequalities on the remaining coordinates.

There is, however, one serious difficulty with this simple grid : many of the vectors in the list will have identical ith coordinates and the non-degeneracy assumption, which is crucial in demonstrating that the replacement step is unique and therefore that the algorithm does not cycle, will not be satisfied. In order to restore the nondegeneracy assumption we must introduce some systematic procedure for breaking ties and determining which of two vectors in the list with identical ith coordinates should be considered to have the larger one.

In chapter 6 a detailed study will be made of a particular lexicographical procedure (whose origins lie in Hansen's thesis, 1968) for breaking ties with this regular grid. The result will be a version of the algorithm with many virtues, including a very low storage requirement. In this chapter, however, I shall adopt a rather clumsy device for breaking ties, which permits us to display several numerical examples with a minimum of preliminary analysis.

3.1.1. [PRELIMINARY TIE-BREAKING RULE] *Let us keep an explicit record of the components of the vectors x^{j_1}, x^{j_2}, ... in the order in which they are introduced into successive primitive sets. In other words, we construct a* *matrix*

$$X_1 = \begin{bmatrix} 0 & M_2 & \cdots & M_n & x_1^{j_1} & \cdots & x_1^{j_m} \\ M_1 & 0 & \cdots & M_n & x_2^{j_1} & \cdots & x_2^{j_m} \\ \vdots & \vdots & & \vdots & \vdots & & \vdots \\ M_1 & M_2 & \cdots & 0 & x_n^{j_1} & \cdots & x_n^{j_m} \end{bmatrix}$$

in which one additional column is inserted as the last column at each iteration in which the vector brought into the primitive set has not appeared in any previous primitive set. We then adopt the convention that if two columns in this matrix have an identical ith coordinate, the first of these two columns is presumed to have the larger one, and that ties between any column in this matrix and a vector which does not appear in the matrix are broken in favor of the former. Ties between two columns not appearing in the matrix are not resolved—nor need they be—until one of the vectors is introduced into a primitive set in the course of the algorithm.

Since this rule gives an unambiguous procedure for resolving ties between any two vectors that arise in the course of the computation, the arguments of the preceding chapter demonstrate that the algorithm cannot cycle and must terminate with a primitive set of the desired type. Moreover the replacement operation does not require a search through the entire grid $x^{n+1}, \ldots, x^k$, but only through the list of vectors which have already been introduced in one of the previous primitive sets—to allow for the possibility that such a vector may be reintroduced.

A numerical example with $n = 4$ and a denominator of 100 should illustrate the method sufficiently. The first four columns in the following matrix refer to the sides of the simplex and the fifth column is that vector in the list—other than the first four—with the highest first coordinate (only the numerators are recorded):

	x^1	x^2	x^3	x^4	x^5	
	0	102	101	100	97	
	103	0	101	100	1	
	103	102	0	100	1	···
	103	102	101	0	1	
Label	1	2	3	4	3	

The initial primitive set consists of x^2, x^3, x^4, x^5 and for the purpose of the illustration we assume that x^5 has received the label 3. The third slack vector must therefore be removed from the primitive set; in order to do this we follow our customary rules.

In the submatrix

$$
\begin{array}{cccc}
x^2 & x^3 & x^4 & x^5 \\
\begin{bmatrix}
102 & 101 & 100 & \underline{97} \\
\underline{0} & 101 & 100 & 1 \\
102 & \underline{0} & 100 & \mathbf{1} \\
102 & 101 & \underline{0} & 1
\end{bmatrix}
\end{array}
$$

$$
\begin{array}{ccccc}
\text{Label} & 2 & 3 & 4 & 3
\end{array}
$$

the second smallest element in row 3 appears in boldface type. We must therefore look for a vector $(m_1, m_2, m_3, m_4)'$, with $m_2 > 0, m_3 > 1, m_4 > 0$, and whose first element is maximal. m_3 must therefore be equal to 2, and the vector to be brought in is the sixth column in the following matrix:

$$
\begin{array}{cccccc}
x^1 & x^2 & x^3 & x^4 & x^5 & x^6 \\
\begin{bmatrix}
0 & 102 & 101 & 100 & 97 & 96 \\
103 & 0 & 101 & 100 & 1 & 1 \\
103 & 102 & 0 & 100 & 1 & 2 \\
103 & 102 & 101 & 0 & 1 & 1
\end{bmatrix} & \cdots
\end{array}
$$

$$
\begin{array}{ccccccc}
\text{Label} & 1 & 2 & 3 & 4 & 3 & 2
\end{array}
$$

Assume that x^6 has been given the label 2. The vector x^2 must therefore be removed from the primitive set displayed by the columns of

$$
\begin{array}{cccc}
x^2 & x^4 & x^5 & x^6 \\
\begin{bmatrix}
102 & 100 & 97 & \underline{96} \\
\underline{0} & 100 & 1 & \mathbf{1} \\
102 & 100 & \underline{1} & 2 \\
102 & \underline{0} & 1 & 1
\end{bmatrix} .
\end{array}
$$

$$
\begin{array}{ccccc}
\text{Label} & 2 & 4 & 3 & 2
\end{array}
$$

The second smallest element in row 2 is set in boldface; the application of our rule will bring into the primitive set the seventh column in the enlarged matrix

$$
\begin{array}{ccccccc}
x^1 & x^2 & x^3 & x^4 & x^5 & x^6 & x^7 \\
\end{array}
$$

$$
\begin{bmatrix}
0 & 102 & 101 & 100 & 97 & 96 & 95 \\
103 & 0 & 101 & 100 & 1 & 1 & 2 \\
103 & 102 & 0 & 100 & 1 & 2 & 2 \\
103 & 102 & 101 & 0 & 1 & 1 & 1 \\
\end{bmatrix} \cdots,
$$

$$
\begin{array}{ccccccc}
\text{Label} \quad 1 & 2 & 3 & 4 & 3 & 2 & 2 \\
\end{array}
$$

which has been given a label of 2.

The vector x^6 must therefore be removed from the primitive set with columns

$$
\begin{array}{cccc}
x^4 & x^5 & x^6 & x^7 \\
\end{array}
$$

$$
\begin{bmatrix}
100 & 97 & 96 & \underline{95} \\
100 & \mathbf{1} & \underline{1} & 2 \\
100 & \underline{1} & 2 & 2 \\
\underline{0} & 1 & 1 & 1 \\
\end{bmatrix} .
$$

$$
\begin{array}{cccc}
\text{Label} \quad 4 & 3 & 2 & 2 \\
\end{array}
$$

A simple calculation will convince the reader that the vector $(96, 2, 1, 1)'$ will be introduced, and we then continue.

This procedure for resolving ties is easy to program for the computer, but it does have the drawback that it requires a search through a matrix whose size is constantly increasing throughout the algorithm. In practice, however, it will generally be adequate to search through a limited number of these vectors—the last hundred or so—since earlier vectors will typically be in a different part of the simplex S and not be candidates for replacement. The procedure can also be used, with very little modification, if the grid size is not uniform throughout the simplex: for example, if the denominator D is selected considerably higher within a given subsimplex in which the answer is expected to lie. Moreover, numerical examples seem to indicate that this method requires substantially fewer iterations than other, more sophisticated, tie-breaking rules.

3.2. AN EXAMPLE OF A PURE EXCHANGE MODEL

If the market excess demand functions are given by $g_1(x), \ldots, g_n(x)$, continuous on the simplex S and satisfying the Walras law, a mapping of the simplex whose fixed points are equilibrium price vectors is given by

$$f_i(x) = \frac{x_i + \max[0, g_i(x)]}{1 + \sum_l \max[0, g_l(x)]}.$$

A particular vector in the list $x^{n+1}, \ldots, x^k$ is given a label corresponding to a coordinate that is nondecreasing under the mapping at that point, i.e., $f_i(x) \geq x_i$, or

$$x_i + \max[0, g_i(x)] \geq x_i \left\{ 1 + \sum_l \max[0, g_l(x)] \right\}.$$

It is clearly sufficient to label the vector x with an index i for which $g_i(x)/x_i$ is maximal. As before, the first n vectors are given the labels $1, 2, \ldots, n$, respectively.

Our example will involve 10 commodities and 5 consumers, each of whom has a stock of commodities $w = (w_1, \ldots, w_{10})$ prior to trade and a utility function

$$u(y) = \sum_{i=1}^{10} a_i^{1/b} y_i^{1 - 1/b}$$

for final consumption. Both the parameters of the utility functions and the initial stock of commodities will differ for each of the five consumers. For any vector of prices x the demands of a typical consumer are obtained by maximizing $u(y)$, subject to his budget constraint $\sum_1^{10} x_i y_i \leq \sum_1^{10} x_i w_i$; for this particular class of utility functions the *excess* demand functions may be written explicitly as

$$y_i = \frac{a_i \sum_1^{10} x_l w_l}{x_i^b \sum_1^{10} x_l^{1-b} a_l} - w_i, \qquad \text{for } i = 1, \ldots, 10.$$

The market excess demand functions are obtained by the summation of these five distinct sets of individual excess demand functions, with different parameters a_i, w_i, and b appearing in each set.

In order to specify the problem, we need to describe for each consumer his stock of commodities prior to trade and the parameters of his utility function.

Initial stock of commodities

Consumer

1	0.6	0.2	0.2	20.0	0.1	2.0	9.0	5.0	5.0	15.0
2	0.2	11.0	12.0	13.0	14.0	15.0	16.0	5.0	5.0	9.0
3	0.4	9.0	8.0	7.0	6.0	5.0	4.0	5.0	7.0	12.0
4	1.0	5.0	5.0	5.0	5.0	5.0	5.0	8.0	3.0	17.0
5	8.0	1.0	22.0	10.0	0.3	0.9	5.1	0.1	6.2	11.0

The numbers in these tables have been selected more or less randomly and have no economic significance other than representing fairly disparate vectors of initially owned stocks.

Utility parameters a

Consumer

1	1.0	1.0	3.0	0.1	0.1	1.2	2.0	1.0	1.0	0.7
2	1.0	1.0	1.0	1.0	1.0	1.0	1.0	1.0	1.0	1.0
3	9.9	0.1	5.0	0.2	6.0	0.2	8.0	1.0	1.0	0.2
4	1.0	2.0	3.0	4.0	5.0	6.0	7.0	8.0	9.0	10.0
5	1.0	13.0	11.0	9.0	4.0	0.9	8.0	1.0	2.0	10.0

Utility parameters b

Consumer

1	2.0
2	1.3
3	3.0
4	0.2
5	0.6

The parameters a_i describe the intensity of preference for each of the commodities: the higher the value of a_i, the more of this commodity will be demanded. The parameter b represents the degree of substitutability between commodities: if b is close to zero, the consumer will demand a commodity bundle close in its proportions to $(a_1, a_2, \ldots, a_{10})$ independently of relative prices; if b is unity, the fraction of income spent on each commodity will be proportional to this vector; and if b is greater than unity, there will be considerable substitution, depending on relative prices.

In this example the grid of prices on the simplex S will consist of all vectors $(m_1/250, \ldots, m_{10}/250)$, with m_i representing positive integers summing to 250. There are some $.8 \times 10^{16}$ such possible vectors and a vastly larger number of primitive sets. The algorithm began at the primitive set containing the sides $x^2, \ldots, x^{10}$ and one additional vector. It terminated after only 468 iterations, taking approximately 1 minute of computation time on an IBM 7094, with the following primitive set of vectors:

$$
\begin{bmatrix}
45 & 51 & 48 & 50 & 50 & 47 & 48 & 46 & 49 & 52 \\
28 & 27 & 28 & 28 & 28 & 28 & 28 & 28 & 28 & 27 \\
25 & 25 & 24 & 24 & 25 & 25 & 25 & 25 & 25 & 25 \\
11 & 11 & 11 & 10 & 11 & 11 & 11 & 11 & 11 & 11 \\
27 & 26 & 27 & 27 & 26 & 27 & 27 & 27 & 27 & 26 \\
20 & 19 & 19 & 19 & 19 & 19 & 19 & 20 & 19 & 19 \\
30 & 29 & 30 & 29 & 29 & 30 & 29 & 30 & 29 & 29 \\
26 & 25 & 25 & 25 & 25 & 25 & 25 & 25 & 25 & 25 \\
25 & 24 & 25 & 25 & 24 & 25 & 25 & 25 & 24 & 24 \\
13 & 13 & 13 & 13 & 13 & 13 & 13 & 13 & 13 & 12
\end{bmatrix},
$$

the ith column having the label i.

In order to obtain a definite answer, the 10 vectors in the primitive set were averaged to provide an initial value for the price vector, and a variation of Newton's method was employed. The following price vector, normalized to lie on the simplex, and excess demands were obtained:

$$x = (.187, .109, .099, .043, .117, .077, .117, .102, .099, .049),$$

$$g(x) = (.00, .00, .00, .00, .00, .00, .00, .00, .00, .00).$$

There is no doubt, as this example indicates, that the algorithm can be applied successfully to problems of reasonable size.

3.3. AN INTERSECTION THEOREM

In the previous example, and in many others, the transition to the algorithm by means of Brouwer's theorem is somewhat artificial. The essential aspect of the algorithm is that each vector in the dense grid $x^{n+1}, \ldots, x^k$ is labelled with one of the first n integers—the side x^i receiving the label i—and a small subsimplex is then found, with the property that for every label i there is a grid point in the subsimplex with that label. The following theorem, obtained by selecting a convergent subsequence of primitive sets from a finer and finer sequence of grids, displays the essentials of the algorithm in a form possibly more transparent than Brouwer's theorem.

3.3.1. [THEOREM] *Let $C_1, \ldots, C_n$ be closed sets on the simplex S, with the following properties:*

a. *Every vector in S is a member of at least one C_i; and*

b. *every vector on the side $x_i = 0$ is contained in C_i, for $i = 1, \ldots, n$. Then $\cap_1^n C_i$ is not empty.*

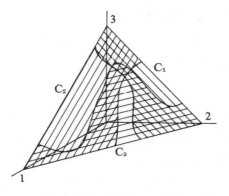

Figure 3.3.1

Figure 3.3.1 illustrates the hypotheses of this theorem for $n = 3$.

The theorem may be demonstrated in a manner virtually identical with that used for Brouwer's theorem. The major difference is that the label associated with a vector x^j in the grid is not based on a mapping, but is taken to be an index i such that $x^j \in C_i$. The algorithm then terminates with a small primitive set that has a nonempty intersection with each one of the closed sets $C_1, \ldots, C_n$. By taking finer and finer grids a limit point may be selected which is contained in each one of these sets.

Theorem 3.3.1 has an obvious resemblance to the Knaster-Kuratowski-Mazurkiewicz lemma (see Hurwicz and Wallman 1941 for a discussion of this classical topological theorem), which provides an alternative set of assumptions guaranteeing that the intersection of n closed sets $C_1, \ldots, C_n$ on the simplex S is not empty. The relationship will be explored in chapter 6, in which our algorithm is compared to the customary approaches to fixed point theorems.

In the application of theorem 3.3.1 to models of exchange the set C_i can be taken to be the union of the side on which $x_i = 0$ and the set of price vectors for which $g_i(x) \geq g_j(x)$, for $j = 1, \ldots, n$.

3.4. AN APPLICATION TO CONVEX PROGRAMMING

Let us consider the convex programming problem

$$\max g_1(x)$$

$$\text{subject to } g_2(x) \le 0$$

(3.4.1)

$$\vdots$$

$$g_n(x) \le 0,$$

$$x \ge 0,$$

in which g_1 is assumed to be concave, and the functions $g_2, \ldots, g_n$ convex. This can be interpreted as a typical problem which involves the production side of the economy alone and in which a conventional price adjustment mechanism is known to converge under certain regularity conditions. However, our algorithm, in the form of theorem 3.3.1 or by means of Brouwer's theorem, can be used equally well to determine the appropriate shadow prices for the constraints and therefore the solution to the constrained maximization problem. (See Wagner 1971 for a similar approach.)

Let us begin with some general considerations. The algorithm will be working in the price simplex

$$S = \{(\pi_1, \ldots, \pi_n) \mid \pi_i \ge 0, \sum_1^n \pi_i = 1\},$$

and we shall make the assumption that for any such price vector the value of x which maximizes the profit function

$$\pi_1 g_1(x) - \sum_2^n \pi_i g_i(x),$$

subject only to the constraints $x \ge 0$, is finite, unique, and a continuous function of π. The present algorithm is to be considered practical only when this function, which we denote by $x(\pi)$, can be obtained in an explicit form. An alternative approach is described in chapter 5 for that class of problems in which profit maximization itself presents serious computational difficulties or in which the profit-maximizing x is not unique.

To apply the algorithm, let us define n closed sets $C_1, \ldots, C_n$ on the simplex S. C_i, for $i = 2, \ldots, n$, is defined to consist of all price vectors π that either have the property $\pi_i = 0$ or satisfy $g_i[x(\pi)] \ge 0$. The set C_1, on the other hand, consists of those vectors with $\pi_1 = 0$ and, in addition, all price vectors for which $g_i[x(\pi)] \le 0$ for $i = 2, \ldots, n$. Under mild assumptions each of these sets is closed, and the two conditions of theorem 3.3.1 are satisfied.

Let π^* be a vector contained in the intersection of $C_1, \ldots, C_n$, and assume for the moment that the first coordinate π_1^* is strictly positive. Then, since $\pi^* \in C_1$, we must have

$$g_i[x(\pi^*)] \leq 0 \qquad \text{for } i = 2, \ldots, n,$$

so that the constraints are all satisfied by $x(\pi^*)$. In addition, since $\pi^* \in C_i$ for $i = 2, \ldots, n$, we must have either $\pi_i^* = 0$ or $g_i[x(\pi^*)] \geq 0$. In other words, $\pi_i^* = 0$ or $g_i[x(\pi^*)] = 0$.

These arguments permit us to demonstrate that $x(\pi^*)$ does indeed solve the constrained maximization problem 3.4.1. For suppose that x is another vector satisfying the constraints $g_i(x) \leq 0$. From the profit-maximizing statement

$$\pi_1^* g_1[x(\pi^*)] - \sum_2^n \pi_i^* g_i[x(\pi^*)] \geq \pi_1^* g_1(x) - \sum_2^n \pi_i^* g_i(x)$$

and the fact that $\Sigma_2^n \pi_i^* g_i[x(\pi^*)] = 0$, we see that

$$\pi_1^* g_1[x(\pi^*)] \geq \pi_1^* g_1(x) - \sum_2^n \pi_i^* g_i(x) \geq \pi_1^* g_1(x),$$

and therefore

$$g_1[x(\pi^*)] \geq g_1(x).$$

This argument depends crucially on the fact that π_1^*—the price of output, so to speak—is strictly positive, a property that can be guaranteed if the following assumption, customarily known as the constraint qualification, is made.

3.4.2. [ASSUMPTION] *There exists a non-negative vector x such that $g_i(x) < 0$ for $i = 2, \ldots, n$.*

Let us then assume that $\pi_1^* = 0$. The fact that $\pi^* \in C_1$ no longer implies that $g_i[x(\pi^*)] \leq 0$ for $i = 2, \ldots, n$. But it is still true that for each $i \geq 2$ either $\pi_i^* = 0$ or $g_i[x(\pi^*)] \geq 0$, so that $\Sigma_2^n \pi_i^* g_i[x(\pi^*)] \geq 0$. This is, however, a contradiction because the vector x will satisfy

$$\pi_1^* g_1(x) - \sum_2^n \pi_i^* g_i(x) > \pi_1^* g_1[x(\pi^*)] - \sum_2^n \pi_i^* g_i[x(\pi^*)]$$

since

$$\pi_1^* = 0, \qquad \sum_2^n \pi_i^* g_i(x) < 0, \quad \text{and} \quad \sum_2^n \pi_i^* g_i[x(\pi^*)] \geq 0.$$

$x(\pi^*)$ is therefore not the profit-maximizing response at prices π^* that it was assumed to be. This demonstrates that $\pi_1^* > 0$ and that our techniques can be applied to this class of nonlinear programming problems.

3.5. AN EXAMPLE OF A NONLINEAR PROGRAMMING PROBLEM

Consider the nonlinear programming problem

$$\max g_1(x) = a \cdot x_1^{\alpha_1} \cdot x_2^{\alpha_2} \cdot \ldots \cdot x_m^{\alpha_m}$$

$$\text{subject to } g_2(x) = b_{21} \cdot x_1 + \ldots + b_{2m} \cdot x_m - c_2 \leq 0$$

$$\vdots$$

$$g_n(x) = b_{n1} \cdot x_1 + \ldots + b_{nm} \cdot x_m - c_n \leq 0,$$

$$x \geq 0,$$

with the following restrictions on the parameters: $\alpha_j > 0$ for all j, $\Sigma_j \alpha_j < 1$, $b_{ij} > 0$ for all i and j, and $c_i > 0$ for all i.

The value of x that maximizes the profit function

$$\pi_1 g_1(x) - \sum_{i=2}^{n} \pi_i g_i(x)$$

is given by

$$x_j(\pi) = \frac{a^\alpha \cdot \pi_1^\alpha}{q_j \{q_1^{\alpha_1} \cdot q_2^{\alpha_2} \ldots q_m^{\alpha_m}\}^\alpha} ,$$

where $\alpha = 1/(1 - \Sigma_j \alpha_j)$ and

$$q_j = \frac{\left(\sum_{i=2}^{n} \pi_i b_{ij} \right)}{\alpha_j} .$$

Given our assumptions on the parameters and the fact that the vectors π are non-negative and lie on the unit simplex, the functions $x_j(\pi)$ are defined for any vector π whose first coordinate is less than one. Aside from this vector, which will never arise in the computation, the response functions $x_j(\pi)$ have all the desired properties and the algorithm described in the preceding section may be applied.

A numerical example with $n = 6$ and $m = 6$ was computed. We have

$$\max g_1(x) = 5 \cdot x_1^{.05} x_2^{.15} x_3^{.35} x_4^{.05} x_5^{.10} x_6^{.10}$$

subject to

$$g_2(x) = \quad x_1 + \quad x_2 + \quad x_3 + \quad x_4 + \quad x_5 + \quad x_6 - 0.8 \;\leq 0,$$

$$g_3(x) = \quad 2x_1 + 0.5\ x_2 + \quad 3x_3 + 0.8\ x_4 + \quad x_5 + 0.7\ x_6 - 1.0 \;\leq 0,$$

$$g_4(x) = \quad x_1 + 0.4\ x_2 + 0.8\ x_3 + 0.7\ x_4 + 0.3\ x_5 + 0.8\ x_6 - 0.7 \;\leq 0,$$

$$g_5(x) = 0.16x_1 + 0.4\ x_2 + 0.2\ x_3 + 0.4\ x_4 + 0.4\ x_5 + 0.6\ x_6 - 0.3 \;\leq 0,$$

$$g_6(x) = 0.4\ x_1 + 0.13x_2 + 0.08x_3 + 0.16x_4 + 0.26x_5 + 0.28x_6 - 0.14 \leq 0,$$

$$x \geq 0.$$

In this example we used a grid on the simplex S consisting of all vectors $(m_1/100, \ldots, m_6/100)$, with m_i representing non-negative integers summing to 100. The algorithm, which used the tie-breaking rule of chapter 6, terminated after 523 iterations in approximately 10 seconds of computation time on an IBM 360–50. The numerators of the vectors in the final primitive set are represented by the columns of the matrix below:

$$\begin{bmatrix} 40 & 41 & 41 & 41 & 41 & 41 \\ 1 & 0 & 1 & 1 & 1 & 1 \\ 27 & 27 & 26 & 27 & 27 & 27 \\ 1 & 1 & 1 & 0 & 1 & 1 \\ 20 & 20 & 20 & 20 & 19 & 20 \\ 11 & 11 & 11 & 11 & 11 & 10 \end{bmatrix}$$

The vector corresponding to the ith column in the matrix carried the label i.

In order to obtain a definite answer a convex combination of the price vectors in the final primitive set and the associated x vectors were taken as a preliminary approximation of the optimal solution. This solution was then improved upon by a variation of Newton's method based on local linearization of the objective function. The following x vector and price vector (after normalizing with $\pi_1 = 1$) were obtained:

$$\hat{x} = (0.035567, \quad 0.277356, \quad 0.178135, \quad 0.068268, \quad 0.113746, \quad 0.124891)$$

and

$$\hat{\pi} = (1., \quad 0., \quad 0.670600, \quad 0., \quad 0.552120, \quad 0.259342).$$

We have $g_i(\hat{x}) < 0$ for $i = 2$ and 4 and $|g_i(\hat{x})| < 10^{-7}$ for $i = 3, 5, 6$. Further,

$$\left| \frac{\partial g_1}{\partial x_i} - \sum_{j=2}^{n} \pi_j \frac{\partial g_j}{\partial x_i} \right|$$

evaluated at $x = \hat{x}$ and $\pi = \hat{\pi}$ is less than 10^{-7} for all i.

CHAPTER 4

An Extension of the Algorithm

4.1. INTRODUCTION

Brouwer's theorem has a substantial range of applicability in mathematical economics. As we have seen, it can be used to demonstrate the existence of equilibrium prices in an exchange model with single-valued continuous demand functions and is capable of a similar application if a strictly convex production set is introduced to describe the production possibilities open to the economy. The existence of Nash equilibrium points in an n-person game may also be demonstrated by means of Brouwer's theorem if strict convexity assumptions are made about the individual payoff functions. Again, as we have seen in the previous chapter, both the theorem and its associated computational techniques can be applied to the solution of nonlinear programming problems if sufficiently strong convexity assumptions are placed on the problem.

In all of these applications the algorithm attempts to find a set of parameters—prices, strategies, etc.—which are in equilibrium in the sense that the response of the system provides no incentive for a change in these parameters. But this requires that the system respond in a unique, single-valued fashion to any specific choice of parameter values. If, for example, the demand functions in an exchange model are multiple-valued—that is, at certain price vectors a consumer is indifferent among a large range of possible consumption vectors—the mapping to which we have applied Brouwer's theorem can no longer be constructed, and some alternative procedure is required to demonstrate that equilibrium prices exist.

While this is not a serious problem on the demand side of the economy (the assumption of single-valued demand functions is not particularly restrictive) it does offer difficulties if production is assumed to display constant returns to scale. For in this case the supply response to a given vector of prices may very well be ambiguous, at least as far as scale is concerned. The difficulties caused by a nonunique response may be seen most clearly in our application to convex programming; if the supply response $x(\pi)$ is not single-valued, then we cannot say with certainty whether a given excess factor demand $g_i[x(\pi)]$ is positive or negative. There may be a wide range of potential labels for a specific price vector, and our previous algorithm will yield a primitive set unrelated to the solution of the problem.

It is for this reason that Kakutani's theorem—a far-reaching generalization of Brouwer's theorem to the case of multiple-valued mappings—has been used with such frequency in mathematical economics. The purpose of the present chapter is to develop a substantial generalization of our methods that will provide, as one of its many applications, a direct algorithm for Kakutani's theorem.

4.2. THE GENERALIZED THEOREM

Let us begin, as before, with a list of vectors on the simplex, $x^{n+1}, \ldots, x^k$, augmented by the vectors $x^1, \ldots, x^n$ representing the sides of the simplex. In our previous algorithm each one of the vectors was associated with a label equal to one of the first n integers. The algorithm was applied with no restriction on the labelling other than the assumption that the side x^i was given the label i (for $i = 1, \ldots, n$). Of course in any application the specific label would be determined by the characteristics of the problem.

In our present extension the notion of a label is dropped completely. Instead of a label each vector x^j will have associated with it a specific vector a_j, which is also in n-dimensional space, though not necessarily on the simplex. For the purpose of the algorithm this association $x^j \to a_j$ will be completely arbitrary, aside from a specific convention about the vectors to be associated with the sides of S. But, as with the previous labelling, the actual mode of association will be of the greatest significance in any specific application.

4.2.1. [ASSUMPTION] *The sides* $x^1, \ldots, x^n$ *will be associated with unit vectors in the following way:*

$$x^1 \to (1, 0, 0, \ldots, 0)$$
$$x^2 \to (0, 1, 0, \ldots, 0)$$
$$\vdots$$
$$x^n \to (0, 0, 0, \ldots, 1).$$

A convenient way to portray the relationship between x^j and a_j is to construct a matrix A with n rows and k columns, the jth of which contains the coordinates of the vector associated with x^j:

$$
A = \begin{array}{cccccccc}
x^1 & x^2 & \cdots & x^n & x^{n+1} & \cdots & x^j & \cdots & x^k
\end{array}
$$

$$
A = \begin{bmatrix}
1 & 0 & \cdots & 0 & a_{1,n+1} & \cdots & a_{1,j} & \cdots & a_{1,k} \\
0 & 1 & \cdots & 0 & a_{2,n+1} & \cdots & a_{2,j} & \cdots & a_{2,k} \\
\vdots & \vdots & & \vdots & \vdots & & \vdots & & \vdots \\
0 & 0 & \cdots & 1 & a_{n,n+1} & \cdots & a_{n,j} & \cdots & a_{n,k}
\end{bmatrix}.
$$

The number of columns in A is apt to be quite large in any specific application, and it is fortunate that the algorithm to be discussed never requires an explicit representation of this matrix in the memory units of the computer.

In addition let $b = (b_1, \ldots, b_n)$ be a vector all of whose coordinates are non-negative. We shall be concerned with vectors $y = (y_1, \ldots, y_k)$ all of whose coordinates are non-negative and which satisfy the equations $Ay = b$. It will be useful, at this point, to remind the reader of the definition of a feasible basis as it is used in linear programming.

4.2.2. [REMINDER] *The columns $j_1, \ldots, j_n$ of the matrix A form a feasible basis if the equations $Ay = b$ have a unique, non-negative solution with $y_j = 0$ unless $j = j_1, j_2, \ldots, j_n$.*

We are now prepared to state our generalization of theorem 2.5.1, though, of course, at this stage its potential applicability to any problem arising in economics will be unclear.

4.2.3. [THEOREM] *Let x^j be associated with the jth column of the matrix A. Let $b \geq 0$, and assume that the set of non-negative solutions to the equations $Ay = b$ is bounded. Then there exists a primitive set $(x^{j_1}, \ldots, x^{j_n})$ such that the columns $j_1, \ldots, j_n$ form a feasible basis for $Ay = b$.*

There is an illuminating geometrical interpretation of this result in the special case in which the columns of A and the vector b all lie on the simplex whose coordinates are non-negative and sum to unity. The relationship between x^j and a_j may then be looked at as a mapping that takes each of the vectors $x^{n+1}, \ldots, x^k$ on the simplex S into a corresponding vector $a_{n+1}, \ldots, a_k$ lying on some other simplex S' of identical dimension (fig. 4.2.1). Since the vector b also lies in S', a feasible basis for the equations $Ay = b$ consists of n linearly independent vectors $a_{j_1}, \ldots, a_{j_n}$ whose convex hull contains the specific point b. The geometric content of theorem 4.2.3 is therefore that from the list $x^1, \ldots, x^{n+1}, \ldots, x^k$ we may select n vectors, which form a primitive set and are such that the vector b is contained in the convex hull of their images. There is some slight loss in geometric

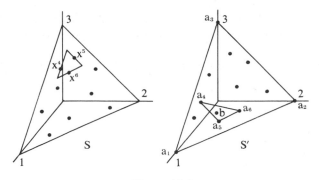

Figure 4.2.1

interpretation when we realize that the entire side of S on which $x_i = 0$ is associated with the single vector a_i, but the suggestion that the theorem is concerned with "inverting" an arbitrary mapping is both accurate and illuminating.

Before describing a proof of this theorem—which I do in the next two sections—it might be appropriate to indicate in precisely what way it represents a generalization of 2.5.1. In that earlier theorem the vector x^j was associated with a specific label selected from the first n integers. To convert this labelling to the present form, let us assume that the jth column of A is a unit vector $(0, \ldots, 1, \ldots, 0)'$ all of whose entries are zero, except for a 1 in the row given by the label associated with x^j. In addition take the vector $b = (1, 1, \ldots, 1)'$.

The hypotheses of theorem 4.2.3 are surely satisfied since any non-negative solution to $Ay = b$ will certainly have $y_j \le 1$ for all j. If we assume the theorem to be correct, the conclusion asserts the existence of a primitive set $x^{j_1}, \ldots, x^{j_n}$ such that the columns $j_1, \ldots, j_n$ form a feasible basis for $Ay = b$. But for this particular system of equations the columns of a feasible basis are the columns of an $n \times n$ unit matrix; therefore the labels associated with different columns in the primitive set must be distinct.

4.3. SOME PRELIMINARY IDEAS FROM LINEAR PROGRAMMING

The basic idea of the algorithm used to demonstrate 4.2.3 is essentially identical with that given in chapter 2. The major modification is to incorporate the concept of a pivot step as used in linear programming. As the reader will remember, the simplex method for the solution of linear programming problems is a systematic procedure for moving through a sequence of feasible bases (for the constraints of the problem) until a feasible basis associated with the highest value of the objective function is found.

Let the constraints of a linear programming problem be represented by $Ay = b$, $y \geq 0$, with

$$
A = \begin{bmatrix} 1 & \cdots & 0 & \cdots & a_{1,j} & \cdots & a_{1,k} \\ \vdots & & \vdots & & \vdots & & \vdots \\ 0 & \cdots & 1 & \cdots & a_{n,j} & \cdots & a_{n,k} \end{bmatrix},
$$

and assume that the columns $j_1, j_2, \ldots, j_n$ represent a feasible basis obtained in some intermediary stage of the simplex method. The method then proceeds by selecting a specific column j^* different from $j_1, \ldots, j_n$ —using a criterion that need not concern us at present—and performing what is known as a pivot step on this column. Explicitly this means the removal of a specific column from the feasible basis so that the remaining $n - 1$ columns plus the column j^* also form a feasible basis.

The actual computations involved in carrying out a pivot step involve expressing both the column to be brought into the basis and the vector b as linear combinations of the n columns $j_1, \ldots, j_n$; the column to be removed from the basis is then determined by a simple examination of certain ratios. Our interest is not, however, in the details of the computation, which may be found in any textbook on linear programming, but rather in the general question of whether a pivot step can be carried out and whether the column to be eliminated is unique.

The answers to these questions are quite well known and will merely be quoted here. First of all, if the set of non-negative vectors y that satisfy the constraints $Ay = b$ forms a bounded set, then the pivot step can always be carried out: there will be at least one vector to be eliminated from the feasible basis such that the remaining $n - 1$ vectors and j^* form a feasible basis. On the other hand, the vector to be eliminated need not be unique unless the following nondegeneracy assumption is made.

4.3.1. [NONDEGENERACY ASSUMPTION] *The vector b cannot be represented as a non-negative linear combination of fewer than n columns of the matrix A.*

We shall, in our discussion of the algorithm for theorem 4.2.3, make this nondegeneracy assumption. One of the standard techniques, such as a perturbation of the vector b or the use of lexicographic rules for breaking ties, can be called upon if the assumption is not naturally satisfied in any given application.

Before proceeding to the algorithm, let us summarize without proof these essential ideas from linear programming.

4.3.2. [THEOREM] *Let the columns $j_1, \ldots, j_n$ form a feasible basis for the equations $Ay = b$. Make nondegeneracy assumption 4.3.1 and assume, in addition, that the set $\{y | y \geq 0, Ay = b\}$ is bounded. Then if j^* is any column other than $j_1, \ldots, j_n$, there is a unique column to be eliminated from this feasible basis so that the remaining $n - 1$ columns and j^* form a new feasible basis.*

The operation of a pivot step should be compared with our replacement operation for primitive sets. In this latter case a specific member of the primitive set is to be eliminated, and a unique replacement is found from the list of vectors not in the primitive set. In a pivot step a specific column not in the feasible basis is to be brought in, and a unique vector to be eliminated is found among one of the n columns in the feasible basis. The operations are in a sense dual to each other—an observation which lies at the heart of the algorithm.

4.4. THE ALGORITHM FOR THEOREM 4.2.3

As in the case of our previous theorem, the algorithm begins at one of the n primitive sets containing $n - 1$ vectors representing the sides of the simplex S. To be definite, let the initial primitive set consist of the vectors $x^2, x^3, \ldots, x^n$ and one additional vector x^j, that vector in the list $x^{n+1}, \ldots, x^k$ with the largest first coordinate. We also remark that since $b \geq 0$, the first n columns of the matrix A form a feasible basis for $Ay = b$. The initial position of the algorithm may then be described as follows:

Primitive Set $2, 3, \ldots, n, j$

Feasible Basis $1, 2, 3, \ldots, n$

The vector x^j will be associated with the jth column of the matrix A. Let us perform a pivot step by introducing the jth column into the feasible basis consisting of the first n columns of A. Under our assumptions this can certainly be carried out and a unique column in this feasible basis will be eliminated. If the first column of A is the one to be eliminated, the problem is over since the vectors $x^2, \ldots, x^n, x^j$ form a primitive set, and the columns $2, \ldots, n, j$ a feasible basis. In general, however, this will not be the case and some column other than the first will be eliminated.

We will then be at a situation that can be described as follows:

$$\text{Primitive Set} \qquad 2, 3, \ldots, \qquad n, j,$$

$$\text{Feasible Basis} \quad 1, 2, 3, \ldots / \ldots, n, j,$$

in which the / refers to that column which has been eliminated by the pivot step.

The algorithm then proceeds by eliminating from the primitive set that vector associated with the column which has just been removed from the feasible basis. A new column j' will then be introduced into the primitive set, and we obtain

$$\text{Primitive Set} \qquad 2, 3, \ldots / \ldots, n, j, j',$$

$$\text{Feasible Basis} \quad 1, 2, 3, \ldots / \ldots, n, j$$

If $j' = 1$, then the problem is clearly over. If j' is different from one, then its corresponding column is brought into the feasible basis by a pivot step, and a column will be eliminated. The vector corresponding to this column is then eliminated from the primitive set, and the algorithm proceeds—alternating between replacement operations on primitive sets and pivot steps on feasible bases.

In general the algorithm will be faced at each iteration with a position which can be described as

$$\text{Primitive Set} \qquad j_1, j_2, \ldots, j_{n-1}, j_n,$$

$$\text{Feasible Basis} \quad 1, j_1, j_2, \ldots, j_{n-1} \quad .$$

The feasible basis will consist of column 1 and $n - 1$ remaining columns of A. The primitive set will contain the $n - 1$ vectors associated with these columns of A and one additional vector x^{j_n} different from x^1. Moreover, the given position will have been attained in one of two possible ways. Either the vector x^{j_n} will have just been introduced into the primitive set, or alternatively the j_nth column of A will have just been eliminated from the feasible basis.

The next step in the algorithm should be quite clear. If x^{j_n} has just been introduced into the primitive set, then introduce the j_nth column of A into the feasible basis by a pivot step. If the first column is eliminated, the algorithm terminates; otherwise it is again in a position with the properties described above. On the other hand, if the j_nth column of A has just been eliminated by a pivot step, then eliminate the vector x^{j_n} from the primitive set. If x^1 is introduced, the algorithm terminates; otherwise we are again in a position with similar properties.

The following hypothetical example illustrates a typical sequence of operations.

1. Primitive Set   2, 3, 4, 5, 18
   Feasible Basis   1, 2, 3, 4, 5
   Step 1. Introduce column 18 into the feasible basis and eliminate, say, column 3.
2. Primitive Set   2, 3, 4, 5, 18
   Feasible Basis   1, 2,   4, 5, 18
   Step 2. Eliminate x^3 from the primitive set, introducing, say, x^{10}.
3. Primitive Set   2, 4, 5, 18, 10
   Feasible Basis   1, 2, 4, 5, 18
   Step 3. Introduce column 10 into the feasible basis, eliminating, say, column 4.
4. Primitive Set   2, 4, 5, 18, 10
   Feasible Basis   1, 2,   5, 18, 10
   Step 4. Eliminate x^4 from the primitive set, and continue.

The algorithm will terminate only if the first column of A is eliminated from the feasible basis, or if x^1 is introduced into the primitive set—in both instances producing an answer of the desired sort. Since there are a finite number of possible positions, theorem 4.2.3 will be demonstrated if we can show, first, that all of the desired replacement operations can be carried out and, secondly, that the algorithm never returns to the same position.

Because of our assumption that the constraint set $\{y|y \geqq 0, Ay = b\}$ is bounded any desired pivot step can be carried out. The algorithm can, therefore, fail only if an impossible replacement step with a primitive set is called for. Can the algorithm be in a position in which the primitive set consists of $n - 1$ vectors representing sides of S, with the remaining vector to be removed. Unless this primitive set were the initial one (in which case cycling would already have occurred), the vector x^1, corresponding to the first side of the simplex, would already be included, and the algorithm would have terminated at some previous iteration.

We need therefore address ourselves only to the question of cycling, and here Lemke's argument may be applied in virtually the identical form as in chapter 2. Each position, other than the initial one, has precisely two adjacent positions, according to the rules of the algorithm. The first position to be revisited, therefore, cannot be one of the intermediary positions. But neither can it be the initial position, for only one operation can be carried out from this point. This concludes the finiteness argument for the algorithm and completes the proof of theorem 4.2.3.

4.5. KAKUTANI'S FIXED POINT THEOREM

As we shall see, theorem 4.2.3 has a number of applications in mathematical economics and related areas. It can be used to provide an alternative algorithm for Brouwer's theorem and an appropriate technique for a class of nonlinear programming problems more general than those we have previously considered. It is applicable to the determination of equilibrium prices and production and distribution plans in a general equilibrium model in which an activity analysis formulation is used to describe the production possibilities open to the economy. And it is also useful in demonstrating existence theorems and providing algorithms for a class of problems in n-person game theory.

All of these applications will be discussed, at one point or another, in the following chapters. At present, in order to give an immediate indication of the algorithm's potential applicability, I shall indicate how it may be used to demonstrate Kakutani's theorem—the generalization of Brouwer's theorem which is concerned with multiple-valued mappings.

Let us return therefore to the simplex S. Every point x in S will now be mapped not into a single point $f(x)$, but rather into a nonempty set of points on the simplex, which we denote by $\Phi(x)$ (fig. 4.5.1). The image of x under the mapping will consist of all of the points in $\Phi(x)$ and no longer be single valued.

We shall be interested in placing on the mapping a set of restrictions that guarantee the existence of a fixed point $\hat{x}$ in the sense that $\hat{x}$ is contained in $\Phi(\hat{x})$. Of course in the case in which $\Phi(x)$ is a single point—for each x—this reduces to the customary definition of a fixed point.

The first condition, which has no immediate analogue for single-valued mappings, is that each $\Phi(x)$ be a closed, convex set. Our methodology will

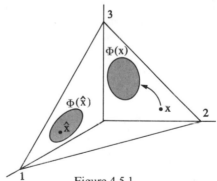

Figure 4.5.1

make use of this assumption in a crucial way, but it can be relaxed in various generalizations of Kakutani's theorem.

As we know, continuity of the mapping is required for Brouwer's theorem, and some version of continuity will be necessary in the generalization of single-valued mappings to set-valued mappings. The appropriate mathematical generalization has been given the name of upper semicontinuity.

4.5.1. [DEFINITION] *A point-to-set mapping* $x \rightarrow \Phi(x)$ *is defined to be upper semicontinuous if the following condition is satisfied: Let* $x^1, x^2, \ldots,$ $x^j \ldots$ *converge to* x. *Let* $\varphi^1 \in \Phi(x^1)$, $\varphi^2 \in \Phi(x^2)$, $\ldots$ *and assume that the sequence* $\varphi^1, \varphi^2, \ldots, \varphi^j, \ldots$ *converges to* φ. *Then* $\varphi \in \Phi(x)$.

The concept of upper semicontinuity will be illustrated by several examples, which display its appropriateness for economic problems. But it can be summarized in the following way. Let the x vectors be conceived of as parameters in an economic system, and for each x let $\Phi(x)$ be, loosely speaking, the set of possible responses to this particular vector of parameters. Then upper semicontinuity is equivalent to the statement: As the x vectors vary, a limit of possible responses is a response to a limiting parameter value.

For example, consider the two-person zero-sum-game with the following payoff matrix for player 1:

$$\begin{bmatrix} 2 & -1 \\ -3 & 4 \end{bmatrix}.$$

Let player 2 adopt a mixed strategy in which the first column is played with probability x and the second column with probability $1 - x$. For each x in $[0, 1]$, let $(\varphi, 1 - \varphi)$ represent the probability distributions on the rows of the matrix that maximize player 1's expected utility (fig. 4.5.2).

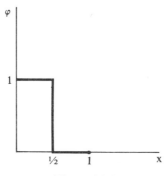

Figure 4.5.2

Clearly if $2x - (1 - x) > -3x + 4(1 - x)$, or equivalently $x > 1/2$, then $\varphi = 1$. If the reverse inequality holds strictly, then $\varphi = 0$. But if $x = 1/2$, so that the two expected payoffs are identical, then any value of φ in the interval $[0, 1]$ will be contained in $\Phi(x)$.

This particular mapping, which is multiple valued only at the point $x = 1/2$, is clearly upper semicontinuous. As another example, let Y be a closed, bounded set in n-dimensional space, conceived of as a set of feasible short-run production plans (fig. 4.5.3). For each price vector x, let $\Phi(x)$ be the set of vectors φ in Y that maximize profit, $x \cdot \varphi$. Then it is easy to demonstrate that this mapping, which may be multiple valued for various xs, is also upper semicontinuous.

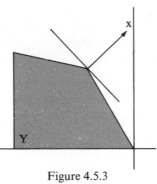

Figure 4.5.3

In order to obtain a point-to-set mapping that is not upper semicontinuous, consider the following example in which the simplex S is the unit interval $[0, 1]$ (fig. 4.5.4). In this example the mapping fails to be upper

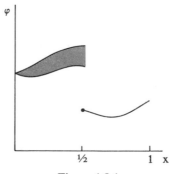

Figure 4.5.4

semicontinuous at the point $x = 1/2$ whose image is a single point—a positive distance away from the sequence of images $\Phi(x)$ for $x \to 1/2$ from below.

4.5.2. [KAKUTANI'S THEOREM] *Let the point-to-set mapping* $x \to \Phi(x)$ *of the simplex S into itself be upper semicontinuous. Assume that for each* x, $\Phi(x)$ *is a nonempty, closed, convex set. Then there exists a fixed point* $\hat{x} \in \Phi(\hat{x})$.

In many of the applications of Kakutani's theorem, the simplex S is replaced by a more general subset E on which the mapping is defined. As the following argument shows, Kakutani's theorem is still valid if the mapping is defined on an arbitrary, closed, bounded, convex subset E of n-dimensional space (fig. 4.5.5). We merely imbed the set E in a simplex S

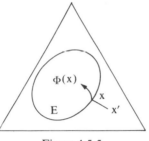

Figure 4.5.5

and define a mapping Φ' of S into itself whose fixed point must be contained in E. If $x \in E$, define $\Phi'(x) = \Phi(x)$. On the other hand, if $x' \in S$ but not in E, let x be that point of E which is closest to x' and define $\Phi'(x') = \Phi(x)$. The fact that E is closed permits x to be defined, and convexity of E implies a unique x for each x' not in E. Since x varies continuously with x', the mapping Φ' is upper semicontinuous if the original mapping was. But the fixed point $\hat{x} \in \Phi'(\hat{x})$ must be in E—since Φ' is in E—and therefore be a fixed point of the mapping Φ. This device, it should be remarked, is also useful in applying the algorithm—to both Brouwer's theorem and Kakutani's theorem—if the mapping is defined on a more general convex set than the simplex.

4.6. THE ALGORITHM FOR KAKUTANI'S THEOREM

In the present section I shall show how an approximate fixed point of a mapping satisfying the conditions of Kakutani's theorem can be obtained by an appropriate specification of the columns of the matrix A

and by the use of theorem 4.2.3. The precise sense in which the solution represents an approximation will be discussed in the following section.

Let the vectors $x^{n+1}, \ldots, x^k$ be a very fine grid on the simplex S; as usual, the list is augmented by the vectors $x^1, \ldots, x^n$ representing the sides of S. We construct the matrix

$$
A = \begin{array}{c}
\begin{array}{ccccccccc} x^1 & \cdots & x^n & x^{n+1} & \cdots & x^j & \cdots & x^k \end{array} \\
\begin{bmatrix}
1 & \cdots & 0 & a_{1,n+1} & \cdots & a_{1,j} & \cdots & a_{1,k} \\
\vdots & & \vdots & \vdots & & \vdots & & \vdots \\
0 & \cdots & 1 & a_{n,n+1} & \cdots & a_{n,j} & \cdots & a_{n,k}
\end{bmatrix}
\end{array}
$$

according to the following rule: For $j = n + 1, \ldots, k$, let $\varphi^j = (\varphi^j_1, \varphi^j_2, \ldots, \varphi^j_n)$ be *any* specific vector contained in the set $\Phi(x^j)$. Then define the jth column of A to be equal to $(\varphi^j_1 - x^j_1 + 1, \varphi^j_2 - x^j_2 + 1, \ldots, \varphi^j_n - x^j_n + 1)'$. Moreover let the vector b be given by $b = (1, 1, \ldots, 1)'$.

In order for theorem 4.2.3 to be applied, we need demonstrate only that the set of non-negative ys satisfying $Ay = b$ is a bounded set. But the jth column of A (for $j > n$) satisfies $\sum_{i=1}^{n} a_{i,j} = n$ (since $\sum_i \varphi^j_i = \sum_i x^j_i = 1$), and by addition of the rows of A we obtain

$$
(4.6.1) \qquad \sum_{1}^{n} y_i + n \sum_{n+1}^{k} y_i = n,
$$

which yields a bounded set for the y vectors.

Theorem 4.2.3 and its associated algorithm will therefore determine for us a primitive set $(x^{j_1}, \ldots, x^{j_n})$ such that the columns $j_1, \ldots, j_n$ form a feasible basis for $Ay = b$. Let us write these equations in the more explicit form

$$
y_1 \qquad + \sum_{j=n+1}^{k} y_j(\varphi^j_1 - x^j_1 + 1) = 1
$$

$$
(4.6.2) \qquad y_2 \qquad + \sum_{j=n+1}^{k} y_j(\varphi^j_2 - x^j_2 + 1) = 1
$$

$$
\qquad\qquad\quad \ddots
$$

$$
y_n + \sum_{j=n+1}^{k} y_j(\varphi^j_n - x^j_n + 1) = 1,
$$

with $y_j \geq 0$ and in fact equal to zero unless $j = (j_1, j_2, \ldots, j_n)$. The slack variable y_i (for $i = 1 \ldots, n$) will, of course, be equal to zero if the ith side of the simplex S is not a member of the primitive set.

As we shall see, if the grid $x^{n+1}, \ldots, x^k$ is sufficiently fine, y_i will be close to zero for $i = 1, \ldots, n$, and the remaining positive y_j will have a sum approximately equal to one. The vector

$$\hat{x} = \sum_{j=n+1}^{k} y_j x^j \Big/ \sum_{j=n+1}^{k} y_j$$

will be an approximate fixed point of the mapping in a sense that will subsequently be made clear. But let us return to this point after investigating the consequences of selecting a finer and finer sequence of grids.

For each such grid a primitive set, a collection of n columns from the matrix A, and a collection of n weights y_{j_i} associated with these columns will be produced by the algorithm. In the limit, as the number of grid points becomes infinite and dense on the simplex, a subsequence of these primitive sets can be selected to satisfy the following conditions:

1. The subsimplices associated with these primitive sets converge to a single vector $\hat{x}$.

2. Each column of A corresponding to a nonslack vector and having a positive weight converges to a vector $(\hat{\phi}_1^j - \hat{x}_1 + 1, \hat{\phi}_2^j - \hat{x}_2 + 1, \ldots, \hat{\phi}_n^j - \hat{x}_n + 1)'$. Moreover, using the upper semicontinuity of the mapping, each $\hat{\phi}^j = (\hat{\phi}_1^j, \ldots, \hat{\phi}_n^j)$ will be contained in $\Phi(\hat{x})$.

3. The positive weights in 4.6.2 converge to a sequence of non-negative weights $\hat{y}$.

In the limit, our equations can now be written as

$$\hat{y}_1 \qquad + \sum_l \hat{y}_{j_l}(\hat{\phi}_1^{j_l} - \hat{x}_1 + 1) = 1$$

(4.6.3) $$\hat{y}_2 \qquad + \sum_l \hat{y}_{j_l}(\hat{\phi}_2^{j_l} - \hat{x}_2 + 1) = 1$$

$$\hat{y}_n + \sum_l \hat{y}_{j_l}(\hat{\phi}_n^{j_l} - \hat{x}_n + 1) = 1,$$

with $\hat{y}_i \geq 0$ and equal to zero if $\hat{x}_i > 0$ (for $i = 1, \ldots, n$), since in this event the ith side of the simplex is not a member of the primitive set for sufficiently fine grids;

$$\hat{\phi}^{j_l} \in \Phi(\hat{x}); \quad \text{and}$$

$$\hat{y}_{j_l} \geq 0.$$

Of course the selection of a subsequence of primitive sets whose associated parameters tend to a limit satisfying equations 4.6.3 is a highly nonconstructive aspect of our argument for Kakutani's theorem. It cannot be carried out on a computer in a finite length of time, and in any specific application an approximation of these equations is the best that can be expected. But let us imagine that we have an exact solution to equations 4.6.3; we shall then argue that $\hat{y}_1 = \hat{y}_2 = \ldots = \hat{y}_n = 0$, that $\hat{y}_{j_1} + \hat{y}_{j_2} + \ldots = 1$, and finally that $\hat{x}$ is contained in $\Phi(\hat{x})$.

In order to obtain first the inequality $\Sigma \hat{y}_{j_i} \geq 1$, let us add together those equations 4.6.3 for which $\hat{x}_i > 0$ and therefore $\hat{y}_i = 0$. If the number of such equations is N (which is positive), we obtain

$$\Sigma \hat{y}_{j_i} \left(\sum_{\hat{x}_i > 0} \hat{\phi}_i^{j_i} - \sum_{\hat{x}_i > 0} \hat{x}_i \right) + N \Sigma \hat{y}_{j_i} = N.$$

But

$$\sum_{\hat{x}_i > 0} \hat{x}_i = 1,$$

and

$$\sum_{\hat{x}_i > 0} \hat{\phi}_i^{j_i} \leq 1.$$

Therefore $N \Sigma \hat{y}_{j_i} \geq N$ and $\Sigma \hat{y}_{j_i} \geq 1$.

The reverse inequality, $\Sigma \hat{y}_{j_i} \leq 1$, is a consequence of 4.6.1, which in our notation states that

$$\hat{y}_1 + \ldots + \hat{y}_n + n(\hat{y}_{j_1} + \hat{y}_{j_2} + \ldots) = n.$$

From this relationship we see that not only

$$\hat{y}_{j_1} + \hat{y}_{j_2} + \ldots = 1,$$

but also

$$\hat{y}_1 = \hat{y}_2 = \ldots = \hat{y}_n = 0.$$

But as a consequence of these two facts, equations 4.6.3 may be written in the simpler form

$$\Sigma \hat{y}_{j_i} \hat{\phi}_1^{j_i} = \hat{x}_1$$
$$\vdots$$
$$\Sigma \hat{y}_{j_i} \hat{\phi}_n^{j_i} = \hat{x}_n.$$

Since $\hat{\phi}^{j_i} \in \Phi(\hat{x})$, by construction, and $\Phi(\hat{x})$ is convex, it follows that $\hat{x} \in \Phi(\hat{x})$, and $\hat{x}$ is the fixed point for which we are searching (fig. 4.6.1).

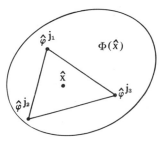

Figure 4.6.1

4.7. THE SENSE OF THE APPROXIMATION*

Kakutani's theorem has now been demonstrated, but the proof, as with Brouwer's theorem, makes use of the nonconstructive step of selecting a subsequence of grids for which a number of relevant variables converge. Because this step is impossible to carry out in practice, we need to inquire as to the type of approximation actually provided by equations 4.6.2.

The algorithm, when applied to a finite grid of vectors on S, will produce a primitive set $(x^{j_1}, x^{j_2}, \ldots)$ and a collection of associated vectors φ^{j_1}, $\varphi^{j_2}, \ldots$ such that

$$\varphi^{j_l} \in \Phi(x^{j_l}) \qquad \text{for } j_l > n.$$

We will also obtain a sequence of non-negative weights $y_{j_1}, y_{j_2}, \ldots$ such that equations 4.6.2 are satisfied. As the grid tends to infinity, the sum of these weights $y_{j_1} + y_{j_2} + \ldots$ has been shown to tend to unity; in a finite grid the weights can be used to average the vectors in the primitive set (other than those representing sides) and their associated images by defining

$$\hat{x} = \sum y_{j_l} x^{j_l} / \sum y_{j_l} \quad \text{and}$$

(4.7.1)

$$\hat{\varphi} = \sum y_{j_l} \varphi^{j_l} / \sum y_{j_l}.$$

Ideally we would like the pair of vectors $(\hat{x}, \hat{\varphi})$ to satisfy two properties that would permit us to regard them as approximations to the fixed point provided by Kakutani's theorem. First of all, we should like them to be quite close if the grid is sufficiently fine. And secondly, we should like $\hat{\varphi}$ to be within a small, preassigned distance of $\Phi(\hat{x})$, the image of $\hat{x}$ under the mapping (fig. 4.7.1). In this statement, by the distance between a point φ and a closed, bounded, convex set Φ we mean the distance between φ

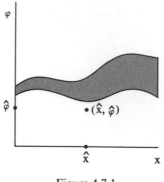

Figure 4.7.1

and the closest point to φ in Φ—using some conventional norm like $\max(|x_1|, \ldots, |x_n|)$ to define distances between pairs of points.

Unfortunately upper semicontinuity is a sufficiently capricious property of mappings that this second property cannot be guaranteed for this particular choice of the vector $\hat{x}$. The best that can be said, without imposing additional conditions on the mapping, is that there will be some vector close to $\hat{x}$ whose distance from its own image set is within a small, preassigned bound. As the following lemma indicates, the first property poses no particular difficulty.

4.7.2. [LEMMA] *If the grid is selected so fine that any two points x and x' in the same subsimplex corresponding to a primitive set satisfy $|x - x'| \leq \varepsilon/n(n - 1)$, then $|\hat{\varphi} - \hat{x}| \leq \varepsilon$.*

In order to demonstrate this inequality, which is considerably poorer than what does occur in practice, let us denote by $x^{i_1}, \ldots, x^{i_m}$ the sides of S that appear in the final primitive set; therefore $y_i = 0$ if $i = 1, \ldots, n$ but is different from $i_1, \ldots, i_m$. Let us add together those $n - m$ equations from 4.6.2 for which $i \neq i_1, \ldots, i_m$. Denoting this index set by T, we have

$$n - m = \Sigma y_{j_l} \sum_{i \in T} (\varphi_i^{j_l} - x_i^{j_l} + 1) \leq (n - m + 1)\Sigma y_{j_l} - \Sigma y_{j_l} \cdot \sum_{i \in T} x_i^{j_l}.$$

But

$$\sum_{i \in T} x_i^{j_l} = 1 - \sum_{i \notin T} x_i^{j_l} \geq 1 - m\varepsilon/n(n - 1),$$

since $x_i^{j_l} \leq \varepsilon/n(n - 1)$ for $i \notin T$. [Remember that the side x^i is in the primitive set for $i \notin T$, and any two points in the same primitive set are separated by a distance less than or equal to $\varepsilon/n(n - 1)$.] The above inequality becomes

$$(n - m) \leq \left(n - m + \frac{\varepsilon \cdot m}{n(n-1)} \right) \Sigma y_{j_l},$$

so that

$$\Sigma y_{j_l} \geq \frac{n - m}{n - m + \dfrac{\varepsilon \cdot m}{n(n-1)}}.$$

Taking $m = n - 1$ (which gives the worst bound), we have

$$\Sigma y_{j_l} \geq \frac{1}{1 + \varepsilon/n}.$$

In order to deduce an upper bound for Σy_{j_l}, we add *all* of the equations 4.6.2. together and obtain $\Sigma y_i + n\Sigma y_{j_l} = n$, from which we see that $\Sigma y_{j_l} \leq 1$, and moreover $y_i \leq n[1 - \Sigma y_{j_l}] \leq \varepsilon/(1 + \varepsilon/n)$.

It can then be shown that 4.6.2 implies that for each i

$$\left| \frac{\Sigma y_{j_l} \varphi_i^{j_l}}{\Sigma y_{j_l}} - \frac{\Sigma y_{j_l} x_i^{j_l}}{\Sigma y_{j_l}} \right| \leq \varepsilon,$$

which is the conclusion of the lemma.

The lemma states that there is a convex combination of the vectors $\varphi^{j_l} - x^{j_l}$ [with $\varphi^{j_l} \in \Phi(x^{j_l})$] that is close to zero in all coordinates. To obtain an intuitive understanding of this statement, let us examine figure 4.7.2 in which $S = [0, 1]$ and the mapping $\Phi(x)$ is given by

$$\begin{aligned}
\Phi(x) &= 1 && \text{if } x < \tfrac{2}{3}, \\
\Phi(x) &= [0, 1] && \text{if } x = \tfrac{2}{3}, \\
\Phi(x) &= 0 && \text{if } x > \tfrac{2}{3}.
\end{aligned}$$

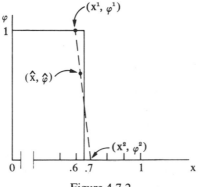

Figure 4.7.2

If the grid consists of all vectors in the unit interval with a denominator of 10, the final primitive set will consist of the pair $x^1 = 6/10$ and $x^2 = 7/10$. x^1 will be associated with the point $\varphi^1 = 1$ and x^2 with $\varphi^2 = 0$. If $\hat{x} = y_1 x^1 + y_2 x^2$ and $\hat{\varphi} = y_1 \varphi^1 + y_2 \varphi^2$, with $y_1 + y_2 = 1$, then the weights y_1 and y_2 may be selected to make $\hat{x}$ and $\hat{\varphi}$ not only close, but actually equal, with a common value of $\hat{x} = \hat{\varphi} = 7/11$. But we cannot say that $\hat{\varphi}$ is actually close to $\Phi(\hat{x})$. The best that can be said is that there is a vector close to $\hat{x}$ (in this case 2/3) which is itself close to its own image set.

The proof that this is a general phenomenon is quite tedious and will be left to the reader who is familiar with arguments of this sort. The basic idea is that upper semicontinuity of the mapping $x \rightarrow \Phi(x)$ is identical with the statement that the set

(4.7.3) $G = \{(x, \varphi)|\varphi \in \Phi(x)\}$

is a closed subset of the product space of the simplex with itself (fig. 4.7.3). Lemma 4.7.2 can then be used to demonstrate the following conclusion.

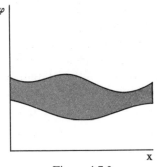

Figure 4.7.3

4.7.4. [LEMMA] *Let δ be an arbitrary positive number. Then there is an $\varepsilon > 0$, with the following property: Take the grid so fine that any two vectors in the subsimplex corresponding to a primitive set have a distance less than or equal to ε. Define $\hat{x}$ and $\hat{\varphi}$ by 4.7.1.*

Then there is a vector x^*, with $|\hat{x} - x^*| \leq \delta$, such that $\hat{\varphi}$ has a distance less than or equal to δ from $\Phi(x^*)$.

Any sense of disappointment with this particular form of our approximation should be balanced by the observation that in most applications the approximation is far better than it might superficially appear to be and corresponds very closely to the needs of the problem. For example, when the algorithm is applied to the general Walrasian model, it will provide us with a price vector $\hat{\pi}$—obtained by averaging the vectors in the final primitive set other than those representing the sides of S—and a corresponding aggregate production plan $\hat{y}$. In the spirit of lemma 4.7.4, the production plan will not necessarily maximize profit at the price vector $\hat{\pi}$ produced by the algorithm, but rather at some neighboring price vector π^*. But this means that the profit achieved by the plan $\hat{y}$ will be very close to the maximum profit that can be achieved at prices $\hat{\pi}$. This is clearly the relevant sense of approximation, since any possible increase in profit obtained by selecting an alternative production plan will be sufficiently small to escape the notice of an entrepreneur motivated by profit maximization.

Moreover, if the grid is sufficiently fine, the discrepancy between supply and the market demand at prices $\hat{\pi}$ will be small for all commodities. Unintended inventories, arising from a price vector that does not clear all markets precisely, will be insufficient to provide a signal for the revision of prices. In this example, and in most others to which the algorithm can be applied, the vector generated by the final primitive set is an adequate approximate solution to the problem.

4.8. AN EXAMPLE OF THE ALGORITHM

Chapter 5 will be devoted to an extensive discussion of several applications of the algorithm, in particular to the computation of equilibrium prices and production plans in a general Walrasian model. In order, however, to provide the reader with a sense of the algorithm's efficiency, I shall include in this chapter a simple numerical application of a problem previously discussed by means of Brouwer's theorem.

Let

$$
B = \begin{bmatrix} b_{11} & \cdots & b_{1n} \\ \vdots & & \vdots \\ b_{n1} & \cdots & b_{nn} \end{bmatrix}
$$

be an arbitrary $n \times n$ matrix. We shall attempt to determine a vector x on the simplex S, and a constant a, such that

$$
\sum_j b_{ij} x_j \geq a,
$$

with the additional proviso that $\sum_j b_{ij} x_j = a$ if $x_i > 0$. Variations of this class of problems can be shown to include the general convex quadratic programming problem and the determination of Nash equilibrium points for a two-person non-zero-sum game.

We construct the mapping whose fixed point gives the required answer in the following simple fashion: For each $x \in S$, let $\Phi(x)$ be the set of all vectors $\varphi = (\varphi_1, \ldots, \varphi_n)$ on the simplex that minimize the linear function $\Sigma_i \varphi_i (\Sigma_j b_{ij} x_j)$. The conditions for Kakutani's theorem are clearly satisfied, and we conclude that there exists an $\hat{x}$ contained in its own image $\Phi(\hat{x})$. In other words, the inequality

$$\sum_i \varphi_i (\sum_j b_{ij} \hat{x}_j) \geq \sum_i \hat{x}_i (\sum_j b_{ij} \hat{x}_j)$$

holds for every vector φ on the simplex. In particular, by selecting φ to have all of its components zero, except for the ith component, we obtain

$$\sum_j b_{ij} \hat{x}_j \geq \sum_i \hat{x}_i (\sum_j b_{ij} \hat{x}_j) = a$$

for $i = 1, \ldots, n$. It then follows trivially that we must have equality if $\hat{x}_i > 0$.

Let us consider the following numerical example in which $n = 5$ and the matrix B is given by

$$B = \begin{bmatrix} 2. & 2. & 1. & -0.3 & -0.8 \\ 2. & 3. & 0. & -0.8 & -0.4 \\ 1. & 0. & 4. & -0.7 & -0.7 \\ 0.3 & 0.8 & 0.7 & 0. & 0. \\ 0.8 & 0.4 & 0.7 & 0. & 0. \end{bmatrix}.$$

The vectors $x^1, \ldots, x^5$ will, as usual, represent the sides of the simplex S; $x^6, \ldots, x^k$ are taken to consist of all vectors of the form $(m_1/100, \ldots, m_5/100)$ with m_i representing positive integers summing to 100. Ties between pairs of vectors with identical coordinates will be broken by the rule to be described in chapter 6.

In order to construct the matrix

$$A = \begin{matrix} & x^1 & \cdots & x^5 & x^6 & \cdots & x^j & \cdots \\ & \begin{bmatrix} 1 & \cdots & 0 & & \cdots & a_{1,j} & \cdots \\ \vdots & & \vdots & & & \vdots & \\ 0 & \cdots & 1 & & \cdots & a_{5,j} & \cdots \end{bmatrix} \end{matrix},$$

we must associate with each vector x^j a specific column a_j, using the mapping to which Kakutani's theorem is applied. For a specific vector x^j we evaluate the five linear functions

$$b_{11}x_1^j + \ldots + b_{15}x_5^j$$
$$\vdots$$
$$b_{51}x_1^j + \cdots + b_{55}x_5^j$$

Let the ith linear function be the smallest; in the event that two or more functions are the smallest, let i be the index corresponding to the first of these. The vector $\varphi^i = (\varphi_1^i, \varphi_2^i, \ldots, \varphi_5^i)'$ whose ith coordinate is unity and whose remaining coordinates are zero will be in $\Phi(x^j)$. The jth column is therefore defined to be $a_j = \varphi^i - x^j + 1$. As before the vector $b = (1, \ldots, 1)'$.

The algorithm terminated after 663 iterations in 6 seconds of computer time on an IBM 360–50. The columns of the matrix below represent the numerators of the vectors in the final primitive set:

$$100 \cdot \pi^{j_1} \quad 100 \cdot \pi^{j_2} \quad 100 \cdot \pi^{j_3} \quad 100 \cdot \pi^{j_4} \quad 100 \cdot \pi^{j_5}$$

$$\begin{bmatrix} 10 & 10 & 10 & 11 & 11 \\ 13 & 13 & 13 & 12 & 13 \\ 14 & 15 & 15 & 15 & 14 \\ 25 & 24 & 25 & 25 & 25 \\ 38 & 38 & 37 & 37 & 37 \end{bmatrix}.$$

The associated feasible basis is given by

$$0.146 \begin{bmatrix} 0 - 0.10 + 1 \\ 0 - 0.13 + 1 \\ 1 - 0.14 + 1 \\ 0 - 0.25 + 1 \\ 0 - 0.38 + 1 \end{bmatrix} + 0.104 \begin{bmatrix} 1 - 0.10 + 1 \\ 0 - 0.13 + 1 \\ 0 - 0.15 + 1 \\ 0 - 0.24 + 1 \\ 0 - 0.38 + 1 \end{bmatrix} + 0.372 \begin{bmatrix} 0 - 0.10 + 1 \\ 0 - 0.13 + 1 \\ 0 - 0.15 + 1 \\ 0 - 0.25 + 1 \\ 1 - 0.37 + 1 \end{bmatrix}$$

$$+ 0.129 \begin{bmatrix} 0 - 0.11 + 1 \\ 1 - 0.12 + 1 \\ 0 - 0.15 + 1 \\ 0 - 0.25 + 1 \\ 0 - 0.37 + 1 \end{bmatrix} + 0.249 \begin{bmatrix} 0 - 0.11 + 1 \\ 0 - 0.13 + 1 \\ 0 - 0.14 + 1 \\ 1 - 0.25 + 1 \\ 0 - 0.37 + 1 \end{bmatrix} = \begin{bmatrix} 1 \\ 1 \\ 1 \\ 1 \\ 1 \end{bmatrix}.$$

Notice that the sum of the weights $.146 + .104 + .372 + .129 + .249$ equals 1.000. (Each of the above columns has a common sum of 5.) These equations may therefore be written as

$$\begin{bmatrix} .104 \\ .129 \\ .146 \\ .249 \\ .372 \end{bmatrix} = \begin{bmatrix} .10 & .10 & .10 & .11 & .11 \\ .13 & .13 & .13 & .12 & .13 \\ .14 & .15 & .15 & .15 & .14 \\ .25 & .24 & .25 & .25 & .25 \\ .38 & .38 & .37 & .37 & .37 \end{bmatrix} \begin{bmatrix} .146 \\ .104 \\ .372 \\ .129 \\ .249 \end{bmatrix},$$

and the vector $(.104, .129, .146, .249, .372)'$ is the approximation $\hat{x}$ referred to in the previous section. It is only an approximation, since

$$B\hat{x} = \begin{bmatrix} 0.2384 \\ 0.2455 \\ 0.2531 \\ 0.2364 \\ 0.2368 \end{bmatrix},$$

and these coordinates are not identical. The correct value of a is 0.2327 and the value of x^* is $(0.102, 0.128, 0.142, 0.263, 0.364)$, which deviates somewhat from the suggested approximation.

The reader should observe that the problem above is equivalent to the quadratic programming problem

$$\max f(z) = -z' \begin{bmatrix} 1.0 & 1.0 & 0.5 \\ 1.0 & 1.5 & 0. \\ 0.5 & 0. & 2.0 \end{bmatrix} z + [1, 1, 1]z$$

subject to $0.3z_1 + 0.8z_2 + 0.7z_3 \geq 1$,
$$0.8z_1 + 0.4z_2 + 0.7z_3 \geq 1,$$
$$z \geq 0.$$

The optimal solution is then given by $\hat{z} = (\hat{x}_1/a, \hat{x}_2/a, \hat{x}_3/a)$ and the associated Kuhn-Tucker multipliers are given by $\hat{x}_4/a, \hat{x}_5/a$.

4.9. A GENERALIZED INTERSECTION THEOREM

In the previous chapter I provided a set of sufficient conditions for n closed sets $C_1, \ldots, C_n$ on the simplex to have a nonempty intersection. The result can be looked upon as a limiting form of the theorem asserting the existence of a primitive set with a distinct set of labels.

The major theorem of the present chapter can also be rephrased in a similar fashion.

4.9.1. [THEOREM] (Scarf 1967b) *Let* $C_1, \ldots, C_n, \ldots, C_k$ *be closed sets on the simplex* S *with the following properties:*

a. $\bigcup_1^k C_i = S$; *and*

b. *every vector on the side* $x_i = 0$ *is contained in* C_i, *for* $i = 1, \ldots, n$. *Let*

$$A = \begin{bmatrix} 1 & \cdots & 0 & a_{1,n+1} & \cdots & a_{1,k} \\ \vdots & & \vdots & \vdots & & \vdots \\ 0 & \cdots & 1 & a_{n,n+1} & \cdots & a_{n,k} \end{bmatrix},$$

and $b = (b_1, \ldots, b_n)'$ *be a non-negative vector such that* $\{y | y \geq 0, Ay = b\}$ *is a bounded set. Then there exist n columns of* A—$j_1, \ldots, j_n$—*which form a feasible basis for* $Ay = b$ *and are such that* $C_{j_1} \cap C_{j_2} \cap \ldots \cap C_{j_n}$ *is not empty.*

The theorem is demonstrated by selecting a fine grid of vectors $x^{n+1}, \ldots$ on the simplex. A matrix with n rows and one column for each such vector is constructed, first by determining a set C_j—say, the one with the smallest index—which contains the given vector and then by associating the vector with the column $(a_{1j}, a_{2j}, \ldots, a_{nj})'$. The hypotheses of theorem 4.2.3 are clearly satisfied and we obtain a primitive set each of whose vectors is contained in a distinct set $(C_{j_1}, C_{j_2}, \ldots, C_{j_n})$ and which is such that the columns $j_1, \ldots, j_n$ of A form a feasible basis for $Ay = b$. The theorem is obtained by a simple passage to the limit.

Even though theorem 4.9.1 seems to require the methods of the present chapter, Kannai (1970) has provided a demonstration that draws only on Brouwer's theorem, in a very subtle and ingenious fashion.

CHAPTER 5

The Computation of Equilibria in a General Walrasian Model and Other Applications

5.1. Statement of the Problem

The present chapter will examine several applications of the methodology embodied in theorem 4.2.3. Perhaps the most interesting application—from an economic point of view—will be to the general Walrasian model, in which an explicit production sector is added to the model of exchange that we have already studied.

As before, each consumer will determine his consumption plan by maximizing utility subject to the constraint that expenditure, at the prevailing set of prices, shall not exceed the income generated by the sale of his productive factors. On the other hand, the independent producing units in the economy are assumed to select production plans that maximize profit, all inputs and outputs being evaluated at the prevailing prices. The vector of prices for all of the goods and services in the economy forms the only link between these independent units and must be selected correctly to lead to mutually consistent decisions. The prices must be such that no producer has a compelling motivation to search for higher profits by the selection of an alternative mode of production. In addition, the discrepancy between supply and demand should be sufficiently small to induce no revision of the list of prices.

In order to display this interaction the Walrasian model distinguishes three basic components of the economic process: the technological possibilities of production, the individual consumer's preferences for consumption, and the distribution of resources among the consumers prior to production. We shall assume that the technology is described by an activity analysis matrix

$$(5.1.1) \qquad B = \begin{bmatrix} -1 & \cdots & 0 & b_{1,n+1} & \cdots & b_{1,m} \\ \vdots & & \vdots & \vdots & & \vdots \\ 0 & \cdots & -1 & b_{n,n+1} & \cdots & b_{n,m} \end{bmatrix}$$

each of whose columns represent a possible production plan with inputs described by negative numbers and outputs by positive numbers. The activities can be operated simultaneously, each at an arbitrary non-negative level, so that the set of production plans available to the economy will be given by the set of vectors $\{By | y \geq 0\}$. It should be remarked that the computational procedure does not require an activity analysis formulation of production; it can be modified quite simply to accommodate the use of production functions or more general production possibility sets if the customary convexity assumptions are made.

On the demand side of the economy, each consumer will be faced with a vector of prices for all of the goods and services available in the economy. His income—or wealth if the model is dynamic—is calculated under the assumption that he can dispose entirely of his initial resource endowment at these prevailing prices. His commodity demands are then represented as a systematic function of all relative prices.

We shall be concerned with the market demand functions $\xi_1(\pi), \ldots,$ $\xi_n(\pi)$ and the vector $w = (w_1, \ldots, w_n)$ describing the total resource endowment of the economy prior to production. The market demands will, in general, be obtained by the summation of individual demand functions, and the vector w by the addition of all stocks of commodities that are privately owned prior to production. Since the demand functions depend only on relative prices, we shall make the customary assumption that prices have been normalized to add up to unity and that the demand functions are continuous on the simplex S. The only additional requirement to be imposed is the Walras law

$$(5.1.2) \qquad \pi_1 \xi_1(\pi) + \ldots + \pi_n \xi_n(\pi) \equiv \pi_1 w_1 + \ldots + \pi_n w_n,$$

the identity obtained by the summation of individual budget constraints.

Aside from continuity and the Walras law, both of which are required for the algorithm to be successful, the demand functions are completely arbitrary. They can, if one prefers, be the result of an econometric study of aggregate responses to changing prices and need not even be based on the summation of individual demand functions. Moreover, none of the stringent assumptions—such as gross substitutability—that are typically assumed in the pure trade case in order to guarantee the global stability of a price adjustment mechanism need be made.

A competitive equilibrium is defined by a vector of prices π^* on the simplex S and a set of non-negative activity levels y^* such that the following two conditions are satisfied:

5.1.3. [DEFINITION] *A price vector π^* and a vector of activity levels y^* constitute a competitive equilibrium if:*

a. *Supply equals demand in all markets, or $\xi(\pi^*) = By^* + w$; and*

b. *production is consistent with profit maximization in the sense that*

$$\sum_i \pi_i^* b_{ij} \leq 0, \qquad \text{with equality if } y_j^* > 0.$$

The existence problem has been one of the major preoccupations of mathematical economists during the last two decades, and, as we now know, if certain relatively mild assumptions are imposed on the model, there will indeed be a competitive equilibrium. In our formulation it is sufficient to assume that the set of activity levels that give rise to a non-negative net supply of all commodities

$$\{y|y \geq 0, \quad By + w \geq 0\},$$

forms a bounded set. We then have the following theorem, for the proof of which an algorithm will be described in the next section.

5.1.4. [THEOREM] *Assume that $\{y|y \geq 0, By + w \geq 0\}$ is a bounded set. Then there exists an equilibrium price vector and production plan.*

Before proceeding to the details of the algorithm, it may be appropriate to indicate at this point why a number of alternative approaches that may seem sound on intuitive grounds cannot be expected to work in general. Consider, first of all, the possibility of deducing the equilibrium price vector from the conditions of zero profitability alone. Figure 5.1.1 illustrates a production possibility set arising from an activity analysis model with three nondisposal activities.

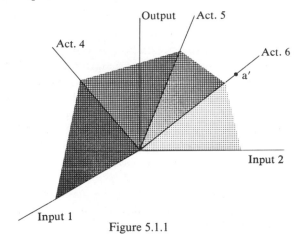

Figure 5.1.1

If it is known that the competitive equilibrium involves a production plan requiring the use of a pair of linearly independent activities such as 5 and 6 (in the general case $n - 1$ activities), then the relative prices can be determined immediately by the condition that each one of these activities shall have a zero profit. From a knowledge of relative prices, the equilibrium activity levels can be obtained by solving the equations

$$(5.1.5) \qquad \xi(\pi^*) - w = By^*$$

under the assumption that the components of y^* are different from zero only for those $n - 1$ activities that have been used to generate the relative prices.

The immediate difficulty, of course, is that the set of $n - 1$ linearly independent activities to be used in equilibrium may have been incorrectly specified. This would reveal itself, first of all, if the relative prices obtained by the zero-profit conditions were not all non-negative. But even if the relative prices were non-negative, a further difficulty would arise if the unique solution of 5.1.5 gave rise to activity levels some of which were negative.

One or the other of these difficulties will arise if the wrong set of $n - 1$ activities is selected. But of course it is too much to require of a computational procedure that it guess the correct set of activities at the outset. Perhaps an algorithm can be constructed by analogy with the simplex method for linear programming: Start with some collection of $n - 1$ linearly independent activities and move to an adjacent collection by some systematic rule should one of the prices or activity levels turn out to be negative.

It needs only a moment's thought, however, to see that no algorithm can be constructed along these lines for there is no difficulty in exhibiting quite reasonable examples in which fewer than $n - 1$ activities are in use in equilibrium—as illustrated by point a' in the figure above. The linear equations arising from the zero profitability conditions would therefore be inadequate to determine relative prices by themselves. In fact the situation may be so extreme that none of the productive activities at all are used in equilibrium: the consumers may prefer merely to trade their initial resources, and the zero-profitability conditions will furnish no information about relative prices.

It should be emphasized that this difficulty is not a question of degeneracy in the sense in which it is used in linear programming. If the data of the problem are perturbed slightly, there is no reason whatsoever to expect a full set of $n - 1$ activities to appear in the solution; after all, there may not even be $n - 1$ activities, other than the disposal activities. We cannot, therefore, expect an algorithm along these lines to be successful in general. Of course there may be specific problems in which several activities can be assumed with great certainty to appear at equilibrium, and computational procedures should make use of information of this sort whenever possible.

Let us turn to an alternative approach of some intuitive appeal—the possibility of converting the search for equilibrium prices and production plans into a nonlinear programming problem. In one sense this can always be done, according to the well-known theorems of welfare economics relating competitive equilibria to Pareto optimal production and distribution plans. In the quite general case in which each utility function is concave, Pareto optimum plans may be obtained by the maximization of a non-negative linear combination of the utilities, subject to the constraints of the technology and total resource endowment. This is a conventional nonlinear programming problem that will generate a vector of shadow prices having many of the required properties of an equilibrium price vector. No activity will make a positive profit at these prices, and the activities in use will, in fact, make a profit of zero. Moreover, no individual consumer will be capable of exchanging the commodity bundle allocated to him by the maximization problem for one of higher utility.

But of course there is a vital drawback to this method. If the utility weights are not correctly selected, the expenditure of each consumer will bear no relationship whatsoever to the income generated from the sale of his productive factors. Unless we are willing to neglect this vital link in the economic system completely, the problem has merely been shifted from the determination of equilibrium prices to the determination of appropriate utility weights, a problem which also requires the use of fixed point techniques.

There may indeed be specific examples for which it is easier to work with mappings in the space of utility weights rather than commodity sectors—problems in which the number of consumers or types of consumers is quite small relative to the number of commodities. An extreme example, in which a nonlinear programming technique should probably be used instead of the algorithm of the next section, arises when the market demand functions themselves may be derived from a single utility function —either because the individual utility functions are capable of aggregation or because we see no great restriction in selecting market demand functions with this property.

The use of a pure price-adjustment mechanism, in which prices are systematically revised based on the discrepancy between supply and demand, is a final candidate for an algorithm to calculate equilibrium prices and production plans. There is a slight technical problem here in the sense that a production possibility set with constant returns to scale does not produce a unique supply response as a function of price; at the least the scale of production is indeterminate. But in practice this should present no serious difficulty since a slight smoothing will produce a strictly convex production set with unique supply functions. The actual difficulty is much more serious: in order to guarantee that a small-step gradient method, such as the Walrasian tâtonnement, does indeed converge, very stringent conditions on the demand functions need to be imposed even in a pure exchange model. And in the case in which there are decreasing returns to scale in production we are unaware of *any* conditions on the utility functions alone that guarantee convergence—other than rather special conditions, such as aggregation into a single utility function. The price-adjustment mechanism has therefore a very limited theoretical basis as an algorithm. And even when it does converge, it may be no more efficient as a computational technique than those we are about to display.

5.2. A COMPUTATIONAL PROCEDURE FOR THE WALRASIAN MODEL

In this section I shall describe one of the several ways in which theorem 4.2.3 can be applied to the computation of equilibrium prices. We begin, as usual, with a very large list of price vectors $\pi^{n+1}, \ldots, \pi^k$ on the simplex S, augmented by the vectors $\pi^1, \ldots, \pi^n$, which represent the sides of the simplex. In order to apply theorem 4.2.3, we need to construct a matrix

$$
\begin{array}{ccccccc}
\pi^1 & \cdots & \pi^n & \pi^{n+1} & \cdots & \pi^j & \cdots & \pi^k
\end{array}
$$

$$
A = \begin{bmatrix}
1 & \cdots & 0 & a_{1,n+1} & \cdots & a_{1,j} & \cdots & a_{1,k} \\
\vdots & & \vdots & \vdots & & \vdots & & \vdots \\
0 & \cdots & 1 & a_{n,n+1} & \cdots & a_{n,j} & \cdots & a_{n,k}
\end{bmatrix}
$$

whose columns are to be associated with the vectors in the list according to some definite rule, and in addition we must specify the non-negative vector b.

5.2.1. [RULE OF ASSOCIATION] (Scarf 1967c) *To construct the column* $(a_{1,j}, \ldots, a_{n,j})'$ *associated with the vector* π^j *(with* $j > n$*), begin by searching through the columns of the activity analysis matrix B to find an activity that maximizes profit at the prices* π^j. *Let this activity be denoted by l:*

if there are several profit-maximizing activities, an arbitrary selection of one of them is made. The maximum profit is therefore given by $p^j = \pi_1^j b_{1,l} + \ldots + \pi_n^j b_{n,l}.$

a. *If* $p^j > 0$, *define*

$$(a_{1,j}, \ldots, a_{n,j})' = -(b_{1,l}, \ldots, b_{n,l})'.$$

b. *If* $p^j \leq 0$, *define*

$$(a_{1,j}, \ldots, a_{n,j})' = [\xi_1(\pi^j), \ldots, \xi_n(\pi^j)]'.$$

The matrix A will be composed of two distinct types of columns: either the negative of an activity in B which maximizes profit at the given set of prices—should this profit be positive—or the market demand evaluated at this price vector. As we shall see, this association, arbitrary as it may seem, leads directly to an approximate equilibrium price vector.

The vector b is defined to be equal to w, the total market supply prior to production. It will be useful for us to assume that w is strictly positive in all coordinates; if this is not the case, the algorithm may be modified by adding a strictly positive vector to b and the same vector to each demand column of A. In order to apply theorem 4.2.3 we need verify only that the set $\{y|Ay = b, y \geq 0\}$ is bounded. This may be shown to be a consequence of our assumption on the activity analysis matrix that $\{y|By + w = 0, y \geq 0\}$ is a bounded set.

The algorithm will terminate with a primitive set $(\pi^{j_1}, \pi^{j_2}, \ldots, \pi^{j_n})$ and a set of non-negative weights $y_1, y_2, \ldots, y_k$ that satisfy

$$\sum_{j=1}^{k} y_j a_{ij} = w_i.$$

y_j will be positive only if the jth column of the matrix A corresponds to a price vector in the final primitive set.

Several of the columns of A that appear with positive weights will be composed of market demands $[\xi_1(\pi^j), \ldots, \xi_n(\pi^j)]'$ evaluated at some specific price vector π^j. Let us—by altering our notation—represent the weights $\{y_j\}$ associated with market demand columns by $\{\alpha_j\}$. The remaining columns of A with positive weights are the negatives of columns in the activity analysis matrix B. By an obvious change of notation, let us represent by y_j the weight associated with the jth activity. Activities that are not associated with any vector in the final primitive set receive a weight of zero. The above equations then become

$$(5.2.2) \qquad \sum_j \alpha_j \begin{bmatrix} \xi_1(\pi^j) \\ \vdots \\ \xi_n(\pi^j) \end{bmatrix} = \begin{bmatrix} w_1 \\ \vdots \\ w_n \end{bmatrix} + \sum_j y_j \begin{bmatrix} b_{1,j} \\ \vdots \\ b_{n,j} \end{bmatrix}.$$

Because of the way in which the columns of A were constructed, we know that a market demand column $[\xi_1(\pi^j), \ldots, \xi_n(\pi^j)]'$ will appear with a positive weight α_j only if π^j belongs to the final primitive set. The demand columns with positive weights are therefore all evaluated at price vectors that are quite close to each other and have their ith coordinates close to zero if the ith side of the simplex belongs to the final primitive set.

In addition, a column of the activity analysis matrix B will appear with a positive weight on the right-hand side of 5.2.2 only if it maximizes profit at some price vector in the primitive set and if this maximum profit is positive. On the other hand, the appearance of a market demand column with a positive weight implies that the maximum profit—for all activities in B—is nonpositive when evaluated at the associated price vector.

If the grid $\pi^{n+1}, \ldots, \pi^k$ is sufficiently fine, the n vectors in the final primitive set will be close to each other. The assumption of continuous market demand functions would then permit us to rewrite the above equations in the form

$$(5.2.3) \qquad (\Sigma \alpha_j) \begin{bmatrix} \xi_1(\pi) \\ \vdots \\ \xi_n(\pi) \end{bmatrix} \sim \begin{bmatrix} w_1 \\ \vdots \\ w_n \end{bmatrix} + \Sigma y_j \begin{bmatrix} b_{1j} \\ \vdots \\ b_{nj} \end{bmatrix},$$

with π an arbitrary vector in the subsimplex corresponding to the final primitive set. If it could be demonstrated that $\Sigma \alpha_j$ is close to unity, then that equilibrium condition asserting the equality between supply and demand in all markets would be approximately described by equations 5.2.3.

This is indeed correct; I shall subsequently exhibit explicit bounds for the deviation between supply and demand as a function of the grid size. Before doing this, however, it may be best to examine the argument as an increasingly finer sequence of grids is used, eventually becoming everywhere dense on the simplex. As we have done several times earlier, we use a standard argument to assert the existence of a sequence of grids for which the nonslack vectors in the primitive sets converge to a limit $\hat{\pi}$, the demand functions converge to $\xi(\hat{\pi})$, and the weights $\{\alpha_j\}$ and $\{y_j\}$

converge to $\{\hat{\alpha}_j\}$ and $\{\hat{y}_j\}$. If we denote $\Sigma_j \hat{\alpha}_j$ by $\hat{\alpha}$, then 5.2.3 becomes

$$(5.2.4) \qquad \hat{\alpha} \begin{bmatrix} \xi_1(\hat{\pi}) \\ \vdots \\ \xi_n(\hat{\pi}) \end{bmatrix} = \begin{bmatrix} w_1 \\ \vdots \\ w_n \end{bmatrix} + \sum_j \hat{y}_j \begin{bmatrix} b_{1j} \\ \vdots \\ b_{nj} \end{bmatrix}.$$

In order to demonstrate that $\hat{\alpha} = 1$ and that $\hat{\pi}$ and the production plan whose activity levels are given by $\{\hat{y}\}$ do indeed represent a competitive equilibrium, we must recall that way in which price vectors are associated with the columns of 5.2.4, taking into account the fact that we have passed to the limit:

1. An activity column $(b_{1,j}, \ldots, b_{n,j})'$ will appear in 5.2.4 with a positive weight only if it maximizes profit at the price vector $\hat{\pi}$ and if this maximum profit is non-negative;

2. $\hat{\alpha}$ will be strictly positive only if the maximum profit $\max_j(\hat{\pi}_1 b_{1j} + \ldots + \hat{\pi}_n b_{nj})$, evaluated at the prices $\hat{\pi}$, is nonpositive (in other words, if all activities make a profit less than or equal to zero).

Let us first argue that $\hat{\alpha}$ is strictly positive, so that the second of these conditions does indeed apply. If this were not so, then equations 5.2.4 would imply

$$0 = \sum_i \hat{\pi}_i w_i + \sum_j \hat{y}_j (\sum_i \hat{\pi}_i b_{ij}).$$

But every term on the right-hand side of this equality is non-negative since $\hat{y}_j > 0$ implies, by the first condition, that $\Sigma_i \hat{\pi}_i b_{ij} \geq 0$. Moreover, the term $\Sigma_i \hat{\pi}_i w_i$ is strictly positive since we have assumed that $w_i > 0$ for all i. This contradiction permits us to conclude that $\hat{\alpha} > 0$ and that conditions 1 and 2 both apply. Taken together, however, they imply the following property:

3. At the prices $\hat{\pi}$, *all* activities in B make a profit less than or equal to zero, and those activities with positive weights $\hat{y}_j$ make a profit of zero.

This is of course the second major condition to be satisfied at equilibrium: that the production decision be consistent with profit maximization at prices $\hat{\pi}$. In order to finish the proof that we have found a competitive equilibrium, we need only demonstrate that $\hat{\alpha} = 1$. But this follows immediately from

$$\hat{\alpha} \sum_i \hat{\pi}_i \xi_i(\hat{\pi}) = \sum_i \hat{\pi}_i w_i + \sum_j \hat{y}_j (\sum_i \hat{\pi}_i b_{ij})$$

$$= \sum_i \hat{\pi}_i w_i$$

when we apply the Walras law. We have therefore demonstrated that theorem 4.2.3 and the algorithm behind it may be used, at least in the limit, to obtain an equilibrium price vector and production plan.

It should be clear that a suitable approximation may be obtained by selecting a fine grid without a passage to the limit. The reader who is satisfied about this on intuitive grounds may prefer to skip the following analysis, which relates the degree of approximation to the size of the grid, and go directly to the examples of the next section.

Let c be a constant greater than the sum of the absolute values of all of the entries in the activity analysis matrix B. Since the set of non-negative vectors $y = (y_1, \ldots, y_m)$ with $By + w \geq 0$ is assumed to be bounded, we can find a second constant c' such that any such y satisfies $\Sigma y_j \leq c'$. Also since the demand functions are continuous on the simplex S, we can assume that $|\xi(\pi)| \leq c''$ and that for any $\delta > 0$. there is an $\varepsilon > 0$ such that $|\pi - \pi'| \leq \varepsilon$ implies $|\xi(\pi) - \xi(\pi')| \leq \delta$. Furthermore, assume that $\varepsilon < \min_i(w_i)/cc'$ and $\delta < \min_i(w_i)$. A set of bounds on the degree of approximation obtained in a finite grid—far worse than what occurs in practice—can now be stated in terms of these quantities.

5.2.5. [LEMMA] *Let the grid be selected so fine that any two vectors in the geometric subsimplex corresponding to the final primitive set are within ε of each other in each coordinate. Let π be any vector in this subsimplex, and $y_1, \ldots, y_m$ the activity levels determined by the algorithm (equations 5.2.2). Then*

a. $\displaystyle\sum_i \pi_i b_{ij} \leq \varepsilon c$ for $j = 1, \ldots, m;$ *and*

b. $\displaystyle\sum_i \pi_i b_{ij} \geq -\varepsilon c$ if $y_j > 0.$

Moreover,

c. $\displaystyle\left| \xi_i(\pi) - w_i - \sum y_j b_{ij} \right| \leq \frac{\varepsilon cc'c'' + \delta(\pi w + c'') + \pi \varepsilon cc'}{\pi \cdot w - \delta}.$

We begin with 5.2.5b which is quite simple, since if $y_j > 0$, there must be some vector π^{ji} in the final primitive set that produces a positive profit for the jth activity. π is within ε of this vector in each coordinate and therefore $\Sigma \pi_i b_{ij} \geq -\varepsilon c$.

Let us then show that

$$\sum_j \alpha_j \geq \frac{\pi \cdot w - \varepsilon cc'}{\pi \cdot w + \delta},$$

which is strictly positive by our assumption on ε. To see this we first argue that

$$\left| \left(\sum_j \alpha_j \right) \xi_i(\pi) - \sum_j \alpha_j \xi_i(\pi^j) \right| \leq \delta \, \Sigma \alpha_j \qquad \text{for } i + 1, \ldots, n,$$

where the terms $\alpha_j \xi_i(\pi^j)$ appear only if $\alpha_j > 0$ and π^j is the corresponding vector in the final primitive set. The inequality is then a simple consequence of the fact that π is within ε—in all coordinates—of any vector in the final primitive set and therefore $|\xi_i(\pi) - \xi_i(\pi^j)| \leq \delta$.

The next step is to replace $\Sigma \alpha_j \xi_i(\pi^j)$ by $w_i + \Sigma y_j b_{ij}$ and obtain

(5.2.6) $|(\Sigma \alpha_j) \xi_i(\pi) - w_i - \Sigma y_j b_{ij}| \leq \delta \Sigma \alpha_j \qquad \text{for } i = 1, \ldots, n.$

It follows that

$$\left(\sum_j \alpha_j \right) \pi \cdot \xi(\pi) - \pi \cdot w - \sum_j y_j \left(\sum_i \pi_i b_{ij} \right) \geq -\delta \Sigma \alpha_j.$$

If we apply the Walras law and 5.2.5b we see that

(5.2.7) $(\Sigma \alpha_j)(\delta + \pi \cdot w) \geq \pi \cdot w - \varepsilon c c',$

which is what we wished to demonstrate.

We know now that $\Sigma \alpha_j$, which we may represent by α, is positive. At least one of the vectors in the final primitive set must therefore be associated with a demand column and at that price all activities make a nonpositive profit. Since π is within ε of this price vector, 5.2.6 follows immediately. Using the other half of the inequality 5.2.6, we also see that

$$\alpha \pi \cdot \xi(\pi) - \pi \cdot w - \Sigma y_j \Sigma \pi_i b_{ij} \leq \delta \alpha;$$

from the Walras law and 5.2.5a it then follows that

(5.2.8) $\alpha \leq \dfrac{\pi \cdot w + \varepsilon c c'}{\pi \cdot w - \delta}.$

The two inequalities 5.2.7 and 5.2.8 can be combined as

$$|1 - \alpha| \leq \frac{\varepsilon c c' + \delta}{\pi \cdot w - \delta},$$

and we see that

$$|\xi(\pi) - w - By| \leq |\alpha \xi(\pi) - w - By| + |1 - \alpha| \, |\xi(\pi)|$$

$$\leq \delta \alpha + |1 - \alpha| \, |\xi(\pi)|$$

$$\leq \frac{\varepsilon c c' c'' + \delta(\pi \cdot w + c'') + \delta \varepsilon c c'}{\pi \cdot w - \delta}.$$

This concludes the proof of lemma 5.2.5.

5.3. Some Numerical Examples of the Algorithm

In order to demonstrate that the algorithm may be applied to Walrasian models of reasonable size, two numerical examples will be examined in the present section. The number of iterations required and the time taken by the computation are typical for examples of this size.

Example I. The first problem involves six commodities that may be described as follows:

1. Capital available at the end of the period
2. Capital available at the beginning of the period
3. Skilled labor
4. Unskilled labor
5. Nondurable consumer goods
6. Durable consumer goods

During the particular time period, production may be carried out in each of three sectors: the construction of durable consumer goods, the production of nondurable consumer goods, and a final sector for the production of new capital available at the end of the period. If the six slack vectors representing disposal are omitted, the activity analysis matrix B is given by:

Commodity	\multicolumn{8}{c}{Activities}
	7	8	9	10	11	12	13	14
1	4	4	1.6	1.6	1.6	.9	7	8
2	-5.3	-5	-2	-2	-2	-1	-4	-5
3	-2	-1	-2	-4	-1	0	-3	-2
4	-1	-6	-3	-1	-8	0	-1	-8
5	0	0	6	8	7	0	0	0
6	4	3.5	0	0	0	0	0	0

Activities 7 and 8 describe the durable consumer good sector. In the first of these activities 4 units of consumer durables are produced from 1 unit of unskilled labor, 2 units of skilled labor, and 5.3 units of capital at the beginning of the period. In addition, the 5.3 units of capital are partially depreciated in use and become 4 units at the end of the period.

Activity number 8 is similar, though it permits the substitution of un-skilled for skilled labor.

Activities 9, 10, and 11 represent three procedures for the production of nondurable consumer goods with varying degrees of skilled and un-skilled labor. The final three activities describe the capital goods sector, with activity number 12 representing the natural depreciation of capital stocks should they not be used in production. Of course it cannot be emphasized too strongly that the numbers are essentially arbitrary and bear no relationship to empirically derived magnitudes.

In addition to this activity analysis matrix we shall assume that there are five consumers, each of whom has a distinct set of demand functions and a vector of initial assets. The following matrix describes the initial assets of each consumer:

| | Commodity | | | |
Consumer	2	3	4	6
1	3	5	.1	1
2	.1	.1	7	2
3	2	6	.1	1.5
4	1	.1	8	1
5	6	.1	.5	2

As we see, no consumer owns, prior to production, either nondurable goods or capital available at the end of the period. The remaining four commodities are owned in varying quantities by each of the five consumers.

In order to complete the description of the model the demand functions must be specified. We shall assume that each consumer has demand functions arising from a utility function with a constant elasticity of substitution. This implies that at prices $\pi_1, \ldots, \pi_6$ the ith consumer will demand

$$\xi^i(\pi) = [a_{i1} f_i(\pi)/\pi_1^{b_i}, \ldots, a_{i6} f_i(\pi)/\pi_6^{b_i}],$$

where b_i is the ith consumer's elasticity of substitution, a_{ij} measures the ith consumer's intensity of demand for commodity j, and $f_i(\pi)$ is a complex function of the price vector selected so that the budget constraint is satisfied for each individual. The specific values of a_{ij} are given by the following matrix:

Consumer	Commodity					
	1	2	3	4	5	6
1	4	0	0.2	0	2	3.2
2	0.4	0	0	0.6	4	1
3	2	0	0.5	0	2	1.5
4	5	0	0	0.2	5	4.5
5	3	0	0	0.2	4	2

As we see, no consumer has a demand for capital at the beginning of
the period, though there may be a substantial demand—depending of
course on relative prices—for capital at the end of the period. Since there
is no explicit description of production after the end of the time period,
this is to be interpreted as a demand for savings. It is an unfortunate
aspect of this particular formulation that investment decisions are motivated exclusively by the desire for private savings and do not reflect the
eventual profitability of future capital stocks. This can be avoided either
by making the problem dynamic, so that investment decisions have a
chance to work themselves out, or by introducing expectations concerning
the value of tomorrow's capital stock. Of course, savings are also represented in this model by a demand for consumer durables—a demand
that reflects both current and expected future services.

The entries under the skilled and unskilled labor columns refer to a
demand for leisure, for in this formulation all potential labor services are
evaluated—at the going wage-rate—in the computation of income and
then repurchased in the form of leisure. We have not made that minor
reformulation of the demand functions which insures that no consumer
repurchases more leisure than the stock of labor initially available to him.

Finally, the elasticities of substitution are given by:

Consumer	b_i
1	1.2
2	1.6
3	.8
4	.5
5	.6

In the numerical solution to this problem the set $\pi^7, \ldots, \pi^k$ was taken to consist of all vectors of the form $(m_1/100, m_2/100, \ldots, m_6/100)$, with m_i representing positive integers summing to 100. In order to comply with the nondegeneracy assumption, ties were broken according to the scheme described in chapter 3. The algorithm terminated after only 913 iterations in just over a minute of computing time on an IBM 7094. The following matrix displays the numerators of the vectors in the final primitive set and below them the associated feasible basis:

$$
\begin{bmatrix}
22 & 22 & 22 & 22 & 22 & 23 \\
24 & 21 & 22 & 22 & 22 & 22 \\
19 & 19 & 20 & 19 & 19 & 20 \\
6 & 7 & 7 & 7 & 6 & 7 \\
11 & 12 & 12 & 12 & 12 & 12 \\
18 & 19 & 17 & 18 & 19 & 16
\end{bmatrix}
$$

$$
.969
\begin{bmatrix}
\xi_1(\pi^{j_1}) \\
\cdot \\
\cdot \\
\cdot \\
\cdot \\
\xi_6(\pi^{j_1})
\end{bmatrix}
+.730
\begin{bmatrix}
-4 \\
5.3 \\
2 \\
1 \\
0 \\
-4
\end{bmatrix}
+1.60
\begin{bmatrix}
-1.6 \\
2 \\
2 \\
3 \\
-6 \\
0
\end{bmatrix}
+.894
\begin{bmatrix}
-1.6 \\
2 \\
4 \\
1 \\
-8 \\
0
\end{bmatrix}
+.79
\begin{bmatrix}
-1.6 \\
2 \\
1 \\
8 \\
-7 \\
0
\end{bmatrix}
+.41
\begin{bmatrix}
-7 \\
4 \\
3 \\
1 \\
0 \\
0
\end{bmatrix}
=
\begin{bmatrix}
w_1 \\
w_2 \\
\cdot \\
\cdot \\
\cdot \\
w_6
\end{bmatrix}
$$

Each vector in the primitive set is associated with that column directly below it: the first such vector corresponds to a column of demands and the remaining five vectors to the negatives of that activity which maximizes profit at the respective prices. The first price vector and the above activity levels will therefore serve as an approximate competitive equilibrium. But they can be improved quite substantially by one of several variations of Newton's method modified to accommodate the presence of inequalities. (See, for example, Robinson 1971.) The following prices and activity levels were then obtained:

Commodity	Price	Supply	Demand
1	.22032	11.2342	11.2342
2	.25107	0.	0.
3	.16102	1.1557	1.1557
4	.05494	2.9746	2.9746
5	.10608	23.6834	23.6834
6	.20658	9.3540	9.3540

Activity	Level	Profit
7	0.4635	0.
8	0.	− 0.142
9	3.9392	0.
10	0.0060	0.
11	0.	− 0.008
12	0.	− 0.053
13	0.4383	0.
14	0.	− 0.254

EXAMPLE II.*   In our second example we have four consumers and the following fourteen commodities:

1. Basic agricultural goods
2. Processed food
3. Textiles
4. Housing services and heating
5. Entertainment
6. Housing, end of period
7. Other capital, end of period
8. Steel
9. Coal
10. Lumber
11. Housing, beginning of period
12. Other capital, beginning of period
13. Labor
14. Foreign exchange

The consumers have initially a nonzero holding only of commodities 11–13. The following matrix describes this ownership pattern:

* From Hansen's thesis (1968).

| | Commodity | | |
Consumer	11	12	13
1	20.	30.	6.
2	4.	20.	8.
3	0.	0.	10.
4	8.	75.	6.

The activity analysis matrix is given in tables 5.3.1 and 5.3.2, in which disposal activities have been omitted. Activities 15–26 refer to the production of domestic goods, 27–33 to import activities, and 34–40 to export activities. Only commodities 1–3 and 7–10 enter into international trade, and as the last row of the technology matrix indicates, these commodities enter at predetermined international prices.

Given a non-negative vector of prices π, the demand function of the ith consumer for commodities 1–7 is assumed to be

$$\xi(\pi) = \left(\frac{a_{i1}}{\pi_1} f_i(\pi), \ldots, \frac{a_{i7}}{\pi_7} f_i(\pi)\right),$$

with f_i again an appropriate function of price—in this case linear—in order to place each consumer on his budget constraint. Only commodities 1–7 are demanded by consumers, and the specific values of a_{ij}, which are the percentage of the ith consumer's income spent on the jth good, are given by:

| | Commodity | | | | | | |
Consumer	1	2	3	4	5	6	7
1	0.1	0.2	0.1	0.1	0.1	0.3	0.1
2	0.2	0.2	0.1	0.1	0.1	0.1	0.2
3	0.3	0.2	0.3	0.1	0.1	0.0	0.0
4	0.1	0.2	0.1	0.1	0.1	0.1	0.3

TABLE 5.3.1. DOMESTIC PROCESSES

Commodity	15	16	17	18	19	20	21	22	23	24	25	26
1	5.0	-3.5	-0.1	0.0	-0.7	0.0	0.0	0.0	0.0	0.0	0.0	0.0
2	-0.9	5.0	-0.1	0.0	-0.8	0.0	0.0	0.0	0.0	0.0	0.0	0.0
3	-0.2	-0.5	2.0	-0.1	-0.1	-0.8	-0.4	-0.1	-0.1	-0.1	0.0	0.0
4	-1.0	-2.0	-2.0	2.0	-2.0	-0.4	-1.8	-1.6	-0.8	-0.2	0.0	0.0
5	0.0	0.0	0.0	0.0	4.0	0.0	0.0	0.0	0.0	0.0	0.0	0.0
6	0.0	0.0	0.0	0.32	0.0	0.8	0.0	0.0	0.0	0.0	0.0	0.36
7	0.4	1.3	1.2	0.0	0.0	1.1	6.0	1.8	1.2	0.4	0.9	0.0
8	-0.2	-0.4	-0.2	-0.1	0.0	-1.0	-2.0	2.0	-0.5	-0.2	0.0	0.0
9	-1.0	-0.1	-0.1	-1.0	0.0	0.0	-0.2	-1.0	2.0	-0.2	0.0	0.0
10	-0.5	-0.4	-0.3	-0.3	0.0	-3.0	-0.2	-0.2	-0.5	1.0	0.0	-0.4
11	0.0	0.0	0.0	-0.4	0.0	0.0	0.0	0.0	0.0	0.0	0.0	0.0
12	-0.5	-1.5	-1.5	-0.1	-0.1	-1.5	-2.5	-2.5	-1.5	-0.5	-1.0	0.0
13	-0.4	-0.2	-0.2	-0.02	-0.4	-0.3	-0.1	-0.1	-0.4	-0.4	0.0	0.0
14	0.0	0.0	0.0	0.0	0.0	0.0	0.0	0.0	0.0	0.0	0.0	0.0

TABLE 5.3.2. IMPORT AND EXPORT PROCESSES

Commodity	Import processes										Export processes			
	27	28	29	30	31	32	33	34	35	36	37	38	39	40
1	1.0	0.0	0.0	0.0	0.0	0.0	0.0	-1.0	0.0	0.0	0.0	0.0	0.0	0.0
2	0.0	1.0	0.0	0.0	0.0	0.0	0.0	0.0	-1.0	0.0	0.0	0.0	0.0	0.0
3	0.0	0.0	1.0	0.0	0.0	0.0	0.0	0.0	0.0	-1.0	0.0	0.0	0.0	0.0
4	-0.4	-0.2	-0.2	-0.4	-0.4	-0.4	-0.4	-0.4	-0.2	-0.2	-0.4	-0.4	-0.4	-0.4
5	0.0	0.0	0.0	0.0	0.0	0.0	0.0	0.0	0.0	0.0	0.0	0.0	0.0	0.0
6	0.0	0.0	0.0	1.0	0.0	0.0	0.0	0.0	0.0	0.0	0.0	0.0	0.0	0.0
7	0.0	0.0	0.0	0.0	0.0	0.0	0.0	0.0	0.0	0.0	-1.0	0.0	0.0	0.0
8	0.0	0.0	0.0	0.0	0.0	0.0	0.0	0.0	0.0	0.0	0.0	-1.0	0.0	0.0
9	0.0	0.0	0.0	0.0	1.0	1.0	0.0	0.0	0.0	0.0	0.0	0.0	-1.0	0.0
10	0.0	0.0	0.0	0.0	0.0	0.0	0.0	0.0	0.0	0.0	0.0	0.0	0.0	-1.0
11	0.0	0.0	0.0	0.0	0.0	0.0	1.0	0.0	0.0	0.0	0.0	0.0	0.0	0.0
12	-0.2	-0.1	-0.1	-0.2	-0.2	-0.2	-0.2	-0.2	-0.1	-0.1	-0.2	-0.2	-0.2	-0.2
13	-0.04	-0.02	-0.02	-0.04	-0.04	-0.04	-0.04	-0.04	-0.02	-0.02	-0.04	-0.04	-0.04	-0.04
14	-0.5	-0.4	-0.8	-1.2	-0.6	-0.7	-0.4	0.5	0.4	0.8	1.2	0.6	0.7	0.4

In order to apply the algorithm the vectors $\pi^{15}, \ldots, \pi^k$ were selected to be of the form $(m_1/200, \ldots, m_{14}/200)$, with m_i representing positive integers summing to 200. The breaking of ties was accomplished in this example by the lexicographic procedure to be described in detail in chapter 6. The number of vectors in the grid is of the order of 10^{21}; the algorithm terminated after the examination of approximately 30,000 such vectors in less than 9 minutes of computation time on an IBM 7094—with the columns of the following matrix being the numerators of the fourteen vectors in the final primitive set:

$$
\begin{bmatrix}
11 & 11 & 11 & 11 & 11 & 11 & 11 & 11 & 11 & 11 & 12 & 12 & 12 & 12 \\
11 & 11 & 11 & 11 & 11 & 11 & 11 & 11 & 11 & 12 & 11 & 11 & 11 & 11 \\
19 & 19 & 19 & 19 & 19 & 19 & 19 & 19 & 20 & 19 & 19 & 19 & 19 & 19 \\
13 & 13 & 13 & 13 & 14 & 14 & 14 & 14 & 13 & 13 & 13 & 13 & 13 & 13 \\
12 & 12 & 12 & 13 & 12 & 12 & 12 & 12 & 12 & 12 & 12 & 12 & 12 & 12 \\
13 & 13 & 13 & 12 & 12 & 12 & 12 & 13 & 13 & 13 & 13 & 13 & 13 & 13 \\
15 & 15 & 15 & 15 & 15 & 16 & 16 & 15 & 15 & 15 & 15 & 15 & 15 & 15 \\
19 & 19 & 20 & 20 & 20 & 19 & 19 & 19 & 19 & 19 & 19 & 19 & 19 & 19 \\
18 & 18 & 17 & 17 & 17 & 17 & 17 & 17 & 17 & 17 & 17 & 18 & 18 & 18 \\
16 & 16 & 16 & 16 & 16 & 16 & 16 & 16 & 16 & 16 & 16 & 15 & 16 & 16 \\
12 & 12 & 12 & 12 & 12 & 12 & 12 & 12 & 12 & 12 & 12 & 12 & 11 & 12 \\
14 & 14 & 14 & 14 & 14 & 14 & 15 & 15 & 15 & 15 & 15 & 15 & 15 & 14 \\
7 & 8 & 8 & 8 & 8 & 8 & 7 & 7 & 7 & 7 & 7 & 7 & 7 & 7 \\
20 & 19 & 19 & 19 & 19 & 19 & 19 & 19 & 19 & 19 & 19 & 19 & 19 & 19
\end{bmatrix}
$$

Of these vectors, two were associated with demand columns and twelve with the negatives of profit-maximizing activities. The following prices (normalized to sum to unity) and activity levels were determined by suitable numerical techniques:

Activity	Level	Profitability
15	4.7923	0.
16	0.	−0.2073
17	0.	−0.0342
18	51.9714	0.
19	4.0414	0.
20	0.	−0.4199
21	0.	−0.1422
22	0.	−0.0684
23	30.5004	0.
24	21.1848	0.
25	36.8945	0.
26	28.0286	0.
27	0.	−0.0267
28	44.0441	0.
29	23.6464	0.
30	0.	−0.0849
31	25.6427	0.
32	0.	−0.0172
33	12.0530	0.
34	0.	−0.0582
35	0.	−0.0424
36	0.	−0.0424
37	47.2847	0.
38	0.	−0.0849
39	0.	−0.0677
40	0.	−0.0849

Commodity	Prices	Supply	Demand
1	.06215	21.1327	21.1327
2	.05833	36.4979	36.4979
3	.09545	11.9182	11.9182
4	.07145	14.9002	14.9002
5	.06585	16.1655	16.1655
6	.06245	26.7211	26.7213
7	.06890	32.9116	32.9116
8	.09811	0.	0.
9	.09024	0.	0.
10	.07956	0.	0.
11	.05620	0.	0.
12	.06201	0.	0.
13	.03652	0.	0.
14	.09279	0.	0.

The number of iterations involved in this example is undoubtedly quite large and even though each iteration is taking no more than .02 second, the total computation time might become prohibitively expensive for problems involving 20 or more sectors. Part of this difficulty may be due to the particular lexicographic ordering that has been employed in this example. This procedure, as distinct from the one previously used, has the virtue of minimal storage requirements. It does however—as we shall see—treat n vectors as belonging to a primitive set only if they are very close in the sense of Euclidean distance. For that reason a grid with denominators of 200 gives a considerably finer approximation than a corresponding grid with a different procedure for breaking ties.

But the problem will still remain, regardless of the ordering. Experience indicates that the number of iterations increases quadratically with the size of the problem (with other aspects of the algorithm held constant) and eventually becomes prohibitively large. One alternative might be to begin a large problem with a rather coarse grid in order to estimate the region in which the approximate solution may be expected to lie. The problem is then repeated with a grid that is refined only in this region. Even though the algorithm must begin, as usual, with one of the vertices of the simplex S, it should pass quite rapidly into the relevant region, thereby reducing the number of iterations.

An ingenious alternative, in which the grid size is continually refined in the course of the computation has recently been suggested by Eaves (1972). The computational experience with Eaves' technique is still quite limited, but it appears to be one of the major directions for future research.

Another possibility, which should be examined carefully in any specific application, is that the problem may be capable of a reformulation in which the algorithm can be applied to a simplex of smaller dimension. For example, in our second problem only seven commodities actually appear in the consumer demand functions. As we shall see in the next section, a quite different version of the algorithm can be applied, with $n = 7$ rather than $n = 14$, to precisely the same problem, resulting in a reduction in the number of iterations by over 90 percent. A third algorithm, based on an entirely different principle, may be found in chapter 6.

5.4. An Alternative to Kakutani's Theorem

In the present section our algorithm will be applied to a technique used by Debreu (1959) and others to demonstrate the existence of equilibrium prices and production decisions in a general Walrasian model. The technique is based on a mathematical theorem which, while it can be derived from Kakutani's theorem, has a substantially greater economic appeal.

Let us begin by assuming that each price vector π on the simplex is associated with a set $\Phi(\pi)$ in n-dimensional Euclidean space. In our applications to the Walrasian model the set $\Phi(\pi)$ will consist of all *excess* demand vectors arising from utility maximization by the consumer and some suitably bounded profit-maximizing response by producers. With this interpretation in mind the following assumptions on the mapping are quite natural.

5.4.1. [ASSUMPTIONS]

a. *For each π, $\Phi(\pi)$ is a nonempty, closed, bounded, convex set.*

b. *The mapping $\pi \to \Phi(\pi)$ is upper semicontinuous.*

c. *The mapping is bounded from below, in the sense that there is some positive vector b with $\varphi > -b$ for all $\varphi \in \Phi(\pi)$ and all $\pi \in S$.*

d. *If $\varphi \in \Phi(\pi)$ then $\pi \cdot \varphi \leq 0$.*

The first three of these assumptions are general technical requirements that need no particular comment. The fourth is an analogue of the Walras law stating that the value of excess demand is nonpositive; it is illustrated by figure 5.4.1 for the case in which $n = 2$.

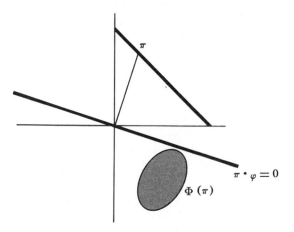

Figure 5.4.1

In our economic applications we are interested in determining a price vector π^* and an associated excess demand $\varphi^* \in \Phi(\pi^*)$, with $\varphi_i^* \leq 0$ for $i = 1, \ldots, n$. It is intuitively plausible that such a price vector will exist in the case in which $n = 2$—since as the π varies on the simplex S, at least one of the sets $\Phi(\pi)$ will necessarily intersect the nonpositive orthant. The general case is covered by the following theorem.

5.4.2. [THEOREM] *Let assumptions 5.4.1 be satisfied. Then there exists a vector π^*, and $\varphi^* \in \Phi(\pi^*)$, with $\varphi^* \leq 0$.*

This result—or a slight variation of it—can be demonstrated directly by means of Kakutani's theorem. (Also see the nonlinear complementarity problem studied by Karamardian 1969, 1971; Habetler and Price 1971; and Eaves 1971b.) Let us assume in addition to 5.4.1 that there is some closed, bounded, convex set Z that contains all of the sets $\Phi(\pi)$. We then construct a mapping of the product space of the simplex S and Z into itself that satisfies the conditions of Kakutani's theorem and whose fixed point is the pair (π^*, φ^*) required in theorem 5.4.2.

To do this, let (π, z) be an arbitrary pair in $S \times Z$. The image of this point, under the mapping to be constructed, will be a set of vectors in the product space $S \times Z$. It will, in this particular instance, be composed of two separate mappings: one in which the vector π is mapped into a subset of Z, and secondly a mapping of the vectors in Z into subsets of the simplex S. To be specific, the vector π is mapped into $\Phi(\pi)$, a subset of Z. To describe the second part of the mapping, let $P(z)$ be defined to be the set of price vectors on the simplex that maximize $\pi_1 z_1 + \ldots + \pi_n z_n$. The mapping on the product space is then given by $(\pi, z) \rightarrow [P(z), \Phi(\pi)]$.

The conditions of Kakutani's theorem are clearly satisfied, and we conclude that there exists a point (π^*, z^*) contained in its own image; in other words, $\pi^* \in P(z^*)$ and $z^* \in \Phi(\pi^*)$. Let us show that $z^* \leq 0$, so that z^* satisfies the conditions of theorem 5.4.2. To see this we notice that $\pi^* \in P(z^*)$ means that

$$0 \geq \sum_1^n \pi_i^* z_i^* \geq \sum_1^n \pi_i z_i^*$$

for any vector $\pi \in S$. But if we take π to have zero for all of its coordinates except the ith, we see that $z_i^* \leq 0$; theorem 5.4.2 is therefore demonstrated.

We have already discussed an algorithm for Kakutani's theorem, and the reader may be curious about why an alternative procedure need be suggested for theorem 5.4.2. But the reasoning here is quite simple: Kakutani's theorem is applied in the product space $S \times Z$, which has essentially twice the dimensionality of the basic simplex. Since a reduction in dimensionality by a factor of two represents a great saving in computation time, it is definitely useful to obtain a direct algorithm for this theorem.

Let us begin the algorithm by selecting, as usual, a fine grid of price vectors $\pi^{n+1}, \ldots, \pi^k$ on the simplex, with $\pi^1, \ldots, \pi^n$ representing the sides. We construct the columns of the matrix A by means of the following simple rule.

5.4.3. [RULE] *Let π^j with $j > n$ be a vector in the list and φ^j an arbitrary member of $\Phi(\pi^j)$. The jth column of the matrix A is then defined by*

$$(\varphi_1^j + b_1, \ldots, \varphi_n^j + b_n)',$$

with $-b$ the vector that strictly bounds all of the sets $\Phi(\pi)$ from below. The vector b is also taken to be the right-hand side for the equations $Ay = b$.

The columns of the matrix A consist simply of an arbitrary image of π^j under the mapping, each column augmented by the same constant vector b to make it strictly positive. The condition that $\{y|Ay = b, y \geq 0\}$ be bounded is clearly satisfied; theorem 4.2.3 can therefore be applied.

We obtain a primitive set $(\pi^{j_1}, \ldots, \pi^{j_n})$ whose associated columns form a feasible basis for $Ay = b$. In other words, the inequalities

$$(5.4.4) \qquad y_{n+1} \begin{bmatrix} \varphi_1^{n+1} + b_1 \\ \vdots \\ \varphi_n^{n+1} + b_n \end{bmatrix} + \ldots + y_k \begin{bmatrix} \varphi_1^k + b_1 \\ \vdots \\ \varphi_n^k + b_n \end{bmatrix} \leq \begin{bmatrix} b_1 \\ \vdots \\ b_n \end{bmatrix}$$

have a non-negative solution that has all of its mass concentrated on columns corresponding to the members of a primitive set. Moreover the ith inequality is in fact an equality unless the ith side—represented by π^i—is a member of the primitive set.

These inequalities may be rewritten as

$$(5.4.5) \qquad y_{n+1} \begin{bmatrix} \varphi_1^{n+1} \\ \vdots \\ \varphi_n^{n+1} \end{bmatrix} + \ldots + y_k \begin{bmatrix} \varphi_1^k \\ \vdots \\ \varphi_n^k \end{bmatrix} \leq (1 - \Sigma y_j) \begin{bmatrix} b_1 \\ \vdots \\ b_n \end{bmatrix}.$$

If it can be shown that $1 - \Sigma y_j \leq 0$—or if positive, quite small—then the vector

$$(y_{n+1}\varphi^{n+1} + \ldots + y_k\varphi^k)/\Sigma y_j$$

will serve as an approximation to the solution required by theorem 5.4.2. As with Kakutani's theorem, there is a somewhat unsatisfactory description of the precise form of the approximation and it may be best at this point to pass directly to the limit.

We take an ever finer sequence of grids for which the subsimplices corresponding to the final primitive sets converge to a vector $\hat{\pi}$, for which the image φ^j (corresponding to nonslack vectors in the primitive sets) converge to limiting vectors $\hat{\varphi}^j$, and for which the positive y_js converge to $\hat{y}_j$. From the upper semicontinuity assumption we have $\hat{\varphi}^j \in \Phi(\hat{\pi})$. The inequalities 5.4.5 become, in the limit,

$$\Sigma \hat{y}_j \hat{\varphi}_i^j \leq b_i(1 - \Sigma \hat{y}_j) \qquad \text{for } i = 1, \ldots, n,$$

with equality unless $\hat{\pi}_i = 0$.

If we multiply the ith of these inequalities by $\hat{\pi}_i$ and sum, we obtain

$$\Sigma \hat{y}_j \left(\sum_i \hat{\pi}_i \hat{\varphi}_i^j \right) = (\Sigma \hat{\pi}_i b_i)(1 - \Sigma \hat{y}_j).$$

But for each j, with $\hat{y}_j > 0$, we have $\hat{\varphi}^j \in \Phi(\hat{\pi})$ so that $\Sigma \hat{\pi}_i \hat{\varphi}_i^j \leq 0$. We may therefore conclude that $\Sigma \hat{y}_j \geq 1$, and as a consequence,

$$\Sigma \hat{y}_j \hat{\varphi}_i^j \leq 0 \qquad \text{for all } i.$$

The vector $\hat{\varphi} = (\Sigma \hat{y}_j \hat{\varphi}^j)/\Sigma \hat{y}_j$, being a convex combination of vectors in $\Phi(\hat{\pi})$, is itself in $\Phi(\hat{\pi})$ and satisfies the conditions of the theorem.

The reader may struggle by himself, following the lines of our argument for Kakutani's theorem, to show that if the grid size is sufficiently small and $\hat{\pi}$ an arbitrary vector in the geometric simplex corresponding to the final primitive set, then $(\hat{\pi}, \Sigma y_j \varphi^j/\Sigma y_j) = (\hat{\pi}, \hat{\varphi})$ represents an approximate answer in the following two senses: (1) The coordinates of $\hat{\varphi}$ are either negative, or if positive, very small; and (2) the pair $(\hat{\pi}, \hat{\varphi})$ is very close to the graph of the mapping, i.e., $\{(\pi, \varphi)|\varphi \in \Phi(\pi)\}$. We shall not pursue this point further but turn instead to an application of the methodology.

5.5. THE WALRASIAN MODEL REVISITED

The purpose of the present section is to use the alternative approach just described to reduce the difficulty of the computation of equilibrium prices under the assumption that some of the commodities do not enter directly into any consumer's utility function. This is a most natural assumption to make because in most examples there will be no direct consumer demand in many sectors, including the initial stocks of capital goods, intermediary goods, and other durable commodities—as distinct from their services.

Let us accordingly group the n commodities into two categories. The first, commodities 1 through l, will contain all of those goods which enter directly into some consumer's utility function, and the second, commodities $l + 1$ through n, those which have no direct consumer demand.

The technology matrix

$$
B = \begin{bmatrix}
-1 & & & & b_{1,n+1} & \cdots & b_{1,m} \\
 & \ddots & & & \vdots & & \vdots \\
 & & -1 & & b_{l,n+1} & \cdots & b_{l,m} \\
 & & & \ddots & \vdots & & \vdots \\
 & & & -1 & b_{n,n+1} & \cdots & b_{n,m}
\end{bmatrix}
$$

is as before, and the vector $w = (w_1, \ldots, w_{l+1}, \ldots, w_n)'$ will represent the total stock of assets prior to production. For the moment, the distribution of ownership of these assets need not be explicitly described, though we shall return to this point in discussing the determination of income.

The algorithm will be applied to a fine grid of vectors on the smaller simplex

$$
S_l = \left\{ \pi = (\pi_1, \ldots, \pi_l) \,\middle|\, \sum_1^l \pi_i = 1, \pi_i \geq 0 \right\}
$$

referring to the prices of goods in the first category alone. The first question to be asked is whether a knowledge of the prices of consumer goods is sufficient to determine the set of excess demand vectors $\Phi(\pi)$.

We begin by assuming that the supply response is obtained by the solution of the linear programming problem

$$
\max\left(\sum_1^l \pi_i b_{i,n+1} \right) y_{n+1} + \cdots + \left(\sum_1^l \pi_i b_{i,m} \right) y_m
$$

(5.5.1)   subject to $-b_{l+1,n+1} y_{n+1} - \cdots - b_{l+1,m} y_m \leq w_{l+1}$

$$
\vdots
$$

$$
-b_{n,n+1} y_{n+1} - \cdots - b_{n,m} y_m \leq w_n,
$$
$$
y_j \geq 0.
$$

In other words, at the price vector $(\pi_1, \ldots, \pi_l)$ the producers maximize the value of the output of consumer goods, subject to the constraint that they make no more net use of goods $l + 1, \ldots, n$ than are initially available. Of course producers can feel free to make full use of the stock of a specific factor only if its supply is inelastic—if it has no alternative use in satisfying demand directly.

In order to guarantee the existence of an optimal solution to this linear programming problem, it is convenient to make the following assumption, which is somewhat stronger than the one described in theorem 5.1.4.

5.5.2. [ASSUMPTION] *The non-negative vectors* $y_{n+1}, \ldots, y_m$ *satisfying the constraints of the linear programming problem*

$$- \sum_{j=n+1}^{m} b_{i,j} y_j \le w_i \qquad \text{for } i = l+1, \ldots, n$$

form a bounded set.

For any price vector $\pi \in S_l$ the linear programming problem will have at least one optimal set of activity levels $(y_{n+1}, \ldots, y_m)$, which will depend of course on π. For any such optimal activity levels, the net supply of consumer goods will be given by

$$s_1 = w_1 + b_{1,n+1} y_{n+1} + \ldots + b_{1m} y_m$$

(5.5.3)
$$\vdots$$

$$s_l = w_l + b_{l,n+1} y_{n+1} + \ldots + b_{l,m} y_m.$$

The optimal activity levels and therefore the net supplies associated with a given price vector π need not be unique but it is easy to see that the set of net supplies is a closed, bounded, convex set that depends in an upper semicontinuous fashion on the price vector π.

In order to determine the demand for consumer goods, each consumer's income must be evaluated as a function of the price vector $(\pi_1, \ldots, \pi_l)$. Consider a typical consumer whose vector of initial assets is given by $w^\alpha = (w_1^\alpha, \ldots, w_l^\alpha, w_{l+1}^\alpha, \ldots, w_n^\alpha)$. That part of his income which derives from his stocks of consumer goods is given by $(\pi_1 w_1^\alpha + \ldots + \pi_l w_l^\alpha)$ and is simple enough to evaluate in terms of the price vector π. But the consumer will typically own some stocks of commodities in category two, and we have as yet no prices for these commodities to calculate their contribution to income.

At this point the duality theorem for linear programming comes to our aid, for in the solution of 5.5.1 a dual vector of prices $\pi_{l+1}, \ldots, \pi_n$ will also be determined. These prices will satisfy the dual linear inequalities

$$- \pi_{l+1} b_{l+1,n+1} - \ldots - \pi_n b_{n,n+1} \ge \sum_{1}^{l} \pi_i b_{i,n+1}$$

$$\vdots$$

$$- \pi_{l+1} b_{l+1,m} - \ldots - \pi_n b_{n,m} \ge \sum_{1}^{l} \pi_i b_{i,m}$$

or, in an alternative form,

(5.5.4) $\displaystyle\sum_{i=1}^{n} \pi_i b_{ij} \leq 0$ for $j = n + 1, \ldots, m$.

Moreover, the duality theorem implies that these inequalities are indeed equalities if $y_j > 0$ and that the value of the dual objective function $\pi_{l+1} w_{l+1} + \ldots + \pi_n w_n$ is equal to the value of the primal objective function

$$\left(\sum_{1}^{l} \pi_i b_{i,n+1} \right) y_{n+1} + \ldots + \left(\sum_{1}^{l} \pi_i b_{i,m} \right) y_m \qquad \text{or}$$

(5.5.5) $$\sum_{i=l+1}^{n} \pi_i w_i = \sum_{i=1}^{l} \pi_i \left(\sum_{j=n+1}^{m} b_{i,j} y_j \right).$$

It is a well-known result in linear programming that the vector of dual prices will be unique if the producer's programming problem is non-degenerate in the customary sense—an assumption that is independent of the consumer goods prices. We shall make this assumption in the remainder of this section. The dual prices may then be used to evaluate that part of the consumer's income deriving from the ownership of goods in the second category. Each consumer's income will then be fully known as a function of consumer goods prices and, therefore, so will his demand for the first l commodities. The market demand functions $\xi_1(\pi_1, \ldots, \pi_l)$, $\ldots, \xi_l(\pi_1, \ldots, \pi_l)$ may then be calculated. They will depend continuously on the price vector $\pi \in S_l$ and satisfy the Walras law, in the form

(5.5.6) $$\sum_{1}^{l} \pi_i \xi_i(\pi) \equiv \sum_{1}^{l} \pi_i w_i + \sum_{l+1}^{n} \pi_i w_i,$$

with the prices for commodities in category two determined by the linear programming problem.

We are now prepared to define the set $\Phi(\pi)$ of market excess demand vectors associated with the price vector $\pi \in S_l$.

5.5.7. [DEFINITION] *The set $\Phi(\pi)$ is defined to consist of all vectors of the form*

$$\varphi_1 = \xi_1(\pi) - w_1 - \sum_{j=n+1}^{m} b_{1,j} y_j$$

$$\vdots$$

$$\varphi_l = \xi_l(\pi) - w_l - \sum_{j=n+1}^{m} b_{l,j} y_j,$$

with $(y_{n+1}, \ldots, y_m)$ *an optimal solution of the linear programming problem* 5.5.1.

With this definition of the mapping, the first three assumptions of 5.4.1 are trivially met. For each π, $\Phi(\pi)$ is a closed, bounded, convex set; as π varies, these sets are uniformly bounded from below (as a consequence of 5.5.2), and they depend upon π in an upper semicontinuous fashion. In order to obtain the remaining condition $\pi \cdot \varphi \leq 0$, we remark that

$$\sum_{i=1}^{l} \pi_i \varphi_i = \sum_{i=1}^{l} \pi_i \xi_i(\pi) - \sum_{i=1}^{l} \pi_i w_i - \sum_{i=1}^{l} \pi_i \left(\sum_{j=n+1}^{m} b_{i,j} y_j \right)$$

$$= \sum_{l+1}^{n} \pi_i w_i - \sum_{i=1}^{l} \pi_i \left(\sum_{j=n+1}^{m} b_{i,j} y_j \right) \quad \text{(by 5.5.6)}$$

$$= 0 \quad \text{(by 5.5.5.)}.$$

Theorem 5.4.2 and the algorithm behind it may therefore be applied. We obtain, in the limit, a price vector $\hat{\pi}$ and a specific excess demand $\hat{\varphi} \in \Phi(\hat{\pi})$ which is nonpositive in all coordinates. $\hat{\varphi}$ is determined by a specific optimal solution $\hat{y}$ of the linear programming problem, so that from 5.5.7 and 5.5.1 we have

$$\xi_1(\hat{\pi}) \leq w_1 + \sum_{j=n+1}^{m} b_{1,j} \hat{y}_j$$

$$\vdots$$

$$\xi_l(\hat{\pi}) \leq w_l + \sum_{j=n+1}^{m} b_{l,j} \hat{y}_j$$

and

$$0 \leq w_{l+1} + \sum_{j=n+1}^{m} b_{l+1,j} \hat{y}_j$$

$$\vdots$$

$$0 \leq w_n + \sum_{j=n+1}^{m} b_{n,j} \hat{y}_j,$$

a form of the correct relationship between supply and demand in all markets. Moreover, if we extend $\hat{\pi}$ to include the imputed prices for commodities in category two, 5.5.4 states that

$$\sum_{i=1}^{n} \hat{\pi}_i b_{ij} \leq 0,$$

with equality if $\hat{y}_j > 0$; production is therefore consistent with profit maximization, and we are indeed at a competitive equilibrium.

I have shown how the algorithm can be applied in a space of substantially lower dimension than the total number of commodities, with a corresponding reduction in the number of iterations. There is, of course, the difficulty that we are required to solve the linear programming problem 5.5.1 at each iteration; this may seem sufficiently costly in computer time to negate the savings obtained by reducing the number of iterations. But this will generally not be so. The only aspect of this linear programming problem that changes in successive iterations is the objective function, which is linear in the consumer goods price vector; the constraints do not vary throughout the course of the algorithm. This implies that for large sequences of iterations the optimal feasible basis and therefore the optimal solution will not change. Of course at each iteration the dual prices $\pi_{l+1}, \ldots, \pi_n$ must be calculated—but they will be simple linear functions of the consumer goods prices as long as the same basis is retained. The optimal basis will be modified in the sequence of iterations only when an activity not in use becomes profitable, and then a few pivot steps—in general only one—will be sufficient to determine the new optimal basis.

Let us see how this version of the algorithm works in practice by returning to the second example of section 5.3, which involves four consumers and fourteen commodities. In this example only the first seven commodities enter into the consumers' utility functions, so the algorithm may be used with $n = 7$. The price vectors $\pi^8, \ldots, \pi^k$ are selected to be all vectors of the form $(m_1/200, \ldots, m_7/200)$ with m_i representing the positive integers summing to 200. There are some 10^{12} such vectors, and the algorithm terminated after 2,867 iterations—in less than 5 minutes of computation time on an IBM 7094—with the following matrix displaying the numerators of the vectors in the primitive set:

$$
\begin{bmatrix}
25 & 25 & 25 & 25 & 25 & 25 & 26 \\
24 & 24 & 24 & 24 & 24 & 25 & 24 \\
39 & 39 & 39 & 39 & 40 & 39 & 39 \\
29 & 30 & 30 & 30 & 29 & 29 & 29 \\
27 & 26 & 27 & 27 & 27 & 27 & 27 \\
26 & 26 & 25 & 26 & 26 & 26 & 26 \\
30 & 30 & 30 & 29 & 29 & 29 & 29
\end{bmatrix}
$$

With each of the vectors in the final primitive set, there is associated a vector of implicit prices for the commodities 8–14 resulting from the linear programming problem 5.5.1. These implicit prices are given below:

$$\begin{bmatrix} 37.0 & 42.0 & 42.0 & 41.3 & 34.3 & 27.5 & 40.9 \\ 36.5 & 37.9 & 37.9 & 37.9 & 36.7 & 37.3 & 38.0 \\ 32.6 & 33.2 & 33.2 & 33.5 & 32.6 & 32.2 & 33.1 \\ 23.4 & 23.4 & 22.5 & 23.5 & 23.4 & 23.4 & 23.4 \\ 27.0 & 27.0 & 27.0 & 26.1 & 27.3 & 31.3 & 26.1 \\ 16.8 & 14.6 & 14.7 & 15.7 & 16.4 & 13.7 & 18.7 \\ 37.9 & 40.0 & 40.0 & 39.0 & 38.9 & 39.5 & 38.8 \end{bmatrix}$$

We have therefore determined seven vectors, each of which assigns a price to all of the fourteen commodities. These prices were then averaged by a suitable numerical procedure. After normalizing the resulting vector by requiring its sum to be unity, a price vector and a set of activity levels virtually identical to those previously found was obtained.

5.6. An Application to Nonlinear Programming

I have, in a previous chapter, discussed the applicability of our technique for Brouwer's theorem to the solution of the nonlinear programming problem

$$\max f_1(x_1, \ldots, x_n)$$

$$\text{subject to } f_2(x_1, \ldots, x_n) \leq 0$$

$$\vdots$$

$$f_m(x_1, \ldots, x_n) \leq 0,$$

$$x \geq 0,$$

under the usual assumptions that f_1 is concave and that each of the functions $f_2, \ldots, f_m$ are convex. In order for this earlier algorithm to be applicable, it was necessary that for any price vector π the value of x which maximizes the Lagrangean

$$\pi_1 f_1(x) - \sum_2^m \pi_i f_i(x)$$

be available in an explicit form.

If the problem of maximizing $\pi_1 f_1(x) - \Sigma_2^m \pi_i f_i(x)$ is in itself difficult, in the sense of requiring iterative methods for its solution, the previous algorithm cannot be expected to perform well. In this section, I shall describe a method suggested by Hansen (1969) that does not require an explicit profit maximization at each iteration. Similar approaches may also be found in Eaves (1971a) and Merrill (1971).

Let us first of all make the notational change of replacing $f_j(x)$ (for $j = 2, \ldots, m$) by $-f_j(x)$ so that the programming problem becomes

$$\max f_1(x_1, \ldots, x_n)$$

$$\text{subject to } f_2(x_1, \ldots, x_n) \geq 0$$

$$\vdots$$

$$f_m(x_1, \ldots, x_n) \geq 0$$

$$x_i \geq 0,$$

with *all* of the functions f_j now concave. We make the following assumptions.

5.6.1. [ASSUMPTIONS]

a. *There is a constant c that satisfies* $0 < c < 1$, *so that if* $x = (x_1, \ldots, x_n)$ *is a non-negative vector satisfying the constraints* $f_j(x) \geq 0$ *for* $j = 2, \ldots, m$, *then* $x_1 + \ldots + x_n \leq c$. (*This is a very minor assumption which merely requires that the constraint set be bounded.*)

b. *There exists a non-negative vector* x^*, *with* $f_j(x^*) > 0$ *for* $j = 2, \ldots, m$. (*This is the customary constraint qualification.*)

c. *The functions* $f_j(x)$ *have continuous partial derivatives in the set* $\{x | x_i \geq 0, \Sigma_1^n x_i \leq 1\}$. *As a notational device we shall represent the partial derivative of* f_j *with respect to* x_i *by* $f_{j,i}(x)$.

In this particular algorithm the concept of a primitive set will be applied to the activity levels x rather than the price vectors. In order to overcome the difficulty that the activity levels bear no natural relation to the simplex $x_1 + \ldots + x_n = 1$ on which primitive sets are defined, we shall introduce an additional coordinate $x_0 = 1 - \Sigma_1^n x_i$ and work with the simplex

$$S = \left\{ x = (x_0, x_1, \ldots, x_n) | x_i \geq 0, \sum_0^n x_i = 1 \right\}.$$

Primitive sets will therefore involve $n + 1$, rather than n, vectors.

As is customary we begin the algorithm with a fine grid $x^0, \ldots, x^n$, $x^{n+1}, \ldots, x^k$ on the simplex—with the understanding that the first $n + 1$

of these vectors represent the sides of S. In order to proceed we need to construct the matrix

$$
A = \begin{array}{ccccccccc}
x^0 & x^1 & \cdots & x^n & x^{n+1} & \cdots & x^j & \cdots & x^k
\end{array}
$$

$$
A = \begin{bmatrix}
1 & 0 & \cdots & 0 & a_{0,n+1} & \cdots & a_{0,j} & \cdots & a_{0,k} \\
0 & 1 & \cdots & 0 & a_{1,n+1} & \cdots & a_{1,j} & \cdots & a_{1,k} \\
\vdots & \vdots & & \vdots & \vdots & & \vdots & & \vdots \\
0 & 0 & \cdots & 1 & a_{n,n+1} & \cdots & a_{n,j} & \cdots & a_{n,k}
\end{bmatrix}
$$

whose columns correspond to the vectors in this list and also the vector $b = (b_0, b_1, \ldots, b_n)'$. The following rule is used.

5.6.2. [RULE OF ASSOCIATION] *Let x be a typical vector in the list, other than one of the first $n + 1$. If all of the constraints $f_2(x) \geq 0, \ldots, f_m(x) \geq 0$ are satisfied by this vector, then*

$$
x \to [1, f_{1,1}(x) + 1, f_{1,2}(x) + 1, \ldots, f_{1,n}(x) + 1]'.
$$

On the other hand, if not all of the constraints are satisfied, then select one, say, f_j, for which $f_j(x) < 0$ and associate

$$
x \to [1, f_{j,1}(x) + 1, f_{j,2}(x) + 1, \ldots, f_{j,n}(x) + 1]'.
$$

The vector b is taken as $(1, 1, \ldots, 1)'$.

In other words, the column associated with a given vector x consists of either the partial derivatives of the objective function—should all of the constraints be satisfied at x—or the partial derivatives of one of the constraints which is not satisfied, all of these entries augmented by unity.

The constraint set $\{y \mid Ay = b, y \geq 0\}$ is clearly bounded since the top row of A has all of its entries equal to one, aside from the first $n + 1$ columns. Theorem 4.2.3 may then be applied and we obtain a primitive set $(x^{j_0}, x^{j_1}, \ldots, x^{j_n})$ whose associated columns form a feasible basis for $Ay = b$;

$$
y_{j_0} \begin{bmatrix} 1 \\ 1 + f_{l_0,1}(x^{j_0}) \\ \vdots \\ 1 + f_{l_0,n}(x^{j_0}) \end{bmatrix} + y_{j_1} \begin{bmatrix} 1 \\ 1 + f_{l_1,1}(x^{j_1}) \\ \vdots \\ 1 + f_{l_1,n}(x^{j_1}) \end{bmatrix} + \cdots \leq \begin{bmatrix} 1 \\ 1 \\ \vdots \\ 1 \end{bmatrix}
$$

with the understanding that we have equality in row i unless the side x^i is a member of the primitive set. As we shall see, if the grid is sufficiently fine on the simplex, the weights $y_{j_0}, y_{j_1}, \ldots$ will permit us to define Lagrange multipliers for the constrained maximization problem.

Let us, as is customary, select a finer and finer sequence of grids for which the vectors in the subsimplices corresponding to the final primitive sets converge to $\hat{x}$ and the corresponding values of y converge to $\hat{y}$. If we use the continuity of the partial derivatives, the above inequalities become

$$(5.6.3) \qquad \hat{y}_{j_0} \begin{bmatrix} 1 \\ 1 + f_{l_0,1}(\hat{x}) \\ \vdots \\ 1 + f_{l_0,n}(\hat{x}) \end{bmatrix} + \hat{y}_{j_1} \begin{bmatrix} 1 \\ 1 + f_{l_1,1}(\hat{x}) \\ \vdots \\ 1 + f_{l_1,n}(\hat{x}) \end{bmatrix} + \ldots \leq \begin{bmatrix} 1 \\ 1 \\ \vdots \\ 1 \end{bmatrix},$$

with equality in the ith row if $\hat{x}_i > 0$. It should be remarked that various columns may be identical if they involve the same instance of the rule of association 5.6.2.

Modifying the notation in an obvious way, we may rewrite these inequalities—with attention to the rules of association 5.6.2—as

$$(5.6.4) \qquad \hat{y}_1 \begin{bmatrix} 1 \\ 1 + f_{1,1}(\hat{x}) \\ \vdots \\ 1 + f_{1,n}(\hat{x}) \end{bmatrix} + \ldots + \hat{y}_m \begin{bmatrix} 1 \\ 1 + f_{m,1}(\hat{x}) \\ \vdots \\ 1 + f_{m,n}(\hat{x}) \end{bmatrix} \leq \begin{bmatrix} 1 \\ 1 \\ \vdots \\ 1 \end{bmatrix},$$

with the following understanding:

5.6.5. [PROPERTIES]

1. *We have equality in the ith row if $\hat{x}_i > 0$;*
2. *$\hat{y}_1 > 0$ implies $f_j(\hat{x}) \geq 0$ for $j = 2, \ldots, m$; and*
3. *$\hat{y}_j > 0$ (for $j = 2, \ldots, m$) implies $f_j(\hat{x}) \leq 0$.*

I shall demonstrate that $\hat{y}_1 > 0$ and that $\Sigma_1^m \hat{y}_j = 1$, which together will imply that $\pi_2 = \hat{y}_2/\hat{y}_1, \ldots, \pi_m = \hat{y}_m/\hat{y}_1$ are the correct Lagrange multipliers for the problem. To obtain these results we shall require the concavity of the functions $f_j(x)$ and the constraint qualifications—namely, the existence of the vector x^* with $f_j(x^*) > 0$ for $j = 2, \ldots, m$.

Let us begin the argument that $\hat{y}_1 > 0$ by multiplying the ith inequality in 5.6.4 by $x_i^* - \hat{x}_i$ and summing, for $i = 0, \ldots, n$. The sense of these inequalities is not changed by this multiplication because if the ith inequality is strict, $\hat{x}_i = 0$ and therefore $x_i^* - \hat{x}_i \geq 0$. We therefore obtain

$$\hat{y}_1 \left\{ \sum_{i=0}^{n} (x_i^* - \hat{x}_i) + \sum_{i=1}^{n} f_{1,i}(\hat{x})(x_i^* - \hat{x}_i) \right\}$$

$$+ \hat{y}_2 \left\{ \sum_{i=0}^{n} (x_i^* - \hat{x}_i) + \sum_{i=1}^{n} f_{2,i}(\hat{x})(x_i^* - \hat{x}_i) \right\} + \ldots \leq \sum_{i=0}^{n} (x_i^* - \hat{x}_i).$$

If we observe that $\Sigma_{i=0}^{n} x_i^* = \Sigma_{i=0}^{n} \hat{x}_i = 1$, this reduces to

$$(5.6.6) \qquad \sum_{j=1}^{m} \hat{y}_j \left[\sum_{i=1}^{n} f_{j,i}(\hat{x})(x_i^* - \hat{x}_i) \right] \leq 0.$$

Now let us make use of the assumption that each of the functions $f_j(x)$ is concave, an assumption which implies that

$$f_j(x^*) - f_j(\hat{x}) \leq \sum_{i=1}^{n} f_{j,i}(\hat{x})(x_i^* - \hat{x}_i).$$

If this inequality is incorporated in 5.6.6, we obtain

$$\sum_{j=1}^{m} \hat{y}_j \left[f_j(x^*) - f_j(\hat{x}) \right] \leq 0, \quad \text{or}$$

$$(5.6.7) \qquad \sum_{j=1}^{m} \hat{y}_j f_j(x^*) \leq \sum_{j=1}^{m} \hat{y}_j f_j(\hat{x}).$$

This latter inequality permits us to deduce that $\hat{y}_1$ is strictly positive, for if $\hat{y}_1 = 0$, then at least one of the remaining $\hat{y}_2, \ldots, \hat{y}_m$ is strictly positive. And moreover $f_j(x^*) > 0$ for $j = 2, \ldots, m$ by the constraint qualification. The left-hand side of 5.6.7 must therefore be strictly positive, and as a consequence so must the right-hand side be. But this contradicts the third part of 5.6.5, which states that $\hat{y}_j > 0$ for $j = 2, \ldots, m$ implies that $f_j(\hat{x}) \leq 0$. This contradiction demonstrates our first conclusion, that $\hat{y}_1 > 0$.

Knowing that $\hat{y}_1 > 0$, we may return to 5.6.5 to deduce that $f_j(\hat{x}) \geq 0$ for $j = 2, \ldots, m$, so that $\hat{x}$ satisfies *all* of the constraints, and moreover $f_j(\hat{x}) = 0$ if $\hat{y}_j > 0$.

To argue that $\Sigma_1^m \hat{y}_j = 1$, we merely notice that since $\hat{x}$ satisfies *all* of the constraints, assumption 5.6.1 implies that $\Sigma_1^n \hat{x}_i \leq c$ and therefore

$\hat{x}_0 \geq 1 - c > 0$. This means that the first inequality in 5.6.4 is indeed an equality; $\Sigma_1^m \hat{y}_j = 1$. The inequalities in 5.6.4 then take the form

$$\sum_{j=1}^{m} \hat{y}_j \frac{\partial f_j}{\partial x_i}(\hat{x}) \leq 0 \qquad \text{for } i = 1, \ldots, n,$$

with equality unless $\hat{x}_i = 0$. Finally if we define the Lagrange multipliers $\pi_2, \ldots, \pi_m$ by $\pi_j = \hat{y}_j / \hat{y}_1$, we see that $f_j(\hat{x}) \geq 0$, with equality if $\pi_j > 0$, and

$$\frac{\partial f_1}{\partial x_i}(\hat{x}) + \sum_{2}^{m} \pi_j \frac{\partial f_j}{\partial x_i}(\hat{x}) \leq 0,$$

with equality if $\hat{x}_i > 0$.

These are the conventional complementarity conditions which imply that the vector $\hat{x}$ is indeed the constrained maximum.

5.7. A NUMERICAL EXAMPLE

To illustrate the working of the algorithm developed in the preceding section let us consider the following nonlinear programming problem:

$$\max f_1(x) =$$
$$(x_1 + 3x_2)^{0.3}(3x_3 + x_4)^{0.2}(2x_5 + 3x_6)^{0.1}(5x_7 + 8x_8)^{0.15}(3x_9 + 4x_{10})^{0.05}$$

subject to

$$
\begin{bmatrix}
1. & 1. & 1. & 1. & 1. & 1. & 1. & 1. & 1. & 1. \\
.5 & 1.5 & .5 & 1.5 & .5 & 1.5 & .5 & 1.5 & .5 & 1.5 \\
2.7 & 2.7 & 1.8 & 1.8 & .9 & .9 & .4 & 1. & 1.5 & .6 \\
1.5 & 1.8 & 1.3 & 1.9 & 4. & 3. & 2. & .9 & 3.2 & 4.1
\end{bmatrix}
x -
\begin{bmatrix}
0.8 \\
0.7 \\
1.1 \\
2.6
\end{bmatrix}
\leq
\begin{bmatrix}
0 \\
0 \\
0 \\
0
\end{bmatrix}.
$$

We have $n = 10$. The vectors $x^{11}, \ldots, x^k$ were selected to be all vectors of the form $(m_0/100, m_1/100, \ldots, m_{10}/100)$ with m_i representing the positive integers summing to 100. The tie-breaking rule to be described in chapter 6 was used. The algorithm then terminated after 2,221 iterations in approximately 20 seconds of computation time on an IBM 360–50 with a primitive set containing the vectors x^1, x^4, x^8, and x^9. The numerators of the remaining seven vectors in the final primitive set are given below:

$$\begin{bmatrix} 20 & 20 & 20 & 20 & 20 & 19 & 19 \\ 1 & 1 & 1 & 1 & 1 & 1 & 1 \\ 17 & 17 & 17 & 17 & 18 & 18 & 18 \\ 18 & 19 & 19 & 19 & 18 & 18 & 18 \\ 1 & 1 & 1 & 1 & 1 & 1 & 1 \\ 6 & 5 & 5 & 5 & 5 & 5 & 6 \\ 5 & 5 & 5 & 6 & 6 & 6 & 5 \\ 25 & 25 & 26 & 25 & 25 & 25 & 25 \\ 1 & 1 & 1 & 1 & 1 & 1 & 1 \\ 1 & 1 & 1 & 1 & 1 & 1 & 1 \\ 5 & 5 & 4 & 4 & 4 & 5 & 5 \end{bmatrix}$$

The vectors in the final primitive set, excluding those representing the sides x^1, x^4, x^8, x^9, were averaged to yield a preliminary approximation of $\hat{x}$. A preliminary approximation of the Lagrangean multipliers π_2, π_3, π_4, π_5 was achieved by (1) obtaining $\hat{y}_1$ by adding the weights of the columns in the final basis corresponding to the derivatives of the objective function, and (2) dividing the other weights by $\hat{y}_1$.

A variation of Newton's method was then used to yield the final approximation, which is given in table 5.7.1.

TABLE 5.7.1. APPROXIMATION OF AN OPTIMAL SOLUTION

$\hat{x}_1$	0.	$f_1(x)$	0.640469
$\hat{x}_2$	0.187846	$f_2(x) - 0.8$	0.
$\hat{x}_3$	0.203826	$f_3(x) - 0.7$	0.
$\hat{x}_4$	0.	$f_4(x) - 1.1$	0.
$\hat{x}_5$	0.042661	$f_5(x) - 2.6$	-0.928465
$\hat{x}_6$	0.062782	π_2	0.190660
$\hat{x}_7$	0.253512	π_3	0.234030
$\hat{x}_8$	0.	π_4	0.178205
$\hat{x}_9$	0.	π_5	0.
$\hat{x}_{10}$	0.049371		

Furthermore, we have

$$(5.7.1) \qquad \frac{\partial f_1(\hat{x})}{\partial x_i} - \sum_{j=2}^{5} \pi_j \frac{\partial f_j(\hat{x})}{\partial x_i} \leq 0, \qquad i = 1, \ldots, 10,$$

with equality if $\hat{x}_i > 0$.

5.8. THE COMPUTATION OF AN INVARIANT OPTIMAL CAPITAL STOCK*

In this section I shall discuss the applicability of our computational methods to an important problem in optimal growth theory, independently explored by Sutherland (1967, 1970) for a very general model and by Koopmans (1971) for an extension of the von Neumann model of proportional capital growth which explicitly incorporates consumption and resources. The application of our methods to this problem was developed by Hansen and is described in a joint paper by Hansen and Koopmans (1972).

Let us begin by considering a technology with l types of capital goods, m additional resources that are spontaneously generated at each moment of time, k consumption goods, and n productive processes that are constant over time and defined by a unit activity. In each period an initial vector of capital stocks z and resources w is transformed into a capital stock z', available at the beginning of the next period, and a stock of nondurable goods ξ, which are consumed during the period in question. The feasible activity levels $x = (x_1, \ldots, x_n)$ are non-negative and constrained by the stocks of capital and other resources in the following fashion:

$$(5.8.1) \qquad \begin{aligned} Bx &\leq z, \\ Dx &\leq w. \end{aligned}$$

B and D are non-negative matrices of order (l, n) and (m, n), respectively. The stocks of new capital and consumer goods are then given by

$$(5.8.2) \qquad \begin{aligned} Cx &\geq z', \\ Ex &\geq \xi', \end{aligned}$$

with C and E also non-negative matrices whose orders are (l, n) and (k, n).

Given an initial capital stock z and a constant stream of resources w—exogenously supplied—the technology may be repeated in each period. In time period t, the activity levels, which may depend on t, will be constrained by w and the capital stock inherited from the past. In this fashion a sequence of consumption vectors $\xi^1, \xi^2, \ldots, \xi^t, \ldots$ consistent with the initial capital stock, resource endowment, and technology will be generated.

There is considerable scope in the selection of the sequence of activity levels, and a variety of different sequences of consumption vectors may be obtained. It is a common practice in optimal growth theory to evaluate such sequences by a social welfare function, in this case taken to be a discounted sum of utilities for consumption in each period:

$$(5.8.3) \qquad u(\xi^1) + \alpha u(\xi^2) + \alpha^2 u(\xi^3) + \ldots$$

The discount factor α is assumed to lie strictly between zero and one, and the common utility function u to be strictly concave and strictly increasing in each argument. We shall also assume, for simplicity, that u has continuous first-order partial derivatives.

For each choice of z—w is taken to be a fixed parameter of the problem —a unique sequence of ξs exist that maximizes 5.8.3, under mild assumptions on the technology matrices B, C, D, and E. This is a conventional nonlinear programming problem which is complicated only by the infinite dimensional set of possible activity levels over time. We can expect that the Kuhn-Tucker theorem applies and that suitable implicit prices (in the sense of present values) exist for each commodity at each moment of time.

The problem will yield not only an optimal sequence of consumption bundles $\xi^1, \xi^2, \ldots$, but also an associated sequence of capital stocks available at the beginning of each time period. Let us focus on the capital stock $z'(z)$ that arises at the beginning of the second period. We explicitly indicate the dependence of the second-period capital on the initial capital stock, other parameters being assumed constant. Our assumptions do not necessarily permit us to argue that z' is a unique function of z; if it is multiple-valued, then the set of z' associated with a given z may easily be shown to be convex.

The first problem, studied by Sutherland, Koopmans, and Hansen and Koopmans, is to demonstrate the existence of an invariant optimal capital stock: a vector z that reproduces itself, in an optimal program, at the beginning of all subsequent time periods. Such a capital stock can be found as a fixed point of the mapping that carries z into the stock of z'. The existence of an invariant optimal capital stock can therefore be demonstrated by a direct application of Kakutani's theorem, assuming that the technical requirements for the theorem are verified.

This particular approach, however, seems impractical for the next problem, that of computing a numerical solution. At each iteration of the algorithm that approximates a fixed point implied by Kakutani's theorem, the infinite dimensional nonlinear programming problem would have to be solved explicitly in order to determine the image of the capital vector in question.

To avoid this difficulty Koopmans has suggested solving instead a nearly equivalent single-period optimization problem, with an additional constraint on the implicit prices, whose solution, as also suggested by Sutherland's earlier work, will provide an invariant optimal capital stock. In order to describe this problem we define

$$(5.8.4) \qquad\qquad v(x) = u(Ex),$$

an induced utility for activity levels. We begin by considering the following nonlinear programming problem in which z is fixed:

$$\max v(x)$$

$$\text{subject to } Bx \le z,$$

$$(5.8.5) \qquad\qquad Cx \ge z,$$

$$Dx \le w,$$

$$x \ge 0.$$

If the Kuhn-Tucker theorem is applied to this problem, we obtain three non-negative vectors of dual variables q^1, q^2, and p corresponding to the three sets of constraints. Given our assumptions, which imply that v has continuous derivatives, we may express the appropriate relationships as follows:

$$\frac{\partial v}{\partial x_j} - \sum_i q_i^1 b_{ij} + \sum_i q_i^2 c_{ij} - \sum_i p_i d_{ij} \le 0 \qquad (= 0, \text{ if } x_j > 0),$$

$$\sum_j b_{ij} x_j \le z_i \qquad (= z_i, \text{ if } q_i^1 > 0),$$

$$(5.8.6) \qquad \sum_j c_{ij} x_j \ge z_i \qquad (= z_i, \text{ if } q_i^2 > 0),$$

$$\sum_j d_{ij} x_j \le w_i \qquad (= w_i, \text{ if } p_i > 0).$$

Of course the activity levels and the implicit prices will depend on the specific choice of z. The following lemma, whose proof may be found in the paper by Hansen and Koopmans, states that z will be an invariant optimal capital stock for the original problem if one additional condition is satisfied.

5.8.7. [LEMMA] *Let x, z, q^1, q^2, and p satisfy 5.8.6. If, in addition $q^2 = \alpha q^1$, then z will be an invariant optimal capital stock.*

The additional condition requires that the shadow prices of the stock of capital goods be identical at the beginning of each period when the discount factor α is used. If we denote q^2 and αq^1 by αq, then 5.8.6 takes the final form on which the computational procedure is based:

$$\frac{\partial v}{\partial x_j} - \sum_i q_i(b_{ij} - \alpha c_{ij}) - \sum_i p_i d_{ij} \leq 0 \qquad (= 0, \text{ if } x_j > 0),$$

(5.8.8)
$$\sum_j (b_{ij} - c_{ij})x_j \leq 0 \qquad (= 0, \text{ if } q_i > 0),$$

$$\sum_j d_{ij}x_j \leq w_i \qquad (= 0, \text{ if } p_i > 0).$$

In this set of conditions the second and third inequalities of 5.8.6 have been combined and the vector z eliminated.

The problem of determining vectors x, p, q that satisfy 5.8.8 may seem to be virtually identical with the Kuhn-Tucker complementary slackness conditions for the nonlinear programming problem

$$\max v(x)$$

$$\text{subject to } (B - C)x \leq 0,$$

$$Dx \leq w,$$

$$x \geq 0.$$

If this were correct, the methods of the previous two sections could be applied with no change. Unfortunately this is not so; the presence of the discount factor α in the first line of 5.8.8 removes our problem from the realm of conventional nonlinear programming problems. In order to employ theorem 4.2.3, the rules of association used in defining the matrix A will be of a more complex sort.

As in section 5.6 let us begin with the following assumptions.

5.8.9. [ASSUMPTIONS]

a. *There exists a c, with $0 < c < 1$, such that the non-negative solutions of $(B - C)x \leq 0$, $Dx \leq w$ satisfy $x_1 + \ldots + x_n \leq c$.*

b. *There exists a non-negative vector x^* such that $(B - \alpha C)x^* < 0$ and $Dx^* < w$. Since C is non-negative and $\alpha \leq 1$, the first part of this assumption implies that $\sum_1^n x_i^* < 1$.*

The second of these conditions plays a role similar to the constraint qualification in nonlinear programming. In a similar fashion it will permit us to deduce that a particular price differs from zero.

Again let us introduce an additional coordinate $x_0 = 1 - \Sigma_1^n x_i$, in order to work with the simplex

$$S = \left\{ x \mid x \geq 0, \sum_0^n x_i = 1 \right\},$$

of one higher dimension than usual. Let the first $n + 1$ vectors in the list $x^0, \ldots, x^n, x^{n+1}, \ldots, x^k$ represent the sides of this simplex and the remaining vectors constitute a fine grid on S. In order to apply theorem 4.2.3 we must associate each of these vectors with a column in the matrix A, whose dimensions are now $(n + 1) \times (k + 1)$.

5.8.10. [RULE OF ASSOCIATION] *Let x be a typical vector in the list other than one of the first $n + 1$.*

If $(B - C)x \leq 0$ and $Dx \leq w$, then

$$x \to [1, v_1(x) + 1, \ldots, v_n(x) + 1]',$$

where the subscripts refer to the partial derivatives of v.

If $\Sigma_j(b_{ij} - c_{ij})x_j > 0$ for some index i, then

$$x \to (1, -b_{i1} + \alpha c_{i1} + 1, \ldots, -b_{in} + \alpha c_{in} + 1)'.$$

If this inequality obtains for several rows i, then select a specific one, say, that with the lowest value of i.

If $(B - C)x \leq 0$, and $\Sigma_j d_{ij} x_j > w_i$, then

$$x \to (1, -d_{i1} + 1, \ldots, -d_{in} + 1)',$$

with a similar remark if several rows are possible. The vector b is taken as $(1, \ldots, 1)'$.

The constraint set $\{y \mid y \geq 0, Ay = b\}$ is clearly bounded, and theorem 4.2.3 may be applied. We obtain a primitive set $(x^{j_0}, \ldots, x^{j_n})$ whose associated columns form a feasible basis for $Ay = b$:

$$y_{j_0} \begin{bmatrix} a_{0j_0} \\ \vdots \\ a_{nj_0} \end{bmatrix} + \ldots + y_{j_n} \begin{bmatrix} a_{0j_n} \\ \vdots \\ a_{nj_n} \end{bmatrix} = \begin{bmatrix} 1 \\ \vdots \\ 1 \end{bmatrix},$$

with $y_{j_0}, \ldots, y_{j_n} \geq 0$.

In order to argue that we have obtained an approximate solution to 5.8.8, we consider a finer and finer sequence of grids. We select a subsequence for which the nonslack vectors in the final primitive sets converge to $\hat{x}$, the columns of A in the final feasible bases converge, and the corresponding weights y converge to $\hat{y}$.

The limiting columns will be of three types:

$$[1, v_1(\hat{x}) + 1, \ldots, v_n(\hat{x}) + 1]',$$

$$[1, -b_{i1} + \alpha c_{i1} + 1, \ldots \quad]', \quad \text{or}$$

$$[1, -d_{i1} + 1, \ldots \quad\quad]'.$$

Let us make a notational change in the above equations by using $\hat{\lambda}$ for the total weight associated with columns of the first type, $\hat{\varepsilon}_i$ for a weight associated with a column of the second type in which an index i appears, and $\hat{\delta}_i$ for a corresponding column of the third type. The above equations take the form

$$(5.8.11) \quad \hat{\lambda}
\begin{bmatrix} 1 \\ 1 + v_1(\hat{x}) \\ \vdots \\ 1 + v_n(\hat{x}) \end{bmatrix}
+ \sum_i \hat{\varepsilon}_i
\begin{bmatrix} 1 \\ 1 - b_{i1} + \alpha c_{i1} \\ \vdots \\ 1 - b_{in} + \alpha c_{in} \end{bmatrix}
+ \sum_i \hat{\delta}_i
\begin{bmatrix} 1 \\ 1 - d_{i1} \\ \vdots \\ 1 - d_{in} \end{bmatrix}
\leq
\begin{bmatrix} 1 \\ 1 \\ \vdots \\ 1 \end{bmatrix}.$$

The rules of association imply the following:

5.8.12. [PROPERTIES]
a. *We have equality in the ith row if $\hat{x}_i > 0$.*
b. *If $\hat{\lambda} > 0$, then $(B - C)\hat{x} \leq 0$, and $D\hat{x} \leq w$.*
c. *If $\hat{\varepsilon}_i > 0$, then $\sum_j (b_{ij} - c_{ij})\hat{x}_j \geq 0$.*
d. *If $\hat{\delta}_i > 0$, then $(B - C)\hat{x} \leq 0$ and $\sum_j d_{ij}\hat{x}_j \geq w_i$.*

We shall demonstrate that $\hat{\lambda} > 0$, and that $\hat{\lambda} + \Sigma\hat{\varepsilon}_i + \Sigma\hat{\delta}_i = 1$. This will permit us to show that $\hat{x}$, $\hat{p}$, and $\hat{q}$ defined by $\hat{p}_i = \hat{\varepsilon}_i/\hat{\lambda}$, $\hat{q}_i = \hat{\delta}_i/\hat{\lambda}$ satisfy conditions 5.8.8.

Let x^* be the non-negative vector previously referred to (in 5.8.9), which satisfies $(B - \alpha C)x^* < 0$ and $Dx^* < w$. We multiply the jth inequality of 5.8.11 by $x_j^* - \hat{x}_j$ and sum for $j = 0, \ldots, n$. (We define $x_0^* = 1 - \Sigma_1^n x_j^*$.) The sense of the inequality is not changed, since if the jth inequality is strict, then $x_j^* - \hat{x}_j = x_j^* \geq 0$. We obtain

$$\hat{\lambda}\left\{\sum_0^n (x_j^* - \hat{x}_j) + \sum_1^n (x_j^* - \hat{x}_j)v_j(\hat{x})\right\}$$

(5.8.13)
$$+ \Sigma\hat{\varepsilon}_i\left\{\sum_0^n (x_j^* - \hat{x}_j) - \sum_1^n (b_{ij} - \alpha c_{ij})(x_j^* - \hat{x}_j)\right\}$$

$$+ \Sigma\hat{\delta}_i\left\{\sum_0^n (x_j^* - \hat{x}_j) - \sum_1^n d_{ij}(x_j^* - \hat{x}_j)\right\} \leq \sum_0^n (x_j^* - \hat{x}_j).$$

If we observe that $\Sigma_0^n x_j^* = \Sigma_0^n \hat{x}_j = 1$, this becomes

$$\hat{\lambda} \sum_1^n (x_j^* - \hat{x}_j)v_j(\hat{x})$$

(5.8.14)
$$- \Sigma\hat{\varepsilon}_i \sum_1^n (b_{ij} - \alpha c_{ij})(x_j^* - \hat{x}_j)$$

$$- \Sigma\hat{\delta}_i \sum_1^n d_{ij}(x_j^* - \hat{x}_j) \leq 0.$$

Now let us assume that $\hat{\lambda} = 0$ and attempt to obtain a contradiction. At least one of the $\hat{\varepsilon}_i$ or $\hat{\delta}_i$ must be strictly positive. But for each $\hat{\delta}_i$ that is positive we must have $\Sigma d_{ij}\hat{x}_j \geq w_i$. Since $\Sigma d_{ij}x_j^* < w_i$, we obtain

$$- \Sigma\hat{\delta}_i \sum_1^n d_{ij}(x_j^* - \hat{x}_j) \geq 0,$$

and strictly so if one of the $\hat{\delta}_i$ is greater than zero.

On the other hand, $\hat{\varepsilon}_i > 0$ implies $\Sigma_j(b_{ij} - c_{ij})\hat{x}_j \geq 0$; and because C is non-negative and $\alpha \leq 1$, it follows that $\Sigma(b_{ij} - \alpha c_{ij})\hat{x}_j \geq 0$. Since $\Sigma_j(b_{ij} - \alpha c_{ij})x_j^* < 0$, we must have

$$- \Sigma\hat{\varepsilon}_i \sum_1^n (b_{ij} - \alpha c_{ij})(x_j^* - \hat{x}_j) \geq 0,$$

and strictly so if one of the $\hat{\varepsilon}_i > 0$.

These two statements combine to provide our first results, i.e., $\hat{\lambda} > 0$. We may then deduce from 5.8.12 that $(B - C)\hat{x} \leq 0$ and $D\hat{x} \leq w$, so that all of the required constraints are satisfied by the limiting vector $\hat{x}$. From the first part of assumption 5.8.9 we see that $\hat{x}_1 + \ldots + \hat{x}_n \leq c < 1$ and therefore $\hat{x}_0 > 0$.

The observation that $\hat{x}_0 > 0$ permits us to conclude that the first inequality of 5.8.11 is, in fact, an equality:

$$\hat{\lambda} + \sum_i \hat{\varepsilon}_i + \sum_i \hat{\delta}_i = 1;$$

and this permits us to replace 5.8.11 by the simpler form

$$\hat{\lambda} \begin{bmatrix} v_1(\hat{x}) \\ \vdots \\ v_n(\hat{x}) \end{bmatrix} - \Sigma\hat{\varepsilon}_i \begin{bmatrix} b_{i1} - \alpha c_{i1} \\ \vdots \\ b_{in} - \alpha c_{in} \end{bmatrix} - \Sigma\hat{\delta}_i \begin{bmatrix} d_{i1} \\ \vdots \\ d_{in} \end{bmatrix} \leq \begin{bmatrix} 0 \\ \vdots \\ 0 \end{bmatrix}.$$

Dividing by $\hat{\lambda}$, we have

$$\frac{\partial v}{\partial x_j} - \sum_i \left(\frac{\hat{\varepsilon}_i}{\hat{\lambda}}\right)(b_{ij} - \alpha c_{ij}) - \Sigma\left(\frac{\hat{\delta}_i}{\hat{\lambda}}\right)d_{ij} \leq 0,$$

the first inequality of 5.8.8. In addition, all of the required complementary slackness conditions have been built into the computational procedure. Assuming the validity of lemma 5.8.7, we have therefore determined an invariant optimal capital stock.

The reader may refer to the paper by Hansen and Koopmans for an explicit numerical example.

CHAPTER 6

A Procedure for Resolving Degeneracy

6.1. A LEXICOGRAPHIC TIE-BREAKING RULE

In virtually all of the numerical applications of our class of algorithms the most convenient grid of vectors on the simplex is the regular one consisting of all vectors of the form $(m_1/D, m_2/D, \ldots, m_n/D)$, with m_i representing non-negative integers summing to D. The grid provides a uniform coverage of the simplex so that a preliminary estimate of the answer is not required and the vectors in the grid can be remembered without storing them in the computer.

But, as we have previously mentioned, this particular grid raises serious problems of degeneracy, which must be resolved if our computational algorithms are not to cycle. In an earlier chapter I suggested a preliminary rule for breaking ties which could be used for problems of moderate size but whose storage requirements rose rapidly with the dimension of the problem. The present chapter will be devoted to an extensive analysis of a particular procedure for resolving degeneracy when the vectors x^{n+1}, $\ldots, x^k$ form a regular grid. The lexicographic tie-breaking rule to be proposed leads to a remarkably simple characterization of those collections of n vectors that form a primitive set and to a series of algorithms whose storage requirements are negligible for any practical application that might seriously be considered. In the third section I shall apply this characterization of primitive sets to the construction of an algorithm for determining equilibrium prices and activity levels that has some features in common with the decomposition method for linear programming.

But the reader should be alerted to the fact that this technique for solving degeneracy is useful not only in problems of numerical analysis and the design of efficient computational procedures. With this tie-breaking rule, primitive sets will be seen in the next chapter to have an intimate connection with simplicial subdivisions of the simplex and therefore with conventional procedures for establishing fixed point theorems. These observations will lead to another interpretation of our class of algorithms, which is capable of an independent generalization and which the reader may prefer on the grounds of familiarity and geometric intuition.

Let us then consider the list $x^{n+1}, \ldots, x^k$ consisting of all vectors of the form $(m_1/D, \ldots, m_n/D)$, with m_i representing non-negative integers summing to D (fig. 6.1.1). In order to overcome the problem of degeneracy,

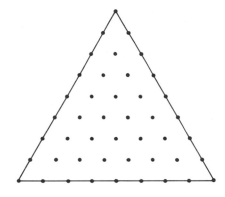

Figure 6.1.1

some systematic rule must be proposed which permits us to decide which of the two vectors

$$(m_1/D, m_2/D, \ldots, m_n/D) \text{ and}$$

$$(m'_1/D, m'_2/D, \ldots, m'_n/D)$$

has the larger ith coordinate should these two coordinates be numerically equal. For the algorithm to be successful the ordering of the ith coordinates must be complete—so that ties are strictly broken between any pair of vectors—and transitive, in the customary sense. The following lexicographic rule, which provides a different tie-breaking procedure for each coordinate, will have these two properties.

6.1.1. [DEFINITION] *Let*

$$x = (m_1/D, m_2/D, \ldots, m_n/D) \quad and$$

$$x' = (m'_1/D, m'_2/D, \ldots, m'_n/D)$$

be an arbitrary pair of vectors in the regular grid. We define an ordering on the ith coordinates of these vectors by saying that $x_i > x_i'$ if and only if the vector

$$(m_i, m_{i+1}, \ldots, m_n, m_1, \ldots, m_{i-1})$$

is lexicographically larger than

$$(m_i', m_{i+1}', \ldots, m_n', m_1', \ldots, m_{i-1}').$$

We also stipulate that the ith coordinate of any vector in the regular grid is to be considered strictly larger than the ith coordinate of the side of the simplex x^i.

The concept of a lexicographic ordering used in this definition is the conventional one: the vector $a = (a_1, a_2, \ldots, a_n)$ is lexicographically larger than $b = (b_1, b_2, \ldots, b_n)$ if the first nonzero element in the sequence $a_1 - b_1, a_2 - b_2, \ldots, a_n - b_n$ is positive. For example, the vector (3, 5, −1, 0, −50) is lexicographically larger than (3, 5, −2, 15, 75).

It is important, however, to stress that the definition 6.1.1 employs a different lexicographic ordering for each coordinate, so that n distinct orderings are involved. Consider, for example, the two vectors

$$x = (.10, .20, .05, .25, .40) \quad \text{and}$$

$$x' = (.09, .20, .07, .24, .40)$$

in the regular grid with $n = 5$ and $D = 100$. The definition implies that $x_2' > x_2$ since the vector (20, 7, 24, 40, 9) is lexicographically larger than (20, 5, 25, 40, 10). On the other hand, $x_5 > x_5'$ because ties in this coordinate are broken by a lexicographic ordering that begins with the fifth coordinate followed by the first, second, third, and fourth coordinates. Strictly speaking, we are dealing with n distinct orderings on the vectors in the regular grid, rather than on their coordinates. But the two concepts are interchangeable once the specific list of vectors is explicitly given.

The reader should have no difficulty in verifying that each of these orderings is complete and transitive, the two properties required for our class of algorithms to be successful. The arguments of chapter 2, which were described in terms of the conventional ordering of strict inequality between real numbers, can easily be extended to an arbitrary complete ordering of the components of the grid vectors such as that afforded by 6.1.1. Primitive sets can be defined as in 2.2.6 and the replacement operation will have uniqueness properties identical with those described in section 2.4.

Consider, for example, a matrix

$$M = \begin{bmatrix} m_{11} & \cdots & m_{1,n-l} \\ m_{21} & \cdots & m_{2,n-l} \\ \cdot & & \\ \cdot & & \\ \cdot & & \\ m_{n1} & \cdots & m_{n,n-l} \end{bmatrix}$$

with n rows and $n - l$ columns. The entries of M are assumed to be non-negative integers and the column sums are equal to D, so that the $n - l$ vectors

$$(m_{11}/D, \ldots, m_{n1}/D)$$

$$\vdots$$

$$(m_{1,n-l}/D, \ldots, m_{n,n-l}/D)$$

lie on the unit simplex. These vectors, along with the sides $s^{i_1}, \ldots, s^{i_l}$, will form a primitive set if the following conditions are met:

6.1.2. [DEFINITION] *For each row i of the matrix M, other than rows $i_1, \ldots, i_l$, let the lexicographically smallest element lie in column j_i. The columns of M—after division by D—form a primitive set, along with the sides $s^{i_1}, \ldots, s^{i_l}$, if there is no vector $m = (m_1, \ldots, m_n)$ with non-negative integer entries summing to D, such that*

$$(m_i, m_{i+1}, \ldots, m_1, \ldots, m_{i-1})$$

is lexicographically larger than

$$(m_{i,j_i}, m_{i+1,j_i}, \ldots, m_{1,j_i}, \ldots, m_{i-1,j_i})$$

for all $i \neq i_1, \ldots, i_l$.

6.2. A CHARACTERIZATION OF PRIMITIVE SETS

It is, of course, interesting that the lexicographic ordering introduced in the previous section is sufficient to eliminate degeneracy. The replacement step will always result in a unique replacement, and each of the algorithms previously discussed can be applied without any concern about cycling. But it would seem, at first glance, that this complex ordering has no particular properties that permit the replacement step to be carried out simply—without an exhaustive search through all of the vectors in the list. This is, however, not the case.

The specific ordering has been selected not only to resolve degeneracy, but also because it permits a direct characterization of those sets of n vectors which form a primitive set. Let

$$M = \begin{bmatrix} m_{11} & m_{12} & \cdots & m_{1n} \\ m_{21} & m_{22} & \cdots & m_{2n} \\ \vdots & \vdots & & \vdots \\ m_{n1} & m_{n2} & \cdots & m_{nn} \end{bmatrix}$$

be the numerators of n vectors in the regular grid other than the first n vectors that represent the sides of S. Each of the entries in M is a non-negative integer and the column sums are all equal to D. The following theorem provides a simple explicit condition which guarantees that these vectors form a primitive set.

6.2.1. [THEOREM] *The vectors associated with the columns of M form a primitive set if and only if there is a rearrangement of these columns and a permutation $\{I(j)\}$ of the integers $1 \ldots, n$, such that:*

a. *The jth column of M is identical with column $j - 1$, except for the two rows $I(j) - 1$ and $I(j)$; and*

b. $m_{i,j} = m_{i,j-1} + 1$ *for* $i = I(j) - 1$,
$m_{i,j} = m_{i,j-1} - 1$ *for* $i = I(j)$.

In statements a and b all subscripts are to be interpreted modulo n.

This class of matrices first appears in Hansen (1968) and with a simple change of coordinates in Kuhn (1968). As we move from a column to its neighbor on the right—the column to the right of column n is the first column—only two changes take place: a specific element is increased by one unit and the element immediately below it is decreased by a single unit. Moreover, for different columns the decreases shall occur in different rows. This property is illustrated by the following example in which $n = 5$ and $D = 100$:

$$\begin{bmatrix} \underline{10} & 10 & 10 & 11 & 11 \\ 20 & 20 & 21 & \underline{20} & 20 \\ 30 & 31 & \underline{30} & 30 & 30 \\ 10 & \underline{9} & 9 & 9 & 10 \\ 30 & 30 & 30 & 30 & \underline{29} \end{bmatrix}$$

The permutation $\{I(j)\}$ describes the row in which a decrease occurs in passing from column $j - 1$ to column j; in this example it is given by the following table:

j	$I(j)$
1	1
2	4
3	3
4	2
5	5

In the course of the algorithm the matrix M will be present on each iteration and varied systematically as the replacement steps are carried out. There will be no necessity to apply theorem 6.2.1 in order to recognize the primitive sets, for the replacements will automatically generate a sequence of matrices satisfying these conditions. This compact description of the vectors generating a primitive set is also capable of a remarkable and far-reaching geometrical interpretation—originally proposed by Kuhn —which will be explored in the subsequent chapter.

Let us begin with a proof of the necessity of these conditions that proceeds through a sequence of three lemmas, each providing additional properties of the matrix M under the assumption that its columns represent a primitive set of vectors. Assume first that the columns of M are rearranged in such a way that the first coordinates of the vectors are lexicographically increasing as we read from column 1 to column n.

Since the vectors form a primitive set, each column of M will contain precisely one entry that is the minimum element in its row—in the sense of the cyclic lexicographical ordering which begins in that row (lemma 2.2.3). For column j let the row with this property be denoted by $I(j)$, thereby defining the permutation required by theorem 6.2.1. In the example above in which $n = 5$, the smallest element in row 4 appears in column 2, since the sequence of vectors

$$\begin{bmatrix} 9 \\ 30 \\ 10 \\ 20 \\ 31 \end{bmatrix} \begin{bmatrix} 9 \\ 30 \\ 10 \\ 21 \\ 30 \end{bmatrix} \begin{bmatrix} 9 \\ 30 \\ 11 \\ 20 \\ 30 \end{bmatrix} \begin{bmatrix} 10 \\ 29 \\ 11 \\ 20 \\ 30 \end{bmatrix} \begin{bmatrix} 10 \\ 30 \\ 10 \\ 20 \\ 30 \end{bmatrix}$$

is lexicographically increasing.

6.2.2. [LEMMA] *The entries in the first row of M are not all equal.*
The proof depends merely on the observation that if

$$M = \begin{bmatrix} m_1 & m_1 & \cdots & m_1 \\ m_{21} & m_{22} & \cdots & m_{2n} \\ \vdots & \vdots & & \vdots \\ m_{n1} & m_{n2} & & m_{nn} \end{bmatrix}$$

the lexicographic ordering of the second row would be identical with that of the first, and both rows would have their lexicographic minima appearing in the same column—a situation inconsistent with the definition of a primitive set.

6.2.3. [LEMMA] *The elements in the first row of M cannot differ by more than one.*

The proof of this lemma is most easily seen by reference to a special case, say, $n = 5$. Let

$$M = \begin{bmatrix} \underline{m_1} & m_1 & m_1 + 1 & m_1 + 1 & m_1 + 2 \\ m_{21} & m_{22} & \underline{m_{23}} & m_{24} & m_{25} \\ m_{31} & m_{32} & m_{33} & m_{34} & \underline{m_{35}} \\ m_{41} & \underline{m_{42}} & m_{43} & m_{44} & m_{45} \\ m_{51} & m_{52} & m_{53} & \underline{m_{54}} & m_{55} \end{bmatrix},$$

in which the minimum element in each row—according to the lexicographical ordering appropriate to that row—has been underlined.

Consider the vector

$$m' = \begin{bmatrix} m_1 + 1 \\ m_{25} \\ m_{35} \\ m_{45} \\ m_{55} + 1 \end{bmatrix},$$

all of whose entries are non-negative and whose column sum is identical with those of M. This vector obviously has its first entry larger than the minimum entry in row 1. But we can say even more. The ith entry of m' (for $i \geq 2$) is lexicographically larger than the ith entry in column 5, and therefore it is lexicographically larger than the minimum entry in the ith row. This contradicts the definition of a primitive set and demonstrates the lemma.

Both of these lemmas are applicable to any row of M and demonstrate that within a row the elements are not identical nor can they differ by more than one. The first two rows of M must therefore have the form

$$
M = \begin{bmatrix}
\underline{m_1} & m_1 & & m_1 & m_1 + 1 & & m_1 + 1 & \cdots & m_1 + 1 \\
m_2 & m_2 & m_2 + 1 & m_2 + 1 & \underline{m_2} & m_2 & m_2 + 1 & \cdots & m_2 + 1 \\
\vdots & & & & \vdots & & & & \vdots \\
m_{n1} & & & & m_{nj^*} & & & & m_{nn}
\end{bmatrix} .
$$

(with j^* labeling the fifth column)

In this matrix the appearance of the second row is required by the assumption that the first row is arranged in a lexicographically increasing order. The second row must be lexicographically increasing as we move from column 1 to column $j^* - 1$, and also as we move from column j^* to column n.

As we have written it, the second row seems to have a more complex structure than the first: its entries are permitted to increase twice and decrease twice as read in a cyclic fashion starting with column j^* and proceeding to the right, rather than the single increase and decrease predicted by theorem 6.2.1. The following lemma shows that a special form for row 2 must prevail, in which this multiple fluctuation does not occur.

6.2.4. [LEMMA] *The entries in row 2 are also lexicographically increasing if we read in a cyclic fashion starting with column j^* and proceed to the right, ending with $j^* - 1$.*

The entries in the second row of M are clearly lexicographically increasing as we move from column 1 to column $j^* - 1$ and also as we move from column j^* to column n. The difficulty arises in moving from column n to column 1. What we must demonstrate is that if the second row does indeed end with $m_2 + 1$ (rather than m_2), then the string that starts with m_2 in column 1 cannot appear.

To see this, consider the vector

$$m' = \begin{bmatrix} m_1 \\ m_2 + 1 \\ m_{3n} \\ \vdots \\ m_{nn} + 1 \end{bmatrix},$$

whose entries are non-negative and sum to D. Clearly this vector has its first entry lexicographically larger than the first entry of column 1. And its ith entry (for $i \geq 2$) is also lexicographically larger than the ith entry of column n. Since the ith entry of column n is lexicographically no less than the minimum entry in the ith row of M, we obtain a contradiction that demonstrates lemma 6.2.4.

This series of lemmas now permits us to say that M has the form

$$
\overset{\displaystyle j^*}{M = \begin{bmatrix} m_1 & \cdots & m_1 & m_1 + 1 & \cdots & m_1 + 1 & \cdots & m_1 + 1 \\ m_2 + 1 & \cdots & m_2 + 1 & m_2 & \cdots & m_2 + 1 & \cdots & m_2 + 1 \\ \vdots & & \vdots & \vdots & & \vdots & & \vdots \end{bmatrix}}
$$

and that the predicted change in passing from column $j^* - 1$ to column j^* —an increase by one unit in a particular row followed by a decrease of one unit in the succeeding row—does appear in the first two rows. Moreover, no other increase appears in row 1 and no other decrease in row 2. But since row 2's elements are now known to be lexicographically increasing (starting with j^*), the identical arguments can now be applied to this row, then to row 3, etc., and finally to row n. The special relationship between the first two rows will therefore prevail in any pair of successive rows of the matrix including row n followed by the first row. This demonstrates that half of theorem 6.2.1 which states that the matrix M must have the required form if its columns represent a primitive set.

The remaining half of the theorem—that a matrix with these properties will always generate a primitive set of vectors—can be argued quite easily by means of induction on the size of the matrix. It is clearly true for $n = 2$. Let us assume that we are given a matrix

$$
M = \begin{bmatrix}
m_{11} & m_{12} & \cdots & m_{1n} \\
m_{21} & m_{22} & \cdots & m_{2n} \\
\vdots & \vdots & & \vdots \\
m_{n1} & m_{n2} & \cdots & m_{nn}
\end{bmatrix}
$$

having non-negative integral entries and column sums equal to D and satisfying the conditions of theorem 6.2.1. If this does not represent a primitive set, then there must be a vector $(m_1, m_2, \ldots, m_n)$ whose coordinates are also non-negative integers summing to D and which has its ith coordinate lexicographically larger than the lexicographic minimum in row i for $i = 1, \ldots, n$. In other words, we must have for each i

(6.2.5) $(m_i, m_{i+1} \ldots m_n, m_1 \ldots) \succ (m_{ij}, m_{i+1,j} \ldots m_{n,j}, m_{1,j} \ldots)$

for that j with $I(j) = i$.

I shall show that this leads to a contradiction by constructing an $(n - 1) \times (n - 1)$ matrix that satisfies the conditions of theorem 6.2.1, but does not represent a primitive set. If we assume that the theorem is correct for matrices of size $n - 1$, this contradiction will demonstrate its validity for matrices of size n. Let us begin by making the observation that for some row i we must have

$$m_i = \min[m_{i1}, m_{i2}, \ldots, m_{in}].$$

For if this were not true, we would have $m_i \geq \min[m_{i1}, m_{i2}, \ldots, m_{in}] + 1$ for all i. Now take an arbitrary column of M, say, the first. We must certainly have $\min[m_{i1}, m_{i2}, \ldots, m_{in}] + 1 \geq m_{i1}$, since no two elements in the ith row differ by more than one. And this inequality must be strict for $i = I(1)$. We therefore conclude that $m_i \geq m_{i1}$ for all i, with at least one strict inequality. This contradicts the assumption that $\Sigma m_i = D = \Sigma m_{i1}$ and shows that $m_i = \min[m_{i1}, m_{i2}, \ldots, m_{in}]$ for at least one i. There is no loss in generality in assuming this row to be the first:

(6.2.6) $m_1 = \min[m_{11}, m_{12}, \ldots, m_{1n}].$

Now let us construct the matrix with $n - 1$ rows and $n - 1$ columns that exhibits the contradiction. Suppose that the unique increase in the first row of M occurs between columns $j^* - 1$ and j^*; row 2 will therefore decrease by one unit between these two columns so that $I(j^*) = 2$:

$$\begin{bmatrix} \cdots & m_{1,j^*-1} & m_{1,j^*-1}+1 & \cdots \\ \cdots & m_{2,j^*-1} & m_{2,j^*-1}-1 & \cdots \\ & \vdots & \vdots & \end{bmatrix}$$

The remaining entries in columns $j^* - 1$ and j^* are, of course, identical.

If we then form a new matrix with $n - 1$ rows and n columns by adding together the first two rows of M

(6.2.7)

$$\begin{bmatrix} m_{11}+m_{21} & \cdots & m_{1j}+m_{2j} & \cdots & m_{1n}+m_{2n} \\ m_{31} & & m_{3j} & & m_{3n} \\ \vdots & & \vdots & & \vdots \\ m_{n1} & & m_{nj} & & m_{nn} \end{bmatrix},$$

columns $j^* - 1$ and j^* will be identical. One of them may be deleted and we obtain an $(n - 1) \times (n - 1)$ matrix M' which also satisfies the conditions of theorem 6.2.1 and which, by the induction assumption, must represent a primitive set. Our contradiction will be obtained by showing that for each $i = 3, \ldots, n$ and for that j with $I(j) = i$

(6.2.8) $(m_i, \ldots, m_n, m_1 + m_2, \ldots) \succ (m_{ij}, \ldots, m_{n,j}, m_{1j} + m_{2j}, \ldots).$

We consider the two cases which can occur:

1. $m_1 = m_{1j} - 1$. In this case the ties in the inequality 6.2.5 must be broken by some coordinate between i and n. But this means that the ties in 6.2.8 are broken in the same way.

2. $m_1 = m_{1j}$. This implies that the ties in 6.2.5 do not involve a comparison between m_1 and m_{1j}; the tie is broken by some other coordinate, and in 6.2.8 the tie will be broken in the same way. This latter argument also demonstrates that

$$(m_1 + m_2, m_3, \ldots) \succ (m_{1j} + m_{2j}, m_{3j}, \ldots) \qquad \text{for } I(j) = 1.$$

We have therefore exhibited a contradiction to the induction assumption that theorem 6.2.1 is valid for matrices of size $(n - 1) \times (n - 1)$ and have established the validity of the theorem in general.

Before proceeding to the description of the replacement step, let us complete this section by extending theorem 6.2.1 to the case in which the primitive set contains vectors $x^{i_1}, x^{i_2}, \ldots, x^{i_l}$ representing sides of the simplex S. The matrix M will be modified to consist only of the nonslack vectors:

$$
M = \begin{bmatrix}
m_{11} & \cdots & m_{1,n-l} \\
m_{21} & \cdots & m_{2,n-l} \\
\vdots & & \vdots \\
m_{n1} & \cdots & m_{n,n-l}
\end{bmatrix}
$$

6.2.9. [THEOREM] *The columns of M and the slack vectors* $x^{i_1}, \ldots, x^{i_l}$ *form a primitive set if and only if:*

a. *The entries in rows* $i_1, \ldots, i_l$ *are all zeros, and*

b. *the* $(n - l) \times (n - l)$ *submatrix of M obtained by deleting rows* $i_1, \ldots, i_l$ *represents a primitive set of dimension* $n - l$.

As an illustration, consider the matrix

$$
\begin{bmatrix}
0 & 0 & 0 \\
49 & 49 & 50 \\
0 & 1 & 0 \\
0 & 0 & 0 \\
15 & 14 & 14
\end{bmatrix}.
$$

Rows 1 and 4 consist entirely of zeros, and the submatrix

$$
\begin{bmatrix}
49 & 49 & 50 \\
0 & 1 & 0 \\
15 & 14 & 14
\end{bmatrix}
$$

represents a primitive set with $n = 3$; the three columns of the matrix therefore represent a primitive set in conjunction with the first and fourth slack vectors.

Let us demonstrate first that a matrix of this form does indeed generate a primitive set. We shall assume, in order to illustrate the proof, that

$$
M = \begin{bmatrix}
0 & 0 & 0 \\
m_{21} & m_{22} & m_{23} \\
m_{31} & m_{32} & m_{33} \\
0 & 0 & 0 \\
m_{51} & m_{52} & m_{53}
\end{bmatrix}.
$$

The submatrix obtained by deleting rows 1 and 4, by hypothesis, represents a primitive set for $n = 3$. Now let $(m_1, m_2, \ldots, m_5)'$ be a vector which has non-negative integral entries, whose coordinates sum to the common column sums of M, and which has its ith coordinate (for $i = 2, 3, 5$) lexicographically larger than the minimum element in the ith row of M, according to the lexicographic ordering appropriate to that row. We may assume that $m_1 = 0$, for if $m_1 > 0$, the vector $(0, m_1 + m_2, m_3, m_4, m_5)'$ would have the same properties. Similarly, m_4 can be taken to be zero. But then the vector $(m_2, m_3, m_5)'$ has each of its elements strictly larger than the minimum element—according to the appropriate lexicographic order—in the corresponding row of

$$\begin{bmatrix} m_{21} & m_{22} & m_{23} \\ m_{31} & m_{32} & m_{33} \\ m_{51} & m_{52} & m_{53} \end{bmatrix},$$

which is a contradiction.

To demonstrate the remaining half of this theorem—that a primitive set must be generated by a matrix of this form—we begin by arguing that the entries in those rows corresponding to slack vectors must be zero. For example, let the columns of

$$\begin{bmatrix} m_{11} & m_{12} & m_{13} \\ m_{21} & m_{22} & m_{23} \\ m_{31} & m_{32} & m_{33} \\ m_{41} & m_{42} & m_{43} \\ m_{51} & m_{52} & m_{53} \end{bmatrix}$$

generate a primitive set in conjunction with the first and fourth slack vectors. If one of the elements in the first row—say, m_{13}—is strictly greater than zero, we merely argue that the vector

$$(m_{13} - 1, m_{23}, m_{33}, m_{43}, m_{53} + 1)'$$

has all of its coordinates strictly larger than the appropriate row-minima because its first and fourth entries are lexicographically positive and its remaining entries lexicographically larger than the corresponding row-minima of M.

In order to complete the demonstration of theorem 6.2.9, we merely apply 6.2.1 to the square matrix obtained by deleting from M those rows corresponding to slack vectors.

6.3. The Replacement Step

The previous section has exhibited the characterization of primitive sets when the cyclic lexicographic ordering is applied to the grid of vectors whose components are rational numbers with a fixed denominator. As the following theorem indicates, the replacement step itself also has a remarkably simple form.

6.3.1. [THEOREM] (Hansen 1968, Hansen and Scarf 1969) *Let M represent a primitive set with no slack vectors. Then the unique replacement for column j is given by*

$$m'_{ij} = m_{ij} + 1 \quad for \ i = I(j) \quad and \quad I(j+1) - 1,$$

$$m'_{ij} = m_{ij} - 1 \quad for \ i = I(j) - 1 \quad and \quad I(j+1),$$

$$m'_{ij} = m_{ij} \quad otherwise.$$

If $I(j) = I(j+1) - 1$, then $m'_{ij} = m_{ij} + 2$ for this common value of i, and as before for the other rows. If $I(j) - 1 = I(j+1)$, then $m'_{ij} = m_{ij} - 2$ for this common row, and as before for the other rows. In this latter case if $m'_{ij} = -1$, the ith slack vector is the replacement for column j.

In order to show that this is the correct form of the replacement rule it is sufficient to demonstrate that the new matrix obtained by the rule satisfies the conditions of theorem 6.2.9 and is therefore a new primitive set. The argument depends on examining the three columns $j - 1, j$, and $j + 1$ (modulo n) in order to verify that after replacement each of these columns differs from its predecessor in the required fashion.

The three columns are all identical except for the elements in rows $I(j) - 1$, $I(j)$, $I(j+1) - 1$, and $I(j+1)$. If we assume for the moment that these four rows are distinct, the submatrix of M consisting of these four rows and three columns is given by

$$
\begin{array}{c}
I(j) - 1 \\
I(j) \\
I(j+1) - 1 \\
I(j+1)
\end{array}
\begin{bmatrix}
a & a+1 & a+1 \\
b+1 & b & b \\
c & c & c+1 \\
d+1 & d+1 & d
\end{bmatrix},
$$
$$
\quad\quad\quad\quad j-1 \quad\ j \quad\ j+1
$$

with a, b, c, and d representing non-negative integers. The suggested replacement for column j will produce a new submatrix given by

$$
\begin{array}{c}
I'(j+1)-1 \\
I'(j+1) \\
I'(j)-1 \\
I'(j)
\end{array}
\begin{bmatrix}
a & a & a+1 \\
b+1 & b+1 & b \\
c & c+1 & c+1 \\
d+1 & d & d
\end{bmatrix},
$$
$$
\begin{array}{ccc}
j-1 & j & j+1
\end{array}
$$

which clearly satisfies the conditions of 6.2.1 if the new permutation I' is defined by $I'(j) = I(j+1)$ and $I'(j+1) = I(j)$ and is equal to I elsewhere.

In the case in which $I(j) = I(j+1) - 1$, the three columns differ only in three elements, and the appropriate submatrix of M is

$$
\begin{array}{c}
 \\
I(j)-1 \\
I(j) \\
I(j+1)
\end{array}
\begin{array}{ccc}
j-1 & j & j+1
\end{array}
$$
$$
\begin{array}{c}
I(j)-1 \\
I(j) \\
I(j+1)
\end{array}
\begin{bmatrix}
a & a+1 & a+1 \\
b+1 & b & b+1 \\
c+1 & c+1 & c
\end{bmatrix}.
$$

The replacement rule produces a submatrix

$$
\begin{array}{ccc}
j-1 & j & j+1
\end{array}
$$
$$
\begin{array}{c}
I'(j+1)-1 \\
I'(j+1) \\
I'(j)
\end{array}
\begin{bmatrix}
a & a & a+1 \\
b+1 & b+2 & b+1 \\
c+1 & c & c
\end{bmatrix},
$$

again satisfying the conditions of 6.2.1 with the same new permutation as before.

The third possibility, $I(j+1) = I(j) - 1$, presents us with

$$
\begin{array}{ccc}
j-1 & j & j+1
\end{array}
$$
$$
\begin{array}{c}
I(j+1)-1 \\
I(j+1) \\
I(j)
\end{array}
\begin{bmatrix}
a & a & a+1 \\
b & b+1 & b \\
c+1 & c & c
\end{bmatrix},
$$

and after replacing column j, we obtain

$$
\begin{array}{cc}
 & \begin{array}{ccc} j-1 & j & j+1 \end{array} \\
\begin{array}{c} I'(j)-1 \\ I'(j) \\ I'(j+1) \end{array} &
\left[\begin{array}{ccc}
a & a+1 & a+1 \\
b & b-1 & b \\
c+1 & c+1 & c
\end{array}\right].
\end{array}
$$

Again we satisfy the conditions of theorem 6.2.1, with the same modified permutation. The only difficulty arises if $b = 0$, for in this case the new vector has an entry of -1 in row $I'(j)$. But in this case the remaining entries in row $I'(j)$ are all zero, and appealing to theorem 6.2.9 we see that a primitive set will result if column j is replaced by the ith slack vector with $i = I'(j)$. This demonstrates theorem 6.3.1.

The following examples of the replacement operation may be useful. If the second column is removed in

$$
\begin{bmatrix}
\underline{10} & 10 & 10 & 11 & 11 \\
20 & 20 & 21 & \underline{20} & 20 \\
30 & 31 & \underline{30} & 30 & 30 \\
10 & \underline{9} & 9 & 9 & 10 \\
30 & 30 & 30 & 30 & \underline{29}
\end{bmatrix},
$$

we obtain

$$
\begin{bmatrix}
\underline{10} & 10 & 10 & 11 & 11 \\
20 & 21 & 21 & \underline{20} & 20 \\
30 & \underline{29} & 30 & 30 & 30 \\
10 & 10 & \underline{9} & 9 & 10 \\
30 & 30 & 30 & 30 & \underline{29}
\end{bmatrix};
$$

and if the first column is subsequently removed from this latter matrix, we have

$$
\begin{bmatrix}
11 & \underline{10} & 10 & 11 & 11 \\
21 & 21 & 21 & \underline{20} & 20 \\
\underline{29} & 29 & 30 & 30 & 30 \\
10 & 10 & \underline{9} & 9 & 10 \\
29 & 30 & 30 & 30 & \underline{29}
\end{bmatrix}.
$$

We shall turn in a moment to the modifications of the replacement step required by the presence of slack vectors in the primitive set. The reader should, however, be aware of the great simplicity of theorem 6.3.1 and the ease with which the replacement step can be carried out. Regardless of the size of the problem each iteration requires a change in no more than four entries of column j, two of which increase by one unit and two of which decrease by a single unit. The permutation $[I(1), \ldots, I(n)]$ is then modified by interchanging $I(j)$ and $I(j + 1)$. A possibly simpler description, which the reader may prefer, is that the replacement for column j equals the sum of columns $j - 1$ and $j + 1$ minus column j itself.

The only parameters requiring storage in the application of our algorithms are therefore the matrix M and the permutation I, at least insofar as primitive sets are concerned. The required operations can easily be programmed for a high-speed computer and carried out with considerable rapidity, so that no serious difficulties are encountered should a problem involve even as many as 10,000 iterations. Whatever time constraints do arise in an actual application will be due entirely to the numerical evaluation of functions or linear programming pivot steps necessary to determine the sequence of vectors to be replaced, not in the mechanics of the replacement step itself.

If slack vectors are involved in the primitive set, the replacement operation need only be modified slightly. If a nonslack vector is removed from M, the replacement operation is carried out on the square submatrix representing a primitive set of dimension $n - l$. A new slack vector will be introduced only if the incoming column has a component of -1, and in this case the number of columns in M shrinks by one. This occurs, for example, if the middle column is removed in the matrix

$$\begin{bmatrix} 0 & 0 & 0 \\ 49 & 49 & 50 \\ 0 & 1 & 0 \\ 0 & 0 & 0 \\ 15 & 14 & 14 \end{bmatrix},$$

yielding a new matrix

$$\begin{bmatrix} 0 & 0 \\ 49 & 50 \\ 0 & 0 \\ 0 & 0 \\ 15 & 14 \end{bmatrix}$$

whose two columns form a primitive set along with the first, third, and fourth slack vectors.

If, on the other hand, a slack vector is removed from a primitive set, the number of columns in M increases by one. The operation is the reverse of deleting the middle column in the case

$$\begin{bmatrix} a & a & a+1 \\ 0 & 1 & 0 \\ b+1 & b & b \end{bmatrix}$$

and this determines precisely the location of the incoming nonslack column. To be more specific, let x^{i*} be a slack vector which is to be removed from the primitive set. The incoming column is then placed immediately after that column with the lexicographically largest element in row $i*$.

For example, if the first slack vector is deleted in

$$\begin{bmatrix} 0 & 0 \\ 49 & 50 \\ 0 & 0 \\ 0 & 0 \\ 15 & 14 \end{bmatrix},$$

we obtain the matrix

$$\begin{bmatrix} 0 & 0 & 1 \\ 49 & 50 & 49 \\ 0 & 0 & 0 \\ 0 & 0 & 0 \\ 15 & 14 & 14 \end{bmatrix};$$

and if the third slack vector is then eliminated, the resulting matrix is

$$\begin{bmatrix} 0 & 0 & 0 & 1 \\ 49 & 49 & 50 & 49 \\ 0 & 1 & 0 & 0 \\ 0 & 0 & 0 & 0 \\ 15 & 14 & 14 & 14 \end{bmatrix}.$$

This completes our discussion of the replacement step. A FORTRAN program for the replacement operation may be found in appendix 1.

6.4. AN APPLICATION TO THE COMPUTATION OF EQUILIBRIUM PRICES*

The characterization of primitive sets that contain slack vectors—given by theorem 6.2.9—can be used to construct a powerful variant of our basic algorithm for the computation of equilibrium prices when production is described by a finite list of activities. As before, let the activity analysis matrix be

$$
B = \begin{bmatrix}
-1 & 0 & \cdots & 0 & b_{1,n+1} & \cdots & b_{1,m} \\
0 & -1 & \cdots & 0 & b_{2,n+1} & \cdots & b_{2,m} \\
\vdots & \vdots & & \vdots & \vdots & & \vdots \\
0 & 0 & \cdots & -1 & b_{n,n+1} & \cdots & b_{n,m}
\end{bmatrix},
$$

and, changing our previous notation slightly, let

$$
\xi(\pi) = [\xi_1(\pi), \ldots, \xi_n(\pi)]
$$

represent *excess* demand functions for the consumer side of the economy. The system of functions is homogeneous of degree zero, continuous on the simplex $\{\pi | \pi_i \geq 0, \Sigma_1^n \pi_i = 1\}$, and satisfies the Walras law in the form $\pi_1 \xi_1(\pi) + \ldots + \pi_n \xi_n(\pi) \equiv 0$.

The algorithms of chapters 4 and 5 may be used to calculate a competitive price vector π^* and a list of non-negative activity levels y^* such that

$$
\xi(\pi^*) = By^*, \quad \text{and}
$$

$$
\pi^* B \leq 0.
$$

As we have seen, there is no difficulty in implementing the algorithm, at least for problems in which the number of commodity sectors is sufficiently small that the time of computation is not excessive.

One of the major reasons for the large number of iterations required by problems in which the number of rows of B are fairly substantial—say, 30 or 40—is that the algorithm of chapter 5 always begins at a vertex of the price simplex, even though there may be definite a priori information about the region in which the equilibrium price vector is expected to lie. For example, the property that each activity make a profit less than or equal to zero at equilibrium,

$$\sum_{i=1}^{n} \pi_i b_{ij} \leq 0 \qquad (\text{for } j = 1, \ldots, m),$$

defines a convex polyhedron on the price simplex which contains the equilibrium price vector and which may—in many problems—be quite small. In particular, if the model is of the Leontief type with relatively little substitution in the production of commodities, the equilibrium price vector may virtually be determined by the condition that each activity in use make a zero profit.

The algorithm of the present section is designed to take advantage of information about relative prices afforded by the activity analysis matrix itself. If this information is fairly restrictive, the present algorithm can be expected to terminate in a far smaller number of iterations than one which begins at a vertex of the price simplex. For example, the second problem of section 5.3 with 14 commodities and 40 activities required approximately 30,000 basic iterations and 9 minutes of computation time on an IBM 7094. The same problem was solved by the algorithm about to be described in approximately 100 iterations with a total computation time of less than 10 seconds. Of course the special features of this example may be quite misleading as an indication of the algorithm's performance: there is no substitution in production other than through the export and import sectors. But this may be characteristic of equilibrium models that emphasize international trade, and for these problems the present algorithm may be a substantial improvement over the previous ones.

The set of price vectors π for which $\pi B \leq 0$ is the dual cone of the production set described by the activity analysis matrix B. We are interested in the convex polyhedron that is the intersection of this cone and the unit simplex and specifically in the finite list of vertices $\pi^1, \ldots, \pi^k$ that span this polyhedron (fig. 6.4.1). The actual calculation of the list of extreme vectors may be extremely tedious in any particular application, and it is important to stress that this is never required by our algorithm. In much the same way as the decomposition method for linear programming, the extreme vectors will be generated one at a time as the computation proceeds; not even which of these is to be called π^1 or π^2, etc., need be known in advance.

The major idea of the algorithm is that the equilibrium prices and activity levels may be found by solving an associated pure trade model that has as many commodities as there are extreme price vectors $\pi^1, \ldots, \pi^k$.

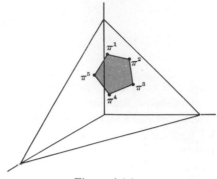

Figure 6.4.1

6.4.1. [DEFINITION OF THE ASSOCIATED PROBLEM] *Let* $T = \{\alpha = (\alpha_1, \ldots, \alpha_k) | \alpha_i \geq 0, \Sigma_1^k \alpha_i = 1\}$. *Define the functions* $f_1(\alpha), \ldots, f_k(\alpha)$, *for* α *in* T, *by*

$$f_1(\alpha) = \pi^1 \cdot \zeta(\alpha_1 \pi^1 + \ldots + \alpha_k \pi^k)$$
$$\vdots$$
$$f_k(\alpha) = \pi^k \cdot \zeta(\alpha_1 \pi^1 + \ldots + \alpha_k \pi^k).$$

The evaluation of these functions seems to require an explicit determination of the extreme prices in the dual cone—a point to which we shall return subsequently. Aside from this, however, the functions have many of the properties of market excess demand functions for a pure trade model: they are homogeneous of degree zero in α, continuous on the simplex T, and satisfy the identity

(6.4.2) $\alpha_1 f_1(\alpha) + \ldots + \alpha_k f_k(\alpha) \equiv 0,$

the analogue of the Walras law.

This artificial market economy falls under the class of problems studied in chapters 2 and 3 and will have an equilibrium α^* for which

$$f_1(\alpha^*) \leq 0$$
$$\vdots$$
$$f_k(\alpha^*) \leq 0.$$

To see that such an equilibrium is useful in solving our original problem, we define

$$\pi^* = \alpha_1^* \pi^1 + \ldots + \alpha_k^* \pi^k$$

and notice that the inequalities above become

$$\pi^1 \cdot \xi(\pi^*) \leq 0$$
$$\vdots$$
$$\pi^k \cdot \xi(\pi^*) \leq 0.$$

In other words, the value of excess demand at the prices π^*, computed using any extreme vertex of the dual cone, is nonpositive. But this implies that $\pi \cdot \xi(\pi^*) \leq 0$ for *any* price vector π with $\pi B \leq 0$. A simple application of the duality theorem for linear programming—or the well known Farkas lemma—is then sufficient to show that $\xi(\pi^*) = By^*$ for some non-negative vector of activities y^*. This is the first of the two conditions characterizing a competitive equilibrium. The second condition, that $\pi^* B \leq 0$, is of course immediate, since π^* is a convex combination of $\pi^1, \ldots, \pi^k$, each of which has this property.

We can therefore focus our attention on using Brouwer's theorem and the techniques of chapter 3 to determine an equilibrium vector $\alpha^* = (\alpha_1^*, \ldots, \alpha_k^*)$ for the associated pure trade model, hopefully without the specific evaluation of all of the extreme price vectors $\pi^1, \ldots, \pi^k$. We begin by selecting a denominator D and consider all vectors α on the simplex T that are of the form $\alpha = (m_1/D, m_2/D, \ldots, m_k/D)$, with m_i representing integers summing to D. At each stage of the algorithm we shall be working with a specific primitive set consisting of, say, the slack vectors

$$x^{i_1}, x^{i_2}, \ldots, x^{i_l}$$

and $k - l$ nonslack vectors, the numerators of which are displayed in the following matrix with k rows and $k - l$ columns:

(6.4.3)
$$M = \begin{bmatrix} m_{11} & \cdots & m_{1,k-l} \\ m_{21} & & m_{2,k-l} \\ \vdots & & \\ m_{k1} & & m_{k,k-l} \end{bmatrix}.$$

According to theorem 6.2.9 the entries in rows $i_1, i_2, \ldots, i_l$ are all zero, and the $(k - l) \times (k - l)$ submatrix of M obtained by deleting these rows satisfies the conditions of theorem 6.2.1.

Typically, at each iteration of the algorithm, most of the vectors in the primitive set will be slack vectors. To be specific, let us assume that there is an integer q such that the slack vectors $x^{q+1}, \ldots, x^k$ are *all* contained in the primitive set in question; the rows $q + 1, \ldots, k$ of the matrix M therefore consist entirely of zeros. We shall now make the assumption that the first q extreme vectors $\pi^1, \pi^2, \ldots, \pi^q$ have been explicitly evaluated in some previous iteration of the algorithm.

How do we then proceed? One of the columns—say, the first—of M has just been introduced into the primitive set and corresponds to a specific vector $\alpha = (m_{11}/D, \ldots, m_{q1}/D, 0, \ldots, 0)$. In order to continue we must associate a label with this column; it is sufficient to use as a label an integer i for which the excess demand

$$f_1(\alpha) \ldots f_i(\alpha) \ldots f_k(\alpha)$$

is maximal. To do this we first determine the price $\tilde{\pi} = (m_{11}/D)\pi^1 + \ldots + (m_{q1}/D)\pi^q$ which corresponds to α and merely requires for its evaluation the knowledge of the first q extreme price vectors $\pi^1, \ldots, \pi^q$. We then calculate $\xi_1(\tilde{\pi}), \ldots, \xi_n(\tilde{\pi})$ and attempt to determine an extreme price vector $\pi^i = (\pi^i_1, \ldots, \pi^i_n)$ that maximizes

$$\pi^i_1 \xi_1(\tilde{\pi}) + \ldots + \pi^i_n \xi_n(\tilde{\pi}).$$

This latter step may be done quite simply by solving the linear programming problem

$$\max \pi_1 \xi_1(\tilde{\pi}) + \ldots + \pi_n \xi_n(\tilde{\pi})$$

subject to $\pi_1 b_{11} \quad + \ldots + \pi_n b_{n1} \le 0$

(6.4.4)

$$\vdots$$

$$\pi_1 b_{1m} \quad + \ldots + \pi_n b_{nm} \le 0,$$

$$\pi_1 \qquad + \ldots + \pi_n \quad = 1.$$

The programming problem, which depends on $\tilde{\pi}$ and therefore on the column just brought into the primitive set, will have a solution at some vector that is an extreme price of the dual cone. To determine the appropriate label for the column in question we merely compare the solution of this linear programming problem with the vectors $\pi^1, \ldots, \pi^q$ that have already been calculated. If it is equal to one of these, say, the ith, then the column is given the label i. If it is different from all of these vectors, then the solution of the programming problem is *defined* to be π^{q+1}, and the column in question is given the label $q + 1$. This concludes the discussion of the labelling process, which involves the solution of a linear programming problem on each iteration of the algorithm.

For example, let us imagine that after a number of iterations of the basic algorithm, five distinct extreme price vectors $\pi^1, \pi^2, \ldots, \pi^5$ have already been evaluated and that the numerators of the vectors in the current primitive set are given by

$$M = \begin{bmatrix} 30 & 30 & 29 & 29 \\ 0 & 0 & 0 & 0 \\ 4 & 5 & 5 & 5 \\ 1 & 0 & 0 & 1 \\ 5 & 5 & 6 & 5 \\ 0 & 0 & 0 & 0 \\ & & \vdots \end{bmatrix} \begin{matrix} \pi^1 \\ \pi^2 \\ \pi^3 \\ \pi^4 \\ \pi^5 \\ \\ \vdots \end{matrix}.$$

The slack vectors x^2 and $x^6, x^7, \ldots, x^k$ are also contained in the primitive set. Suppose, in addition, that the final column of this matrix has just been brought into the primitive set, so that we are required to associate an integer label with it. To do this we compute

$$\tilde{\pi} = \tfrac{29}{40} \pi^1 + \tfrac{5}{40} \pi^3 + \tfrac{1}{40} \pi^4 + \tfrac{5}{40} \pi^5$$

and then evaluate the demand functions $\xi_1(\tilde{\pi}), \ldots, \xi_n(\tilde{\pi})$. The linear programming problem 6.4.4. is solved, yielding a specific extreme price vector π'. If π' is equal to one of the first five vectors, its label is then determined. If π' is a new extreme vector, we define $\pi^6 = \pi'$ and give the last column of M the label 6.

In this latter case the label 6 appears on two distinct members of the primitive set, column 4 and the sixth slack vector. On the next iteration the sixth slack vector must be removed from the primitive set, and according to the discussion of the previous section, this results in a new matrix:

$$M^1 = \begin{bmatrix} 30 & 30 & 29 & 29 & 29 \\ 0 & 0 & 0 & 0 & 0 \\ 4 & 5 & 5 & 5 & 5 \\ 1 & 0 & 0 & 0 & 1 \\ 5 & 5 & 5 & 6 & 5 \\ 0 & 0 & 1 & 0 & 0 \\ \vdots & \vdots & \vdots & \vdots & \vdots \end{bmatrix} \begin{matrix} \pi^1 \\ \pi^2 \\ \pi^3 \\ \pi^4 \\ \pi^5 \\ \pi^6 \\ \\ \end{matrix}.$$

The third column of this matrix is the one which has just been introduced into the primitive set and for which a label must be found on the next iteration of the algorithm.

An initial extreme vector π^1 must be selected in order to begin the algorithm—in much the same way that an initial vertex of the price simplex must be selected in our previous techniques. This choice may be put to good use if there is sufficient information to enable an informed guess about π^1 that is close to the actual equilibrium price vector. The better the guess, the smaller will be the number of iterations before the algorithm terminates.

Let us see how the method works in example II of section 5.3. D, the denominator of the vectors in a typical primitive set, will be selected to be 50, a number which is much smaller than that required for comparable accuracy with our previous methods. The initial extreme price vector $\pi^1 = (\pi^1_1, \ldots, \pi^1_{14})$ was chosen to be

$$(.031, .038, .057, .273, .052, .044, .042, .033, .245, .047, .000, .064).$$

The algorithm terminated after 76 iterations, in approximately 8 seconds of computing time. During the course of the algorithm, three additional extreme price vectors π^2, π^3, and π^4 were determined:

$\pi^2 =$
$(.066, .071, .118, .076, .070, .000, .095, .119, .094, .078, .000, .086, .010, .118),$

$\pi^3 =$
$(.070, .066, .109, .079, .074, .000, .079, .111, .102, .090, .000, .071, .042, .106),$

$\pi^4 =$
$(.032, .029, .046, .042, .036, .295, .030, .049, .047, .040, .266, .027, .016, .044).$

The final primitive set consisted of the first two slack vectors and two additional vectors whose numerators are the columns of

$$
M = \begin{bmatrix} 0 & 0 \\ 0 & 0 \\ 39 & 40 \\ 11 & 10 \end{bmatrix} \begin{matrix} \pi^1 \\ \pi^2 \\ \pi^3 \\ \pi^4 \end{matrix} .
$$

In this particular application the algorithm terminated by bringing the first slack vector into the primitive set; on the last iteration of the algorithm the demand functions were evaluated at the price vector

$$\tilde{\pi} = \tfrac{39}{50}\,\pi^3 + \tfrac{11}{50}\,\pi^4$$

or

$$\tilde{\pi} =$$

(.062, .058, .095, .071, .066, .065, .069, .098, .090, .079, .059, .062, .036, .092),

which is very close to the equilibrium price vector given in section 5.3. The linear programming problem 6.4.4. produced a value of .07 for the maximum of $\pi \cdot \xi(\tilde{\pi})$ as π ranges over all prices in the dual cone whose coordinates are normalized to sum to unity. The optimal dual variables for this linear programming problem will therefore yield a set of activity levels providing a discrepancy between supply and demand of no more than .07 and an aggregate profit of no less than $-.07$. Of course these differences can be made even smaller if suitable numerical techniques are used.

CHAPTER 7

Algorithms Based on Simplicial Subdivisions

7.1. THE RELATION BETWEEN PRIMITIVE SETS AND SIMPLICIAL SUBDIVISIONS

The customary proofs of Brouwer's theorem make use of a combinatorial theorem known as Sperner's lemma, similar in many respects to our theorem 2.5.1 but based on the concept of a simplicial subdivision of the simplex, rather than that of a primitive set. The present chapter will explore the relationship between these two constructions and suggest an alternative version of our major computational technique—theorem 4.2.3—in terms of this more conventional topological framework.

Consider an arbitrary simplex contained in S with linearly independent vertices $v^1, v^2, \ldots, v^n$. The simplex consists of those vectors x which can be written as a convex combination

$$x = \alpha_1 v^1 + \alpha_2 v^2 + \ldots + \alpha_n v^n$$

of the n vertices, with $\alpha_i \geq 0$ and $\Sigma_{i=1}^n \alpha_i = 1$. The orientation of a simplex defined in this fashion is considerably more general than those arising in the study of primitive sets; in particular, the sides of the simplex need not be parallel to the coordinate hyperplanes (fig. 7.1.1).

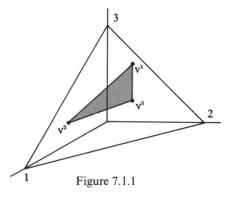

Figure 7.1.1

The simplex has n sides, each defined by requiring a specific weight, say, α_i, to be equal to zero and permitting the remaining weights to vary arbitrarily subject to the condition that they be non-negative and sum to unity. In figure 7.1.1 the side connecting v^1 and v^3 is obtained by requiring that $\alpha_2 = 0$.

In addition to these n faces the simplex will have a number of faces of smaller dimension in which two or more weights are required to be equal to zero.

7.1.1. [DEFINITION] *Consider a simplex with vertices* $v^1, v^2, \ldots, v^n$. *A face of this simplex is defined to be the convex hull of any subset of the vertices.*

Now let us consider a collection of simplices $S^1, S^2, \ldots, S^k$ each contained in our large simplex S. We make the assumption that each vector in S is contained in at least one simplex in the collection. An arbitrary pair of these simplices may be disjoint or they may intersect in a variety of ways.

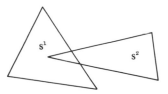

Figure 7.1.2

They may, as figure 7.1.2 indicates, have interior points in common, or their intersection may not be an entire subface of both simplices (fig. 7.1.3). Even more elaborate possibilities are available in higher dimensions.

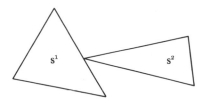

Figure 7.1.3

The conventional treatment of fixed point theorems relies on the notion of a simplicial subdivision of the simplex S; a collection of simplices whose union covers the entire simplex and which has the property that the intersection of any pair in the collection is either empty or an entire face of both simplices. In contrast to the previous figures the following three simplices (fig. 7.1.4) do satisfy this second condition. The intersection of S^1 and S^2 is a line segment that is a proper face of both simplices, and the intersection of S^1 and S^3 is a single vertex of both—itself a proper face.

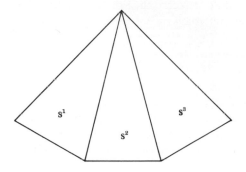

Figure 7.1.4

7.1.2. [DEFINITION] *A collection of simplices* $S^1, S^2, \ldots, S^k$ *is a simplicial subdivision of S if:*

a. $\bigcup_{1}^{k} S^i = S$, *and*

b. *the intersection of any pair* S^i *and* S^j *is either empty or a proper face of both.*

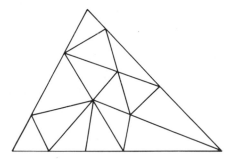

Figure 7.1.5

In general, simplicial subdivisions bear no particular relationship to the concept of primitive sets on which we have based our computational procedures—even in the case in which the vertices of the simplices in the subdivision form the grid $x^{n+1}, \ldots, x^k$ used in the construction of primitive sets. There is, however, one important instance in which these two concepts coincide. Consider the regular grid of vectors $(m_1/D, m_2/D, \ldots, m_n/D)$, with m_i representing arbitrary non-negative integers whose sum is D. Let ties be broken by the cyclic lexicographic ordering of the previous chapter. We have seen how to describe the sets of n vectors $x^{j_1}, \ldots, x^{j_n}$ that form a primitive set using this rule for the resolution of degeneracy. On the other hand, each such collection of n vectors may be used to define a simplex contained in S by constructing its convex hull. Let us formalize this definition in the following way.

7.1.3. [DEFINITION] *Let $x^{j_1}, \ldots, x^{j_n}$ be n nonslack vectors forming a primitive set using the regular grid and the cyclic lexicographic ordering 6.1.1. We define the simplex $S_{j_1,\ldots,j_n}$ to be the convex hull of the vectors $x^{j_1}, \ldots, x^{j_n}$.*

In the remainder of this section I shall demonstrate that the collection of simplices defined above forms a simplicial subdivision. The argument, based on the work of Harold Kuhn (1960, 1968), begins by considering a matrix

$$
M = \begin{bmatrix} m_{11} & \cdots & m_{1n} \\ m_{21} & \cdots & m_{2n} \\ \vdots & & \vdots \\ m_{n1} & \cdots & m_{nn} \end{bmatrix}
$$

whose columns are the numerators of n vectors that form a primitive set according to theorem 6.2.1. There is, therefore, a permutation of the integers $I(j)$ such that the jth column of M is identical with column $j - 1$ except for the rows $I(j) - 1$ and $I(j)$,

$$
m_{i,j} = m_{i,j-1} + 1 \qquad \text{for } i = I(j) - 1, \quad \text{and}
$$

$$
m_{i,j} = m_{i,j-1} - 1 \qquad \text{for } i = I(j).
$$

In all cases the subscripts are interpreted modulo n.

We shall see that the columns of M are linearly independent; an arbitrary vector $x = (x_1, \ldots, x_n)$ on the simplex will therefore have a unique representation as

$$
x_i = \sum_j \alpha_j m_{ij}/D,
$$

with α_j summing to unity. If the weights α_j are non-negative, then the vector x is contained in the simplex generated by the columns of M. In order to demonstrate that x is contained in at least one simplex in the collection $\{S_{j_1,\ldots,j_n}\}$ it is useful to find an explicit representation of the weights $\alpha_1, \ldots, \alpha_n$ in terms of the coordinates of x.

7.1.4. [THEOREM] *Let M satisfy the conditions of theorem 6.2.1 and let $I(j^*) = 1$. Then any vector $x = (x_1, \ldots, x_n)$ with $\Sigma_1^n x_i = 1$ has a unique representation of the form*

$$x_i = \sum_j \alpha_j m_{ij}/D.$$

The weights α_j are given by

$$\alpha_j = \sum_{I(j)}^{I(j+1)-1} (m_{ij^*} - Dx_i),$$

with the understanding that if the upper limit in this summation is smaller than the lower limit, the summation is over the index set $i = [I(j), \ldots, n, 1, \ldots, I(j+1) - 1]$. Finally, if $j = j^*$, the expression for α_j should be increased by unity.

Let us consider a specific example in which

$$M = \begin{bmatrix} 11 & \underline{10} & 10 & 11 & 11 \\ 21 & 21 & 21 & \underline{20} & 21 \\ 29 & 29 & 30 & 30 & \underline{29} \\ 10 & 10 & \underline{9} & 9 & 9 \\ \underline{29} & 30 & 30 & 30 & 30 \end{bmatrix}.$$

The permutation $I(j)$ describes the row whose lexicographic minimum falls in column j and is therefore given by:

j	$I(j)$
1	5
2	1
3	4
4	2
5	3

Clearly, $j^* = 2$. According to the theorem, an arbitrary vector $(x_1, \ldots, x_5)$ whose coordinates sum to unity will be represented as a linear combination of the columns of M, with weights α_i/D, where

$$\alpha_1 = [m_{5,2} - 100x_5],$$
$$\alpha_2 = [m_{1,2} - 100x_1] + [m_{2,2} - 100x_2] + [m_{3,2} - 100x_3] + 1,$$
$$\alpha_3 = [m_{4,2} - 100x_4] + [m_{5,2} - 100x_5] + [m_{1,2} - 100x_1],$$
$$\alpha_4 = [m_{2,2} - 100x_2],$$
$$\alpha_5 = [m_{3,2} - 100x_3] + [m_{4,2} - 100x_4].$$

If the specific values of the second column [since $I(2) = 1$] are entered, this representation becomes

$$\alpha_1 = 30 - 100x_5,$$
$$\alpha_2 = 61 - 100(x_1 + x_2 + x_3),$$
$$\alpha_3 = 50 - 100(x_4 + x_5 + x_1),$$
$$\alpha_4 = 21 - 100x_2,$$
$$\alpha_5 = 39 - 100(x_3 + x_4).$$

The reader may then convince himself that

$$
\begin{bmatrix}
11 & 10 & 10 & 11 & 11 \\
21 & 21 & 21 & 20 & 21 \\
29 & 29 & 30 & 30 & 29 \\
10 & 10 & 9 & 9 & 9 \\
29 & 30 & 30 & 30 & 30
\end{bmatrix}
\begin{bmatrix}
.3 - x_5 \\
.61 - x_1 - x_2 - x_3 \\
.5 - x_4 - x_5 - x_1 \\
.21 - x_2 \\
.39 - x_3 - x_4
\end{bmatrix}
\equiv
\begin{bmatrix}
x_1 \\
x_2 \\
x_3 \\
x_4 \\
x_5
\end{bmatrix}
$$

for all vectors x whose coordinates sum to unity.

In order to demonstrate theorem 7.1.4, we begin by assuming that the elements in the top row of M are arranged in lexicographically increasing order—so that $I(1) = 1$ and therefore $j^* = 1$—and we denote the columns of M by the vectors $m^1, m^2, \ldots, m^n$. Let us define the vectors

$$e^k = (0, 0, \ldots, 1, -1, \ldots, 0)'$$

with the $(k - 1)$th coordinate equal to 1, kth coordinate equal to -1, and the remaining entries zero (if $k = 1$, $k - 1$ is interpreted as n). According to theorem 6.2.1, the columns of M bear the following relationship to each other:

$$m^2 = m^1 + e^{I(2)},$$
$$m^3 = m^2 + e^{I(3)},$$
$$\vdots$$
$$m^n = m^{n-1} + e^{I(n)},$$
$$m^1 = m^n + e^{I(1)}.$$

Now let x be a vector whose coordinates sum to unity. For x to be represented as

$$x = \frac{\alpha_1 m^1}{D} + \frac{\alpha_2 m^2}{D} + \ldots + \frac{\alpha_n m^n}{D},$$

we must have

$$x = \frac{\alpha_1}{D} m^1 + \frac{\alpha_2}{D} [m^1 + e^{I(2)}] + \ldots + \frac{\alpha_n}{D} [m^1 + e^{I(2)} + \ldots + e^{I(n)}]$$

$$= \frac{m^1}{D} + e^{I(2)} \frac{(\alpha_2 + \ldots + \alpha_n)}{D} + e^{I(3)} \frac{(\alpha_3 + \ldots + \alpha_n)}{D} + \ldots + e^{I(n)} \frac{\alpha_n}{D}.$$

But these equations can be solved very simply if we add together rows $I(j)$ through n. For each j we have

$$\sum_{i=I(j)}^{n} \left(x_i - \frac{m_i^1}{D} \right) = \left(\frac{\alpha_2 + \ldots + \alpha_n}{D} \right) \sum_{i=I(j)}^{n} e_i^{I(2)}$$

$$+ \left(\frac{\alpha_3 + \ldots + \alpha_n}{D} \right) \sum_{i=I(j)}^{n} e_i^{I(3)}$$

$$+ \ldots + \frac{\alpha_n}{D} \sum_{i=I(j)}^{n} e_i^{I(n)}$$

We then use the fact that for any index $k \geq 2$,

$$\sum_{i=I(j)}^{n} e_i^k = \begin{cases} -1; & I(j) = k \\ 0; & \text{otherwise.} \end{cases}$$

We therefore have

(7.1.5) $$\sum_{i=I(j)}^{n} \left(x_i - \frac{m_i^1}{D} \right) = -\left(\frac{\alpha_j + \alpha_{j+1} + \ldots + \alpha_n}{D} \right)$$

for $j = 2, \ldots, n$.

By subtracting two successive terms of 7.1.5, we obtain

$$\alpha_j = \sum_{i=I(j)}^{n} (m_i^1 - Dx_i) - \sum_{i=I(j+1)}^{n} (m_i^1 - Dx_i)$$

for $j = 2, \ldots, n$. If $I(j + 1) > I(j)$, this reduces to the expression in theorem 7.1.4. On the other hand, if $I(j + 1) < I(j)$, we have

$$\alpha_j = - \sum_{I(j+1)}^{I(j)-1} (m_i^1 - Dx_i),$$

which equals the summation of the terms $(m_i^1 - Dx_i)$ over the index set $[I(j), \ldots, n, 1, \ldots, I(j + 1) - 1]$, since

$$\sum_{1}^{n} (m_i^1 - Dx_i) = 0.$$

The formula for α_1 in theorem 7.1.4 may then be obtained from $\alpha_1 = 1 - \Sigma_2^n \alpha_i$. This demonstrates theorem 7.1.4.

Having obtained this explicit representation, let us now ask whether the simplices obtained from all of the primitive sets by forming their convex hulls cover the entire simplex S. This is equivalent to asking whether an arbitrary vector in S will be contained in at least one of these convex hulls, i.e., has a representation with $\alpha_j \geq 0$.

Consider, for example, the case $n = 5$ and the regular grid with denominators $D = 100$. Can we find a primitive set whose convex hull contains the vector $x = (.205, .376, .031, .125, .263)'$? To answer this question, let us use formula 7.1.5. We notice, first of all, that the partial sums

$$\sum_{i=I(j)}^{5} (m_i^1 - 100x_i)$$

must all lie between zero and one for $j = 2, \ldots, 5$. Whatever be the permutation $I(j)$, as long as $I(1) = 1$, these sums are given by

$$m_2^1 + m_3^1 + m_4^1 + m_5^1 - 79.5,$$

$$m_3^1 + m_4^1 + m_5^1 - 41.9,$$

$$m_4^1 + m_5^1 - 38.8,$$

$$m_5^1 - 26.3.$$

But this tells us immediately that

$$m_2^1 + m_3^1 + m_4^1 + m_5^1 = 80,$$

$$m_3^1 + m_4^1 + m_5^1 = 42,$$

$$m_4^1 + m_5^1 = 39,$$

$$m_5^1 = 27,$$

so that $m^1 = (20, 38, 3, 12, 27)$. To find the permutation $I(j)$ we merely notice from 7.1.5 that the sums

$$\sum_{i=I(j)}^{5} (m_i^1 - 100x_i)$$

must be decreasing in j. Since these partial sums are

$$\sum_{2}^{5} (m_i^1 - 100x_i) = .5,$$

$$\sum_{3}^{5} (m_i^1 - 100x_i) = .1,$$

$$\sum_{4}^{5} (m_i^1 - 100x_i) = .2,$$

$$\sum_{5}^{5} (m_i^1 - 100x_i) = .7,$$

$I(j)$ is given by:

j	$I(j)$
1	1
2	5
3	2
4	4
5	3

The unique representation of x in terms of a primitive set is therefore

$$
\begin{bmatrix} .205 \\ .376 \\ .031 \\ .125 \\ .263 \end{bmatrix}
=
\begin{bmatrix}
\underline{.20} & .20 & .21 & .21 & .21 \\
.38 & .38 & \underline{.37} & .37 & .38 \\
.03 & .03 & .03 & .04 & \underline{.03} \\
.12 & .13 & .13 & \underline{.12} & .12 \\
.27 & \underline{.26} & .26 & .26 & .26
\end{bmatrix}
\begin{bmatrix} .3 \\ .2 \\ .3 \\ .1 \\ .1 \end{bmatrix}.
$$

The method of this example can be generalized with no difficulty to obtain the following theorem.

7.1.6. [THEOREM] *Let* $x = (x_1, \ldots, x_n)$ *be an arbitrary vector on the simplex S. Then x is contained in some simplex* $S_{j_1,\ldots,j_n}$.

To demonstrate this theorem we need find a non-negative integer vector $(m_1, \ldots, m_n)$, the sum of whose components is D, and a permutation $I(j)$ with $I(1) = 1$ such that equations 7.1.5 yield non-negative weights $\alpha_1, \ldots, \alpha_n$. If these equations are written in the form

$$
(7.1.7) \quad \sum_{i=I(j)}^{n} (m_i - Dx_i) = \alpha_j + \alpha_{j+1} + \ldots + \alpha_n \qquad \text{for } j > 1,
$$

we see that

$$
0 \le \sum_{k}^{n} m_i - D \sum_{k}^{n} x_i \le 1 \qquad \text{for all } k > 1.
$$

In general the vector m that satisfies these inequalities need not be unique, but one solution is given by

$$
m_n = \langle Dx_n \rangle \quad \text{and}
$$

$$
m_k = \left\langle D \sum_{k}^{n} x_i \right\rangle - \left\langle D \sum_{k+1}^{n} x_i \right\rangle \qquad \text{for } n > k > 1,
$$

where the symbol $\langle y \rangle$ means the smallest integer greater than or equal to y. m_1 is then determined by the relation $m_1 = D - \sum_{2}^{n} m_i$.

In order to obtain the permutation $I(j)$, we define the sequence $f_1 = 1$ and $f_k = \sum_{k}^{n}(m_i - Dx_i)$ for $k = 2, \ldots, n$. Any permutation consistent with $f_1 \ge f_{I(2)} \ge f_{I(3)} \ge \ldots \ge f_{I(n)} \ge 0$ will permit us to define non-negative αs by means of $\alpha_j = f_{I(j)} - f_{I(j+1)}$ (for $j < n$) and $\alpha_n = f_{I(n)}$, the set of which satisfy the above equations and therefore represent x as a convex combination of the n vectors in the primitive set determined by $(m_1, \ldots, m_n)$ and the permutation $I(j)$. This demonstrates theorem 7.1.6. While it is not part of the proof of theorem 7.1.6, it is interesting to remark that equations 7.1.7 have a *unique* solution if it is known that $\alpha_1 > 0$. Under that condition, we must have

$$\sum_k^n m_i = \left\langle D \sum_k^n x_i \right\rangle$$

for $k = 2, \ldots, n$.

These arguments provide an explicit procedure for determining a simplex $S_{j_1 \ldots j_n}$ that contains a given vector x. It is quite possible, however, that the solution of 7.1.7 is not unique and that there are other simplices that contain the same vector. For example, any vector that is a convex combination of the final four columns of the primitive set represented by

$$\begin{bmatrix} 10 & 10 & 10 & 11 & 11 \\ 20 & 20 & 21 & 20 & 20 \\ 30 & 31 & 30 & 30 & 30 \\ 10 & 9 & 9 & 9 & 10 \\ 30 & 30 & 30 & 30 & 29 \end{bmatrix}$$

will also be in the primitive set obtained by replacing the first of these columns:

$$\begin{bmatrix} 11 & 10 & 10 & 11 & 11 \\ 20 & 20 & 21 & 20 & 20 \\ 31 & 31 & 30 & 30 & 30 \\ 9 & 9 & 9 & 9 & 10 \\ 29 & 30 & 30 & 30 & 29 \end{bmatrix}$$

In this case the two simplices intersect in a full face of each simplex, the convex hull of the final four vectors in each primitive set. In order to complete the demonstration that the collection $\{S_{j_1, \ldots, j_n}\}$ forms a simplicial subdivision we must verify that this is characteristic of the intersection of any pair of simplices.

7.1.8. [THEOREM] *The collection $\{S_{j_1, \ldots, j_n}\}$ forms a simplicial subdivision.*

Let us consider a vector x that is contained in a particular simplex in the collection and therefore represented as

$$
D \begin{bmatrix} x_1 \\ x_2 \\ \vdots \\ x_n \end{bmatrix} = \begin{bmatrix} m_{11} & \cdots & m_{1j*} & \cdots & m_{1n} \\ m_{21} & \cdots & m_{2j*} & \cdots & m_{2n} \\ \vdots & & \vdots & & \vdots \\ m_{n1} & \cdots & m_{nj*} & \cdots & m_{nn} \end{bmatrix} \begin{bmatrix} \alpha_1 \\ \alpha_2 \\ \vdots \\ \alpha_n \end{bmatrix}.
$$

The matrix M satisfies the conditions of theorem 6.2.1 and $\alpha_j \geq 0$ for $j = 1, \ldots, n$. We assume that $I(1) = 1$, so that the columns of M are lexicographically increasing. In general, not all of the weights $\{\alpha_j\}$ will be strictly positive. Let us define $j*$ to be the first column associated with a strictly positive weight. Our argument for theorem 7.1.8 will be based on the observation that this column $(m_{1j*}, m_{2j*}, \ldots, m_{nj*})'$ and its corresponding weight α_{j*} are uniquely determined by the vector x and are fully independent of the integer $j*$ and of the particular simplex in the collection containing x.

Consider first the case in which $j* = 1$, so that the weight α_1 is strictly positive. If we then return to 7.1.5, we see that

$$
(7.1.9) \qquad \sum_{i=I(j)}^{n} (m_{i1} - Dx_i) = \alpha_j + \ldots + \alpha_n
$$

for $j = 2, \ldots, n$. Since α_1 is strictly positive, we must have $\alpha_j + \ldots + \alpha_n < 1$ for $j = 2, \ldots, n$ and therefore

$$
\sum_{i=I(j)}^{n} m_{i1} = \left\langle D \sum_{i=I(j)}^{n} x_i \right\rangle.
$$

The partial sums $\sum_{i=k}^{n} m_{i1}$ are uniquely determined for $k = 2, \ldots, n$ and so, therefore, is the vector $(m_{11}, m_{21}, \ldots, m_{n1})'$. From the equations 7.1.8 we also see that

$$
1 - \alpha_1 = \max_{k} \left\{ \sum_{i=k}^{n} m_{i1} - Dx_i \right\},
$$

which uniquely determines the value of α_1.

Our purpose is now to show that this same vector will occur in column $j*$ if the simplex containing x has $\alpha_1 = \alpha_2 = \ldots = \alpha_{j*-1} = 0$ and $\alpha_{j*} > 0$. In order to do this let us apply the replacement operation of theorem 6.3.1 to column 1 of the matrix M, then to column 2, and continue to column

$j^* - 1$. Each replacement operation will produce a new simplex in the collection that also contains x since we are changing only those columns of M which have a zero weight in the representation of x. Moreover, since the replacement operation on column j produces a new permutation with $I(j)$ and $I(j + 1)$ interchanged, the final matrix will have $I(j^*) = 1$.

In other words, this sequence of replacement operations will produce a new simplex containing x with the property that the old column j^* (with a positive weight α_{j*}) is now the lexicographically smallest column in the new matrix. By the earlier argument, this column and its corresponding weight are identical with that given above.

In order to complete the argument that the collection $\{S_{j_1,\ldots,j_n}\}$ forms a simplicial subdivision, consider a vector x that is contained in a pair of these simplices S and S', with corresponding matrices M and M'. We wish to show that the columns of M and M', which are associated with positive weights, are identical.

The previous argument permits us to conclude that the lexicographically smallest of these columns are identical in both matrices (say, to the common vector v) and have a common weight α. To complete the argument we then form the new vector $(x - \alpha v)/(1 - \alpha)$, which is also contained in the pair of simplices S and S', and continue. This demonstrates theorem 7.1.8.

We have finally arrived at the geometrical interpretation of primitive sets in terms of the standard topological notion of a simplicial subdivision of the simplex—for the specific grid emphasized in this chapter. This also implies a geometrical interpretation of the replacement step, because in removing a vector from a primitive set we must move to the primitive set whose subsimplex contains the remaining $n - 1$ vectors (fig. 7.1.6).

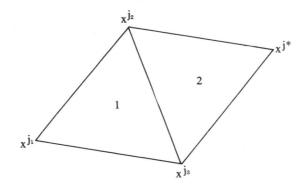

Figure 7.1.6

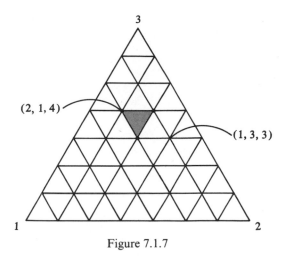

Figure 7.1.7

This is illustrated in figure 7.1.7, in which $n = 3$ and $D = 7$. If the vector $(2, 1, 4)'$ is removed from the shaded triangle that corresponds to

$$\begin{bmatrix} \underline{1} & 2 & 2 \\ 2 & \underline{1} & 2 \\ 4 & 4 & \underline{3} \end{bmatrix},$$

the replacement operation produces the new matrix

$$\begin{bmatrix} \underline{1} & 1 & 2 \\ 2 & 3 & \underline{2} \\ 4 & \underline{3} & 3 \end{bmatrix}$$

corresponding to the adjacent triangle.

The reader should not be misled by the simplicity of this geometrical construction. When $n = 3$, there is only one simplicial subdivision based on the regular grid of vectors. But when $n > 3$, there are many distinct simplicial subdivisions whose vertices are specified by the regular grid. Geometric intuition is misleading for larger values of n, and this accounts for the complexity of our presentation.

7.2. SIMPLICIAL SUBDIVISIONS AND A GENERAL GRID

The geometrical interpretation of primitive sets described in the previous section depended very heavily on the specific properties of the regular grid and the lexicographic procedure for resolving ties. In this section I shall show that a similar geometric interpretation cannot be given for a general grid of vectors $x^{n+1}, \ldots, x^k$ on the simplex. In general, primitive sets as defined in 2.2.6 lead to geometric objects of some novelty that bear no immediate relationship to standard topological constructions.

The simplices $\{S_{j_1,\ldots,j_n}\}$ will be defined as the convex hulls of those primitive sets $\{x^{j_1}, \ldots, x^{j_n}\}$ with no slack vectors and whose members are linearly independent (fig. 7.2.1). Will this family of simplices represent a

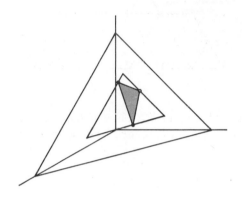

Figure 7.2.1

simplicial subdivision in the sense that its union covers the entire simplex S and that the intersection of any two must be either empty or a common subface of both?

There is one immediate problem that must be resolved before the discussion can begin. Clearly, for a general grid there will be open spaces near the faces that will not be contained in any such simplex. In order to overcome this problem, the definition of the simplices $S_{j_1,\ldots,j_n}$ will be extended to include primitive sets some of whose members are slack vectors.

Let us consider the larger simplex T consisting of all vectors $x = (x_1, \ldots, x_n)$ with $\Sigma_1^n x_i = 1$ and $x_i \leq 1$ (fig. 7.2.2). This simplex will contain S and have as its extreme points the vertices

$$(2 - n, 1, \ldots, 1)'$$

$$\vdots$$

$$(1, 1, \ldots, 2 - n)',$$

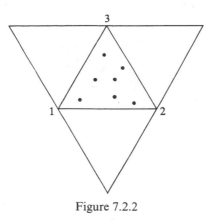

Figure 7.2.2

which can be used in place of the vectors

$$(0, M_1, \ldots, M_1)'$$

$$\vdots$$

$$(M_n, M_n, \ldots, 0)'$$

to represent the slack vectors $x^1, \ldots, x^n$. The matrix that displays the coordinates of the vectors $x^1, \ldots, x^k$ will now have the form

$$
\begin{array}{cccccc}
x^1 & \ldots & x^n & x^{n+1} & \ldots & x^k
\end{array}
$$

$$
\begin{bmatrix}
2-n & \ldots & 1 & x_1^{n+1} & \ldots & x_1^k \\
\vdots & & \vdots & \vdots & & \vdots \\
\vdots & & \vdots & \vdots & & \vdots \\
1 & \ldots & 2-n & x_n^{n+1} & \ldots & x_n^k
\end{bmatrix}.
$$

Our definitions of a primitive set are unchanged since all that was required of the slack vectors was that the diagonal elements be nonpositive and the off-diagonal elements be not less than unity.

This particular form for the slack vectors permits us to extend the definition of the simplex $S_{j_1, \ldots, j_n}$ to include primitive sets with slack vectors.

7.2.1. [DEFINITION] *Let* $x^{j_1}, \ldots, x^{j_n}$ *be n linearly independent vectors that form a primitive set. The simplex* $S_{j_1, \ldots, j_n}$ *is defined to be the convex hull of these n vectors.*

Figure 7.2.3 illustrates the extended definition. We have the following theorem, originally conjectured by Kuhn in an unpublished communication.

7.2.2. [THEOREM] *Every vector in T is a member of at least one simplex* $S_{j_1, \ldots, j_n}$.

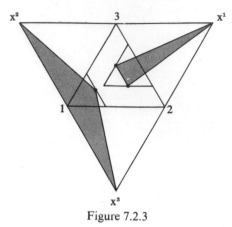

Figure 7.2.3

This theorem, stating that the union of the simplices covers T, is the direct generalization of theorem 7.1.6. In its present generality, however, it does require the algorithm of chapter 4 relating primitive sets and feasible bases for a system of linear inequalities, rather than the explicit procedure used in the special case of the previous section.

Let $c = (c_1, \ldots, c_n)$ be an arbitrary vector in T. We construct a matrix of size $n \times k$, each of whose columns corresponds to one of the vectors in the grid:

$$A = \begin{array}{cccc} x^1 & \cdots & x^n & x^j \\ \begin{bmatrix} 1 & \cdots & 0 & (1 - x_1^j)/(n - 1) & \cdots \\ \vdots & & \vdots & \vdots \\ 0 & \cdots & 1 & (1 - x_n^j)/(n - 1) & \cdots \end{bmatrix} \end{array}.$$

The transformation producing column j is applicable to every column of A, including those representing slack variables.

Also let the non-negative vector b be defined by $b_i = (1 - c_i)/(n - 1)$. The hypotheses of theorem 4.2.3 are satisfied since $\Sigma_i a_{ij} = 1$ and therefore every vector in the set $\{\alpha | A\alpha = b, \alpha \geq 0\}$ satisfies $\Sigma \alpha_j = \Sigma b_i = 1$. The theorem then asserts that there exists a primitive set $(x^{j_1}, \ldots, x^{j_n})$ such that columns $j_1, \ldots, j_n$ form a feasible basis for $A\alpha = b$. In other words,

$$\sum_j \alpha_j (1 - x_i^j)/(n - 1) = (1 - c_i)/(n - 1),$$

with α_j non-negative for all j and different from zero only for $j = j_1, \ldots, j_n$. But since $\Sigma \alpha_j = 1$, it follows that

$$\sum_j x_i^j \alpha_j = c_i,$$

and the vector c is therefore a convex combination of $x^{j_1}, \ldots, x^{j_n}$. This demonstrates theorem 7.2.2.

As this theorem indicates, the simplices $S_{j_1,\ldots,j_n}$, defined to be the convex hulls of primitive sets, do satisfy the first requirement of a simplicial subdivision of T: their union does cover this simplex. Unfortunately the second condition, relating to the intersection of two different simplices, need not be satisfied for a general grid of vectors $x^{n+1}, \ldots, x^k$. As the following example illustrates, it is quite possible, when $n > 3$, for two distinct simplices to have even an interior point in common.

Consider the eight vectors $x^5, \ldots, x^{12}$ given by the columns of the matrix

$$
\begin{array}{cccccccc}
x^5 & x^6 & x^7 & x^8 & x^9 & x^{10} & x^{11} & x^{12}
\end{array}
$$
$$
\begin{bmatrix}
\varepsilon & 1 & 6 & 7 & 2+\varepsilon & 3 & 4 & 5 \\
3 & 2+\varepsilon & 5 & 4 & 1 & \varepsilon & 7 & 6 \\
6 & 7 & \varepsilon & 1 & 4 & 5 & 2+\varepsilon & 3 \\
5 & 4 & 3 & 2+\varepsilon & 7 & 6 & 1 & \varepsilon
\end{bmatrix},
$$

with ε a small positive number. The reader may easily verify that the column sums of this matrix are each $14 + \varepsilon$, so that the vectors x^j lie on the simplex $\Sigma_1^4 x_i = 14 + \varepsilon$. Our grid will lie on this simplex rather than on $\Sigma_1^4 x_i = 1$ and will consist entirely of these eight vectors, augmented by four slack vectors.

It is easy to verify that x^5, x^6, x^7, x^8 form a primitive set for there is no vector x^j in the list with

$$
x_1^j > \min[x_1^5, x_1^6, x_1^7, x_1^8] = \varepsilon,
$$
$$
x_2^j > \min[x_2^5, x_2^6, x_2^7, x_2^8] = 2 + \varepsilon,
$$
$$
x_3^j > \min[x_3^5, x_3^6, x_3^7, x_3^8] = \varepsilon,
$$
$$
x_4^j > \min[x_4^5, x_4^6, x_4^7, x_4^8] = 2 + \varepsilon.
$$

Moreover, for small ε these columns are linearly independent.

The vector

$$
x = \left(\frac{14 + \varepsilon}{4}, \frac{14 + \varepsilon}{4}, \frac{14 + \varepsilon}{4}, \frac{14 + \varepsilon}{4} \right)'
$$

is interior to the convex hull of x^5, x^6, x^7, x^8 since

$$
x = \tfrac{1}{4}x^5 + \tfrac{1}{4}x^6 + \tfrac{1}{4}x^7 + \tfrac{1}{4}x^8,
$$

and its representation has four positive weights.

But the vectors x^9, x^{10}, x^{11}, x^{12} have precisely the same properties. They are linearly independent and form a primitive set whose convex hull contains x as an interior point. The two distinct subsimplices $S_{5,6,7,8}$ and $S_{9,10,11,12}$ therefore have an interior point in common and cannot be part of a simplicial subdivision. We see that primitive sets based on the regular grid and the cyclic lexicographic tie-breaking procedure bear a relationship to simplicial subdivisions that cannot be generalized to an arbitrary grid.

7.3. ALGORITHMS BASED ON SIMPLICIAL SUBDIVISIONS

Even though primitive sets and simplicial subdivisions are distinct geometrical concepts, they do share with each other the feature of a replacement step. Since it is this property—taken in conjunction with pivot steps for a system of linear inequalities—that forms the basis for our algorithms, a similar class of algorithms can be developed using simplicial subdivisions. This approach to computational techniques is the one emphasized by Eaves (1970, 1971a), Kuhn (1968), Shapley (1972), Merrill (1971), Wagner (1971), and Freidenfelds (1971).

If $x^{j_1}, \ldots, x^{j_n}$ are the vectors of a primitive set, then a unique replacement can be found for any of these, assuming that the remaining $n - 1$ vectors are not all slack vectors. For a simplicial subdivision the corresponding property involves the vertices $v^{j_1}, \ldots, v^{j_n}$ of an arbitrary simplex $S_{j_1,\ldots,j_n}$ in the subdivision. In general, if a specific vertex is designated, there will be a unique simplex in the subdivision which has the remaining $n - 1$ vertices in common with $S_{j_1,\ldots,j_n}$ and whose nth vertex is different. In figure 7.3.1 the vertex v^{j^*} is the replacement for v^{j_1}, and the simplex $(v^{j_1}, v^{j_2}, v^{j_3})$ is transformed by the replacement step into $(v^{j^*}, v^{j_2}, v^{j_3})$.

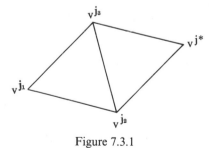

Figure 7.3.1

In a general simplicial subdivision of S—or T—the replacement for a vertex in a simplex can always be found unless the remaining $n - 1$

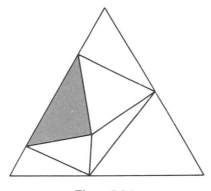

Figure 7.3.2

vertices lie on the boundary. In figure 7.3.2, that vertex of the shaded simplex which is interior to the large simplex cannot be replaced. This permits a clear statement of the circumstances under which a replacement step can be carried out. Unfortunately for the algorithm, however, there are far too many of these circumstances, a fact that may force the algorithm to terminate before a desired solution is obtained. In order to avoid this difficulty we shall focus on the rather special type of simplicial subdivision described in the following definition.

7.3.1. [DEFINITION] *A simplicial subdivision of the simplex* $T = \{(x_1, \ldots, x_n)|x_i \leq 1, \Sigma_1^n x_i = 1\}$ *is defined to be restricted if for each i the face on which* $x_i = 1$ *is contained in a single subsimplex.*

The definition, illustrated by figure 7.3.3, merely requires that those vertices of a simplex in the subdivision which lie on the boundary of

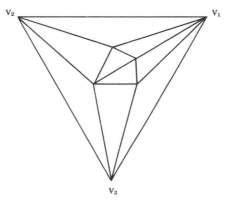

Figure 7.3.3

T must be one of the n vertices whose coordinates are given by the columns of the matrix

$$
\begin{array}{cccc}
v^1 & v^2 & \ldots & v^n
\end{array}
$$

$$
\begin{bmatrix}
2-n & 1 & \ldots & 1 \\
1 & 2-n & \ldots & 1 \\
1 & 1 & \ldots & 1 \\
\vdots & \vdots & & \vdots \\
1 & 1 & \ldots & 2-n
\end{bmatrix}.
$$

If a restricted simplicial subdivision is used, the following simplification occurs in the description of a replacement step.

7.3.2. [THEOREM] *Let $v^1, \ldots, v^n, v^{n+1}, \ldots, v^k$ be the vertices of a restricted simplicial subdivision of T, and let $v^{j_1}, \ldots, v^{j_n}$ be the vertices of a simplex $S_{j_1,\ldots,j_n}$ in this subdivision. If a particular vertex of $S_{j_1,\ldots,j_n}$ is removed, there is a unique replacement producing a new simplex in the subdivision, except in the case in which the remaining $n-1$ vertices of $S_{j_1,\ldots,j_n}$ are all from the set $(v^1, \ldots, v^n)$.*

The reader should be able to supply a proof of this intuitively obvious statement by himself. But it should be clear from the similarity of this statement and theorem 2.3.1 that primitive sets and restricted subdivisions have identical formal properties from the point of view of our algorithms.

For example, let the vertices $v^1, \ldots, v^k$ of a restricted subdivision be given a label from one of the first n integers, and let v^i (for $i = 1, \ldots, n$) be given the label i. Then, by an argument virtually identical to that previously used, we may conclude that there is a simplex in the subdivision all of whose vertices are differently labelled.

We begin the algorithm with the simplex whose vertices are $v^2, \ldots, v^n$ and one additional vertex v^j (fig. 7.3.4). If v^j has been given the label 1, the algorithm terminates, since all of the labels will be distinct. Otherwise v^j will have a label identical with that of one of the vertices $v^2, \ldots, v^n$, and that vertex is removed in order to obtain the next simplex. The algorithm proceeds in this fashion, always removing the vertex whose label is identical with that of the vertex just introduced. Lemke's argument is then available, as in chapter 2, to conclude that the algorithm cannot cycle and must terminate with a simplex of the required type. This demonstrates the following theorem, analogous to theorem 2.5.1.

7.3.3. [THEOREM] *Let the vertices $v^1, \ldots, v^k$ of a restricted simplicial subdivision of T each be assigned a label from the first n integers. Assume*

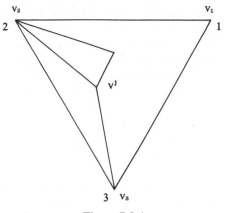

Figure 7.3.4

that v^i (for $i = 1, \ldots, n$) receives the label i. Then there is a simplex of the subdivision all of whose vertices are differently labelled.

The major result of chapter 4, relating primitive sets to the feasible bases of a system of linear equations $Ay = b$, may also be transposed into an analogous form involving simplicial subdivisions, an observation first made by Eaves (1970). As above, the algorithm and the finiteness proof merely use the fact that primitive sets and restricted simplicial subdivisions are formally equivalent. The reader should have no difficulty in constructing a proof of the following theorem.

7.3.4. [THEOREM] *Let $v^1, \ldots, v^k$ be the vertices of a restricted simplicial subdivision of T. Associate with each vertex a column of the matrix*

$$
A = \begin{array}{c} \begin{array}{cccccc} v_1 & \cdots & v_n & v_{n+1} & \cdots & v_k \end{array} \\ \begin{bmatrix} 1 & \cdots & 0 & a_{1,n+1} & \cdots & a_{1,k} \\ \vdots & & \vdots & \vdots & & \vdots \\ 0 & \cdots & 1 & a_{n,n+1} & \cdots & a_{n,k} \end{bmatrix} \end{array}
$$

in such a way that the first n vertices are associated with slack columns. Let $b \geq 0$ and assume that $\{y|Ay = b, y \geq 0\}$ is bounded. Then there exists a subsimplex in the subdivision with vertices $v^{j_1}, \ldots, v^{j_n}$ and such that columns $j_1, \ldots, j_n$ form a feasible basis for $Ay = b$.

Let us conclude this section by showing how the well-known Sperner's lemma can be demonstrated by our methodology (see Cohen 1967, for a similar treatment). This lemma, which has historically formed the basis for fixed point theorems, is rarely required in numerical applications where it can be replaced by the simpler techniques of theorem 2.5.1 and 7.3.3.

Sperner's lemma involves a simplicial subdivision of the simplex S, each of whose vertices is again associated with a label selected from the first n integers. A series of restrictions is then placed on the labels—one such restriction for each subface of S. More specifically a vertex that lies on the face $(x_{i_1} = 0, \ldots, x_{i_l} = 0)$ must be assigned a label *different* from $i_1, \ldots, i_l$. The conclusion is then the familiar one: there exists a simplex in the subdivision all of whose vertices are differently labelled.

The difference between the assumptions of Sperner's lemma and theorem 2.5.1 may be illustrated quite simply by their limiting forms, in which sufficient conditions are given for the intersection of n closed sets $C_1, \ldots, C_n$ (whose union covers S) to be nonempty. The analogue of Sperner's lemma is then the Knaster-Kuratowski-Mazurkiewicz lemma previously mentioned, which requires a separate condition for each face $x_{i_1} = 0, \ldots, x_{i_l} = 0$: namely, that an arbitrary vector in this subface be contained in one of the sets C_j, with $j \neq i_1, \ldots, i_l$. This is to be contrasted with our intersection theorem of chapter 3, which involves n conditions —that x be in C_i if $x_i = 0$—rather than $2^n - 1$ such conditions (fig. 7.3.5).

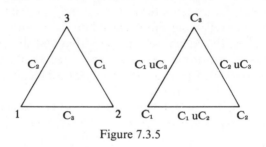

Figure 7.3.5

In order to obtain Sperner's lemma by our methodology we imbed the simplex S properly in the simplex

$$T = \{x | x_i \leq 1 + \varepsilon, \sum_1^n x_i = 1\}.$$

ε is selected to be positive so that S is completely contained in T. The subdivision of S is extended to T as follows: new simplices are formed by taking $n - l$ vertices of a simplex of S which happen to be on the face $x_{i_1} = 0, \ldots, x_{i_l} = 0$ of S and adjoining to them the vertices $v^{i_1}, \ldots, v^{i_l}$ of T.

In this restricted simplicial subdivision of T the vertices of S will retain the labels satisfying the assumptions of Sperner's lemma. The new vertices of T—$v^1, \ldots, v^n$—will be labelled in a somewhat novel fashion: v^i will receive the label $i + 1$ (mod. n) (fig. 7.3.6).

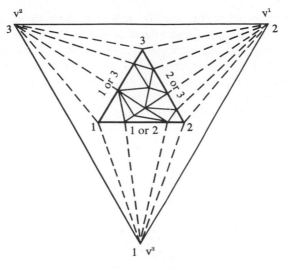

Figure 7.3.6

The algorithm is then applied to T in order to obtain a simplex whose vertices are differently labelled. Sperner's lemma will, of course, be demonstrated if we can show that this simplex must be one of the original simplices of S. Suppose to the contrary that the simplex with distinct labels is formed from $v^{i_1}, \ldots, v^{i_l}$ and $n - l$ vertices lying on the face $x_{i_1} = 0, \ldots, x_{i_l} = 0$. By the assumptions of Sperner's lemma these latter vertices will have labels different from $i_1, \ldots, i_l$; therefore the labels $i_1, \ldots, i_l$ must be associated with the vertices $v^{i_1}, \ldots, v^{i_l}$ in some order. But this is impossible if $l < n$ since v^i has been given the label $i + 1$ (mod. n). The simplex with distinct labels must therefore be one of the original simplices of S, and Sperner's lemma has been demonstrated.

7.4. AN ALTERNATIVE SIMPLICIAL SUBDIVISION*

As we have seen, our class of algorithms can be based either on the notion of primitive sets or on simplicial subdivisions of the simplex S. Any problem amenable to one of these techniques can be analyzed, in a more or less natural fashion, by the other. Can we say which of the techniques is preferable from a computational point of view?

Primitive sets do seem to have one substantial advantage at the outset: they can be based on an arbitrary grid of points $x^{n+1}, \ldots, x^k$ on S as long as the nondegeneracy assumption is satisfied. The points can be selected, for example, to emphasize a region of the simplex in which an approximate solution is expected to lie, thereby reducing the number of iterations. On the other hand, with a general grid of vectors there may be substantial storage requirements and the replacement step itself will involve a search that is expensive in terms of computer time. These considerations seem to suggest either the regular grid with which we have been involved in this chapter or perhaps a simple modification in which the denominators are selected to be much higher within some region of S (fig. 7.4.1). But then

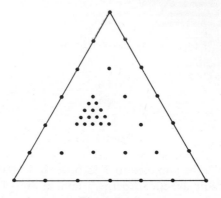

Figure 7.4.1

if the cyclic lexicographic ordering is used to resolve degeneracy and to simplify storage requirements, we are back to a simplicial subdivision.

On the other hand, a restricted simplicial subdivision may always be found with an arbitrary preassigned list of vertices $v^{n+1}, \ldots, v^k$; in fact, a large number of subdivisions will be consistent with a given list of vertices (fig. 7.4.2). This requires, however, that a vast amount of information be

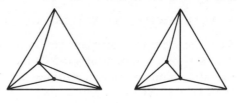

Figure 7.4.2

stored in the computer in order to recognize whether a given collection of n of these vertices corresponds to a simplex in the subdivision. And a search of substantially greater magnitude than that involved with primitive sets will be called for in order to determine the replacement for a given vector. If either primitive sets or simplicial subdivisions are used as the basis of an algorithm, some regularity must be imposed to economize on storage and search.

Shapley (1972) has suggested a compact description of the simplices arising in a barycentric subdivision of the simplex—a particular simplicial subdivision long favored by topologists. We shall discuss this briefly in the present section, though, as we shall see, there are some serious computational costs in its implementation if the grid is fine.

Consider a simplex with vertices $v_1, \ldots, v_n$ consisting of all vectors of the form $\alpha_1 v_1 + \ldots + \alpha_n v_n$ with $\alpha_i \geq 0$ and $\Sigma_1^n \alpha_i = 1$. The first barycentric subdivision of the simplex is a simplicial subdivision consisting of $n!$ subsimplices each one associated with a particular permutation $(i_1, \ldots, i_n)$ of the integers. For each such permutation the subsimplex $S_{i_1, \ldots, i_n}$ is defined to consist of all vectors with $\alpha_{i_1} \geq \alpha_{i_2} \geq \ldots \geq \alpha_{i_n}$.

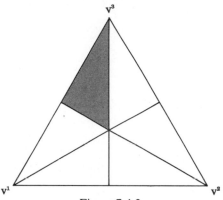

Figure 7.4.3

For example, if $n = 3$, there are six simplices in the barycentric subdivision. The simplex S_{312} consists of all vectors $\alpha_1 v_1 + \alpha_2 v_2 + \alpha_3 v_3$ with $\alpha_3 \geq \alpha_1 \geq \alpha_2$ (fig. 7.4.3). The vertices of S_{312} may easily be seen to be given by

$$v_3' = v_3,$$

$$v_1' = \frac{v_3 + v_1}{2},$$

$$v_2' = \frac{v_3 + v_1 + v_2}{3},$$

since any vector of the form

$$\lambda_3 v_3 + \lambda_1 \left(\frac{v_3 + v_1}{2} \right) + \lambda_2 \left(\frac{v_3 + v_1 + v_2}{3} \right),$$

with $\lambda_i \geq 0$, can be written as

$$\alpha_3 v_3 + \alpha_1 v_1 + \alpha_2 v_2,$$

with $\alpha_3 \geq \alpha_1 \geq \alpha_2 \geq 0$, by means of the formula

$$\alpha_2 = \frac{\lambda_2}{3}, \qquad \alpha_1 = \frac{\lambda_1}{2} + \frac{\lambda_2}{3}, \qquad \alpha_3 = \lambda_3 + \frac{\lambda_1}{2} + \frac{\lambda_2}{3},$$

and vice versa. In the general case the vertices of the subsimplex $S_{i_1, \ldots, i_n}$ are given by

$$v'_{i_1} = v_{i_1}$$

$$v'_{i_2} = \frac{v_{i_1} + v_{i_2}}{2}$$

$$\vdots$$

$$v'_{i_n} = \frac{v_{i_1} + \ldots + v_{i_n}}{n}.$$

We shall be concerned with repeated barycentric subdivisions each obtained from the previous one by subjecting every simplex to a barycentric subdivision. But for the moment let us ask about the replacement operation in the simple case of a single barycentric subdivision. Suppose that $n = 4$ and we wish to remove the vertex v'_4 from the simplex S_{3142} whose vertices are

$$v'_3 = v_3,$$

$$v'_1 = \frac{v_3 + v_1}{2},$$

$$v'_4 = \frac{v_3 + v_1 + v_4}{3},$$

$$v'_2 = \frac{v_3 + v_1 + v_4 + v_2}{4}.$$

Clearly the only other simplex in the subdivision whose vertices are v'_3, v'_1, and v'_2 is given by S_{3124}—based on the new permutation in which 4 and 2 have been interchanged.

This rule may be summarized in the following lemma.

7.4.1. [LEMMA] *Let the simplex be defined by the permutation* $(i_1, i_2, \ldots, i_n)$. *If the vertex* v'_{i_α} *is removed, the unique replacement is determined by the new permutation in which* i_α *and* $i_{\alpha+1}$ *are interchanged. If* $\alpha = n$, *the* $n - 1$ *remaining vertices of the simplex lie on the boundary and no replacement is possible.*

In order to demonstrate the lemma we merely note that the vertices of the two simplices in question are given by

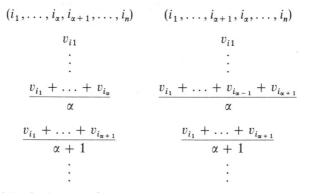

$$(i_1, \ldots, i_\alpha, i_{\alpha+1}, \ldots, i_n) \qquad (i_1, \ldots, i_{\alpha+1}, i_\alpha, \ldots, i_n)$$

$$v_{i1} \qquad\qquad\qquad v_{i1}$$
$$\vdots \qquad\qquad\qquad \vdots$$
$$\frac{v_{i_1} + \ldots + v_{i_\alpha}}{\alpha} \qquad \frac{v_{i_1} + \ldots + v_{i_{\alpha-1}} + v_{i_{\alpha+1}}}{\alpha}$$

$$\frac{v_{i_1} + \ldots + v_{i_{\alpha+1}}}{\alpha + 1} \qquad \frac{v_{i_1} + \ldots + v_{i_{\alpha+1}}}{\alpha + 1}$$
$$\vdots \qquad\qquad\qquad \vdots$$

which are identical except for v'_{i_α}.

The second barycentric subdivision is obtained by subjecting each of the $n!$ simplices $S_{i_1,\ldots,i_n}$ to a further barycentric subdivision. There will be a total of $(n!)^2$ subsimplices in the second barycentric subdivision, each one characterized by a pair of permutations (fig. 7.4.4). The shaded triangle

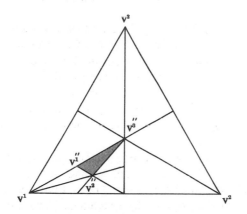

Figure 7.4.4

in figure 7.4.4 is represented, for example, by 123—312, since it is contained in S_{123} of the first subdivision and is based on the subsequent permutation 312.

If the vector v_3'' is removed from this simplex, the replacement is found by the application of lemma 7.4.1 to the last permutation. We replace 312 by 132 and obtain the new simplex 123—132. A slight difficulty arises if we attempt to replace v_2'' instead of v_3'', for this case, which is revealed by the fact that the permutation 312 ends in 2, takes us outside of the simplex 123. We then replace this larger simplex by 132 and arrive at 132—213.

The kth barycentric subdivision will involve $(n!)^k$ subsimplices each defined by k permutations

(7.4.2) $(i_1^1, \ldots, i_n^1), (i_1^2, \ldots, i_n^2), \ldots, (i_1^k, \ldots, i_n^k).$

The vertices are described recursively by means of

$$v_{i_1}^l = v_{i_1}^{l-1},$$

$$v_{i_2}^l = \frac{v_{i_1}^{l-1} + v_{i_2}^{l-1}}{2},$$

$$\vdots$$

$$v_{i_h}^l = \frac{v_{i_1}^{l-1} + \ldots + v_{i_h}^{l-1}}{n};$$

the reader should be alerted to the minor complication that a given vertex may have different subscripts in the several different simplices of which it is a member.

Consider the simplex defined by 7.4.2, and let us attempt to remove the vertex v_x^k with x, an integer between 1 and n. This is done by means of the following rule, whose validity is demonstrated by Shapley (1972).

7.4.3. [RULE] *Find that permutation located farthest to the right for which x is not the last integer (if x is the last integer in every permutation, no replacement can be made). Let this be permutation l, so that $i_\alpha^l = x$ for some $\alpha < n$. Let $y = i_{\alpha+1}^l$. To find the new simplex, interchange x and y in the permutations $l, l+1, \ldots, k$.*

For example, suppose that we attempt to remove the vertex v_3^4 from the simplex 2314—1324—1243—4123. The second permutation is that one farthest to the right for which the integer 3 is not final, and in this permutation it is followed by a 2. We therefore exchange 2 and 3 in the final three permutations, thereby obtaining the simplex 2314—1234—1342—4132.

The method can clearly be programmed for a computer, but it would seem to be less efficient computationally than an algorithm based on the regular grid studied in this chapter. In a problem of size 10, for example, in order to obtain the accuracy corresponding to a D of 500, it may be necessary to have as many as 40 subdivisions, so that each simplex would be represented by a string of 400 integers. Moreover, the coordinates of the new vertex would have to be calculated on each iteration in order to evaluate the mapping or the demand functions, etc. This would impose a computational burden on each iteration substantially larger than that required by the regular grid with the lexicographical ordering and would suggest that barycentric subdivisions provide an inferior algorithm.

CHAPTER 8

Some Applications to *n*-Person Game Theory

8.1. INTRODUCTION

The techniques in the previous chapters were originally designed to provide a numerical procedure for a specific problem in game theory: the computation of an outcome in the core of an *n*-person game (Scarf 1967a). It was not until somewhat later that it became clear that the concept of a primitive set and the associated replacement steps could be applied equally well to the approximation of fixed points of a continuous mapping and to the determination of equilibrium prices and activity levels in a general equilibrium model (Scarf 1967b, 1967c). The present chapter will return to the topic of *n*-person game theory and describe the modifications of our basic algorithm that are required for this class of applications.

Since this monograph is primarily devoted to computational techniques, it would be inappropriate to attempt a summary of the many conceptual innovations introduced into game theory since the pioneering work of von Neumann and Morgenstern (1947). I shall therefore—aside from a few introductory remarks—restrict my attention to a small number of topics which are intimately related to the methodology developed in the earlier chapters.

The customary way of presenting an *n*-person game is in terms of its "normal" form, i.e., a specification of the strategies available to each of the players in the game and a description of the utility or preference indicator for each player as a function of the joint selection of strategies. There are many situations of conflict, which we may wish to examine by means of the concepts of game theory, whose formulation in these strategic terms suggests itself quite readily. For example, the behavior of a small number of firms engaged in producing a common output may be analyzed in terms of a game in which each producer selects as a strategy an output level, or a price for his product, or perhaps a suitable combination of both price and output. The utility function for each producer can then be taken as the difference between the revenue resulting from the sale of his output and the cost of production.

The specification of a game in terms of strategies and utility functions can be contrasted with an alternative formulation, known as the "characteristic" form, in which the basic concept is the set of utility vectors that can be "achieved" by an arbitrary coalition of players. For example, in a model of exchange in which each consumer owns a stock of assets prior to trade and has a conventional utility function for final consumption, the set of utility vectors achievable by a coalition S can be taken most naturally as those arising from an arbitrary redistribution of that coalition's assets. Production can also be introduced in a variety of ways, perhaps the simplest of which is to assume a common production possibility set available to each coalition. The determination of achievable utility vectors for the coalition would then permit—in addition to the exchange of initial assets—the production of new commodities valued by the members of the coalition.

To be specific, let us consider a model of exchange involving three consumers, with utility functions $u_1(x)$, $u_2(x)$, $u_3(x)$ and with vectors of initial holdings w^1, w^2, and w^3. In order to describe the game in characteristic form, the set of achievable utility vectors must be given for each of the seven possible coalitions—the set of all players, the three two-player coalitions, and the three coalitions each consisting of a single player.

Consider first the coalition of all three players whose total assets $w^1 + w^2 + w^3$ can be allocated in an arbitrary fashion x^1, x^2, x^3 among the three members subject only to the constraint $x^1 + x^2 + x^3 \leq w^1 + w^2 + w^3$. For any such allocation, the utility triple (u_1, u_2, u_3), with

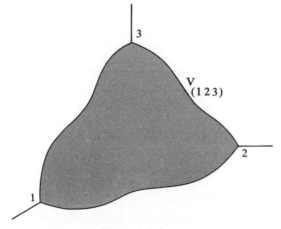

Figure 8.1.1

$u_i = u_i(x^i)$ (for $i = 1, 2, 3$), is obtained; the set of all achievable utility vectors, which we denote by $V_{(123)}$, is then generated by letting the allocations range over all of those consistent with the initial endowment of the coalition (fig. 8.1.1).

For the coalition $(1, 2)$ of the first two players, the set $V_{(12)}$ of achievable utility vectors consists of those utility pairs (u_1, u_2), with $u_1 \leq u_1(x^1)$ and $u_2 \leq u_2(x^2)$ for some x^1, x^2 (with $x^1 + x^2 \leq w^1 + w^2$), and similarly for each of the remaining two-player coalitions (fig. 8.1.2). Each of these sets is contained in the hyperplane whose coordinates corresponding to players not in the coalition are zero. Finally, the single-player coalitions have no strategic possibilities available to them, and the set $V_{(i)}$ (for $i = 1, 2, 3$) may be defined as the set of all points on the i-axis not larger than the utility of the ith player's initial holdings.

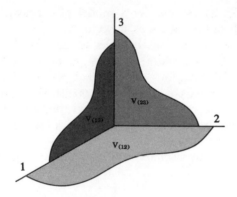

Figure 8.1.2

This example of a three-person exchange economy illustrates the description of a game in characteristic form in terms of the set of achievable utility vectors V_S for each coalition of players. In order to give a formal definition, let us introduce the following notation: The set of n players will be denoted by N and an arbitrary coalition by S. For each S, E^S will mean the Euclidean space of dimension equal to the number of players in S and whose coordinates have as subscripts the integers representing members of S. If u is a vector in E^N, then u^S will be its projection onto E^S.

8.1.1. [DEFINITION] *An n-person game in characteristic form is defined by associating with each coalition S a set of achievable utility vectors V_S, subject to the following conditions:*

a. *For each S, V_S is a closed, nonempty subset of E^S;*
b. *if $u \in V_S$ and $u' \in E^S$ with $u' \leqq u$, then $u' \in V_S$;*
c. *the set V_N is bounded from above.*

The three conditions listed in this definition are all quite minor and need no elaborate justification. The assumption that V_S be a closed set is a continuity assumption; the second condition recognizes that free disposal is incorporated in the definition; and the third, that V_N be bounded from above, states that there are some limitations on the utilities that can be collectively achieved. It may be useful to illustrate the definition by means of several examples.

EXAMPLE I. Let us consider a general model of exchange involving n players, with utility functions $u_1(x), \ldots, u_n(x)$ defined and continuous for all non-negative vectors. The initial assets, prior to trade, are given by the vectors $w^1, w^2, \ldots, w^n$. For any coalition S, the set of achievable utility vectors V_S is then defined by

$$(8.1.2) \qquad V_S = \{u \in E^S | u_i \leq u_i(x^i) \text{ for some } \{x^i\} \text{ with } \sum_S x^i \leqq \sum_S w^i\}.$$

As we see, the formulation of this important class of models as games in characteristic form is quite immediate. On the other hand, it is by no means clear what should be taken as the set of possible strategies for each player if we wish to formulate the exchange model as a game in normal form. I will suggest such a formulation as part of a subsequent example, but at this point it is appropriate to remark that strategies such as the proposal of rates of exchange by each player will yield a determinate outcome of the game in only very special examples.

The easiest way to incorporate production into a model of this form is to assume the existence of a production possibility set Y, summarizing the common technological knowledge available to all coalitions S. The definition of V_S is then modified by permitting $\Sigma_S x^i - \Sigma_S w^i$ to be in Y rather than insisting that net supply be non-negative. It is important to point out that the conventional neoclassical convexity assumptions on preferences and technological possibilities are quite unnecessary for the definition of the game. This observation raises the hope that some of the important variations of the neoclassical model, such as increasing returns to scale in production, may be capable of analysis in game-theoretic terms rather than by more conventional behavioristic assumptions.

EXAMPLE II. Von Neumann and Morgenstern, and many game theorists since them, make use of the assumption of transferable utility in discussing games in characteristic form. Under this assumption the sets V_S are defined by $\{u \in E^S | \Sigma_{i \in S} u_i \leq f_S\}$, with f_S representing a specific number associated with the coalition S. In general, there seems to be no compelling reason for making so drastic an assumption, which can be justified only by requiring utility to be proportional to some tradable commodity, such as money. Nor will the property be preserved under independent monotonic transformations of each player's utility function; even linear transformations require the same scale factor for each player.

Of course there are some examples of n-person games in which appropriate utility transformations may be found so that the sets V_S are each half-spaces, even without making an explicit assumption of transferable utility. In an exchange model, if all players have identical utility functions $u(x)$, which are also assumed to be concave and homogeneous of degree one, it is a simple matter to verify that a vector u is in V_S if and only if $\Sigma_{i \in S} u_i \leq u(\Sigma_{i \in S} w^i)$. But this is a rather extreme case implying, as it does, the possibility of aggregating individual preferences into group preferences.

EXAMPLE III. Let us consider a special case of the problem of reconciling individual preferences by means of majority voting in a framework similar to that introduced by Kenneth J. Arrow (1951). We imagine, for convenience, three players who are faced with the selection of a single social state from a list of four possibilities: states 1, 2, 3, and 4. Each of the three players has a preference ordering over these four states summarized by a table of utilities (table 8.1.1).

TABLE 8.1.1.   UTILITIES

	Player		
State	1	2	3
1	8	3	8
2	5	7	1
3	3	6	10
4	1	4	2

The entries in the table are preference indicators; of any pair of alternatives a player will prefer that one associated with the highest number. Of course the underlying preferences are unchanged if a strictly monotonic transformation is applied to a single player's preference indicator.

Let us assume that a pair of players, since they represent a majority, can select any of the four social outcomes and that a single player by himself has no influence on the outcome. The set $V_{(12)}$ will then consist of four possible utility pairs $(8, 3), (5, 7), (3, 6),$ and $(1, 4)$. Figure 8.1.3 illustrates

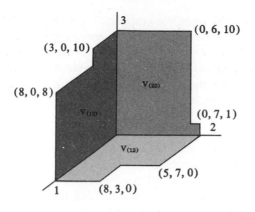

Figure 8.1.3

the three sets V_S for S an arbitrary two-player coalition. Each of these sets, as well as $V_{(123)}$, is defined by a finite list of "corners" rather than being bounded by a smooth curve as is typically the case in a model of exchange.

EXAMPLE IV. As our final example, let us imagine that an n-person game has been presented to us in its normal form, in terms of the strategies available to each player and with a set of utility functions defined for each joint selection of strategies. To be specific, let the set of possible strategies for the ith player be denoted by X^i, and a typical strategy by a lower case x^i. X^i may consist of a finite number of strategies—as in the familiar two-person game—or it may be a continuum, or perhaps an even more general set. For each $x^1 \in X^1, \ldots, x^n \in X^n$, player i's utility indicator is given by $u_i(x^1, x^2, \ldots, x^n)$.

The problem of passing from a game in normal form to the characteristic form is one to which von Neuman and Morgenstern devoted substantial attention. The difficulty resides in the fact that while the members of a coalition may be presumed to have complete freedom in the selection of their own strategies, they have no control over the strategic choices of the complementary coalition. The outcome of the game, and therefore the utility levels obtained by the members of a coalition, will, in general, depend on the collective strategy choices of all players, not only on those made by the coalition. It is therefore by no means clear how to interpret the statement that a vector of utility levels can be achieved by a coalition since the coalition finds it necessary to make some implicit assumption about the actions of the remaining players.

There is, it would seem, no completely satisfactory resolution of this difficulty unless the threats of the complementary coalition are of an exceptionally limited nature, such as their refusal to trade in a model of exchange. The solution originally put forward by von Neumann and Morgenstern—and subsequently modified by Aumann (1961) to avoid the assumption of transferable utility—solves this problem by an extremely conservative treatment of the threats available to the complementary coalition. For them a utility vector is achievable by a coalition S if the members of S have a specific selection of strategies that yield this utility vector regardless of the strategic choices of the remaining players. To take a specific example, the utility vector $(u_1, u_2) \in V_{(12)}$ in a four-player game if there is a pair of strategies x^1 and x^2 such that $u_1 \leq u_1(x^1, x^2, x^3, x^4)$ and $u_2 \leq u_2(x^1, x^2, x^3, x^4)$ for *any* $x^3 \in X^3$ and $x^4 \in X^4$, with a similar definition for an arbitrary coalition.

I shall return to this example in the next several sections, because a rather simple set of conditions on the strategy spaces and utility functions are sufficient to guarantee the existence of an appealing cooperative solution to the game.

8.2. The Core of a Game

The core of an n-person game is a generalization of the contract curve first introduced by Edgeworth in 1881; as a method of solution it is capable of being studied in the context of an arbitrary game in which the utility vectors achievable by a coalition are specified. While the concept does not appear explicitly in the work of von Neumann and Morgenstern, it is intimately related to the notion of dominance, which plays so important a role in their analysis of cooperation solutions.

In order to introduce the concept, we begin with the following formal definition.

8.2.1. [Definition] *A utility vector* $u = (u_1, u_2, \ldots, u_n)$ *is said to be blocked by the coalition S if there exists $u' \in V_S$ with $u'_i > u_i$ for all $i \in S$.*

In this definition the coalition that blocks must be able to provide higher utility levels for all of its members than that prescribed by the vector u; nothing is stipulated about the players who are not members of the coalition. For example, in the voting model of the previous section the utility vector $(8, 3, 8)$ is blocked by the coalition of the second and third players since the vector $(6, 10) \in V_{(23)}$ and it is larger in both of its coordinates than $(3, 8)$. On the other hand, the utility vector $(1, 4, 2)$ associated with the fourth state of the world is blocked by the coalition of all three players because $(3, 6, 10) \in V_{(123)}$, and this latter vector is strictly preferred in all of its coordinates. In the general case any vector that is not a Pareto optimum will be blocked by the coalition of all of the players.

8.2.2. [DEFINITION] *The core of an n-person game is the set of utility vectors $u \in V_N$ that are blocked by no coalition.*

In other words, the core consists of those utility vectors that are, on the one hand, feasible for all of the players acting collectively and, secondly, have the property that no coalition can do better for all of its members.

There are many examples of n-person games in which every utility vector that is collectively feasible can be blocked by some coalition and whose core is therefore empty. The voting example of the previous section illustrates this possibility because—as the reader may verify with no difficulty—the utility vectors associated with each of the four possible outcomes will be blocked by at least one of the two-player coalitions.

On the other hand, games that are based on economic models of exchange and production, in which the customary assumptions of convexity of preference and production sets are maintained, typically do have a nonempty core. I shall provide an argument for this remark in the general existence theorem to be developed subsequently, but it may be appropriate to note at this point that the allocation resulting from a competitive equilibrium provides a utility vector which is in the core.

To see this, let us focus our attention on a model of exchange described by utility functions $u_1(x), \ldots, u_n(x)$ and vectors of initial holdings $w^1, \ldots, w^n$. A competitive equilibrium is then given by a price vector π and an allocation $x^1 + \ldots + x^n = w^1 + \ldots + w^n$ such that x^i maximizes the ith consumer's utility subject to the constraint that he spend no more than $\pi \cdot w^i$. If this allocation is to be blocked by a coalition S, the coalition must have an alternative reallocation of its own resources

$$\sum_{i \in S} y^i = \sum_{i \in S} w^i,$$

with $u_i(y^i) > u_i(x^i)$ for all $i \in S$. But since y^i was not chosen in preference to x^i, it must cost more than $\pi \cdot w^i$; in other words, $\pi \cdot y^i > \pi \cdot w^i$. If these inequalities are added together for all consumers in S, we obtain

$$\pi \sum_{i \in S} w^i = \pi \sum_{i \in S} y^i > \pi \sum_{i \in S} w^i,$$

a contradiction that demonstrates that the competitive allocation is in the core.

The interest that economists have recently shown in the core of an economy derives not only from this observation that the competitive equilibrium is in the core, but also from the fact that if every agent is sufficiently small relative to the collectivity of agents, virtually the only allocations in the core are competitive equilibria. This point may be made either by consideration of a suitable sequence of economies with the number of consumers tending to infinity or else by a direct treatment of exchange economies with an infinite number of agents.

I shall not pursue this line of argument in the present monograph and shall remark merely that it serves as an important justification for a game-theoretic approach to the problem of distribution in an economy.

Even though an n-person game in characteristic form may be used to describe an economy in which the conventional neoclassical assumptions are absent, it is conceivable that the resulting game will have an empty core. This may be seen in an example involving three players and two commodities. The players have identical preferences with the indifference curves displayed in figure 8.2.1. It is a simple matter to verify that if each consumer initially owns one unit of both goods, then every allocation can be blocked by some coalition and the resulting core is empty.

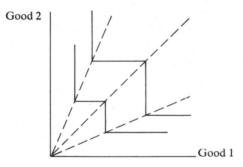

Figure 8.2.1

Illuminating as this example may be in displaying the relevance of convexity to the core, it is not a particularly interesting example of non-convexity from an economic point of view. The more significant deviations from the neoclassical model arise on the production side of the economy in the form of large indivisibilities and increasing returns to scale. But regardless of the specific origins of nonconvexity, their presence is typically sufficient to rule out the existence of a competitive equilibrium and to invalidate that line of argument for the existence of utility vectors in the core. It is because of our hope that game-theoretic analyses may be fruitful for more than the conventional competitive model that we turn, in the next section, to an existence theorem stated in terms of a cooperative game itself, rather than its underlying economic model.

8.3. BALANCED GAMES AND THE EXISTENCE OF A NONEMPTY CORE

The existence theorem that I am about to state makes use of the concept of a *balanced* collection of coalitions, independently introduced by Bondareva (1962) and Shapley (1965) in order to study the core of games with transferable utility.

8.3.1. [DEFINITION] *Let* $N = \{1, 2, \ldots, n\}$. *A collection* $T = \{S\}$ *of subsets of N is called a balanced collection if there are non-negative weights* δ_S *satisfying the equations*

$$\sum_{\substack{S \in T \\ S \supset \{1\}}} \delta_S = 1$$

(8.3.2)
$$\vdots$$

$$\sum_{\substack{S \in T \\ S \supset \{n\}}} \delta_S = 1.$$

The definition can be put in a somewhat different form which may be slightly easier to work with. Define a matrix

$$
(8.3.3) \qquad A =
\begin{array}{c}
\begin{array}{ccccccccc}
(1) & \ldots & (n) & (12) & \ldots & S & \ldots & N
\end{array} \\
\begin{bmatrix}
1 & \ldots & 0 & 1 & \ldots & a_{1,S} & \ldots & 1 \\
0 & \ldots & 0 & 1 & \ldots & a_{2,S} & \ldots & 1 \\
\vdots & & \vdots & \vdots & & \vdots & & \vdots \\
0 & \ldots & 1 & 0 & \ldots & a_{n,S} & \ldots & 1
\end{bmatrix}
\end{array}
$$

with n rows and $2^n - 1$ columns, each column referring to a specific subset of N. The entry in row i and column S will be 1 if player i is a member of the coalition S and 0 if he is not. A collection of coalitions $T = \{S\}$ is then balanced if and only if the equations $A\delta = (1, \ldots, 1)'$ have a non-negative solution with δ_S equal to zero if S is not a member of the collection. In particular, any feasible basis for $A\delta = (1, \ldots, 1)'$ will correspond to n (or less, since the equalities are degenerate) sets of a balanced collection.

Any partition of the set N into disjoint subsets whose union is the full set of players will provide a balanced collection of sets: we need only select $\delta_S = 1$ for S in the partition and $\delta_S = 0$ for the remaining sets. But there are many balanced collections that are far more complex than those arising from partitions. For example, if $n = 3$, the three coalitions $\{(1, 2), (1, 3), (2, 3)\}$ form a balanced collection since

$$\begin{bmatrix} 1 & 1 & 0 \\ 1 & 0 & 1 \\ 0 & 1 & 1 \end{bmatrix} \begin{bmatrix} 1/2 \\ 1/2 \\ 1/2 \end{bmatrix} = \begin{bmatrix} 1 \\ 1 \\ 1 \end{bmatrix}.$$

For $n = 4$ the collection $\{(1, 2), (1, 3), (1, 4), (2, 3, 4)\}$ is balanced with weights $\delta_{(1,2)} = 1/3$, $\delta_{(1,3)} = 1/3$, $\delta_{(1,4)} = 1/3$, $\delta_{(2,3,4)} = 2/3$, as may be seen from the equations

$$\begin{bmatrix} 1 & 1 & 1 & 0 \\ 1 & 0 & 0 & 1 \\ 0 & 1 & 0 & 1 \\ 0 & 0 & 1 & 1 \end{bmatrix} \begin{bmatrix} 1/3 \\ 1/3 \\ 1/3 \\ 2/3 \end{bmatrix} = \begin{bmatrix} 1 \\ 1 \\ 1 \\ 1 \end{bmatrix}.$$

Another example, again with $n = 4$, is given by $(1, 2), (1, 3, 4), (2, 3, 4)$, each of which is associated with the weight $\delta = 1/2$. The number of balanced collections of coalitions, and their diversity, increases rapidly as the number of players becomes large.

In order to state the sufficient conditions for the existence of a nonempty core—which involve the concept of balanced collections—let us make a preliminary modification of the sets V_S. For each proper coalition S this set is contained in the Euclidean subspace whose coordinates refer to the players in S. We extend this set of achievable utility vectors to a full n-dimensional set according to the following definition.

8.3.4. [DEFINITION] *For each S the set $\tilde{V}_S$ consists of all vectors $u = (u_1, \ldots, u_n)$ whose projection u^S is in V_S.*

In other words, the vectors in V_S are filled out by adding arbitrary values for the coordinates corresponding to the players not in S, as figure 8.3.1 illustrates for $n = 3$ and $S = (2, 3)$.

We are now prepared to define a class of n-person games whose importance will be justified by the subsequent theorem.

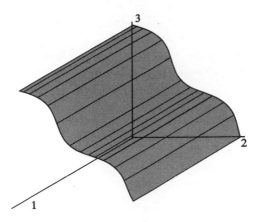

Figure 8.3.1

8.3.5. [DEFINITION] *An n-person game is defined to be balanced if for every balanced collection* $T = \{S\}$ *we have*

$$\bigcap_{S \in T} \tilde{V}_S \subseteq V_N.$$

The obscurity of this definition will hopefully be clarified by a number of examples of balanced games, but let us first state the major theorem of this chapter, the proof of which depends on a slight extension of the concept of primitive sets combined with the algorithmic techniques which we have developed.

8.3.6. [THEOREM] *A balanced n-person game has a nonempty core.*

Before illustrating the range of applicability of this theorem, let us make a few observations which may put it in perspective. For a vector to be in the core of the game it must be contained in V_N and at the same time not be blocked by any coalition S. This latter condition is the same as requiring that the vector not be interior to $\tilde{V}_S$. We are therefore looking for a vector $u \in V_N$ and that is also in the closure of the complement of $\tilde{V}_S$ for every S. The existence of a vector in the core is therefore a theorem about the nonemptiness of the intersection of a number of closed sets.

In various sections of this monograph we have seen how some of the standard intersection theorems (such as the Knaster-Kuratowski-Mazurkiewicz theorem) of combinatorial topology, and also a variety of substantial generalizations, can be derived from our basic methodology. In each of these previous theorems a number of conditions were placed on the family of closed sets in order to guarantee that their intersection be nonempty. In our present theorem the analogous conditions are those which require that the game be balanced.

For example, in a game with three players, there are essentially five such conditions corresponding to the balanced collections:

1. (1), (2), (3)
2. (1, 2), (3)
3. (1, 3), (2)
4. (1), (2, 3)
5. (1, 2), (1, 3), (2, 3)

The conditions are then:

1. $\tilde{V}_{(1)} \cap \tilde{V}_{(2)} \cap \tilde{V}_{(3)} \subseteq V_{(1,2,3)}$
2. $\tilde{V}_{(1,2)} \cap \tilde{V}_{(3)} \subseteq V_{(1,2,3)}$
3. $\tilde{V}_{(1,3)} \cap \tilde{V}_{(2)} \subseteq V_{(1,2,3)}$
4. $\tilde{V}_{(1)} \cap \tilde{V}_{(2,3)} \subseteq V_{(1,2,3)}$
5. $\tilde{V}_{(1,2)} \cap \tilde{V}_{(1,3)} \cap \tilde{V}_{(2,3)} \subseteq V_{(1,2,3)}$

It is easy to verify that the corresponding condition for any other balanced collection will be satisfied if these five conditions obtain. But the first four of them are rather trivial statements of superadditivity—merely requiring that it not be disadvantageous for disjoint coalitions to combine—and would be expected to hold in virtually every game-theoretic situation. It is the last condition that is restrictive and will not be met in every three-person game.

In order to get a sense of this last condition, let us consider a three-person market model with utility functions u_1, u_2, u_3 and vectors of initial holdings w^1, w^2, and w^3. Let u be a vector in $\tilde{V}_{(1,2)} \cap \tilde{V}_{(1,3)} \cap \tilde{V}_{(2,3)}$. Therefore there exist vectors

$$
\begin{aligned}
x^1 + x^2 \quad\;\; &= w^1 + w^2, \\
y^1 \quad\;\; + y^3 &= w^1 \quad\quad\; + w^3, \\
z^2 + z^3 &= \quad\;\; w^2 + w^3,
\end{aligned}
$$

with

$$
\begin{aligned}
u_1(x^1) \geq u_1, &\qquad u_1(y^1) \geq u_1, \\
u_2(x^2) \geq u_2, &\qquad u_2(z^2) \geq u_2, \\
u_3(y^3) \geq u_3, &\qquad u_3(z^3) \geq u_3.
\end{aligned}
$$

Can we infer that the vector u is also in $V_{(1,2,3)}$, or, in other words, that there is an allocation of the total resources $w^1 + w^2 + w^3$ yielding player i (for $i = 1, 2, 3$) a utility of at least u_i? Of course this cannot be done for a general market because the core may be empty if the preferences are not convex. But if the convexity assumption is satisfied, then u is in $V_{(1,2,3)}$ since the allocation

$$\left(\frac{x^1 + y^1}{2}\right) + \left(\frac{x^2 + z^2}{2}\right) + \left(\frac{y^3 + z^3}{2}\right) = w^1 + w^2 + w^3$$

will provide the first player with a utility of $u^1[(x^1 + y^1)/2] \geq u_1$, and similarly for players 2 and 3.

For a three-person exchange economy the convexity of preferences implies that the game is balanced. As the following result indicates, the generalization is valid regardless of the number of players.

8.3.7. [THEOREM] *The game derived from an n-person exchange economy with convex preferences is balanced.*

Let $T = \{S\}$ be a balanced collection with non-negative weights δ_S (for $S \in T$) that satisfy

(8.3.8)
$$\sum_{S \supset \{i\}} \delta_S = 1 \quad \text{for each } i.$$

Also let $u \in \cap_{S \in T} \tilde{V}_S$. We wish to demonstrate that $u \in V_N$.

For each $S \in T$, there is an allocation of that coalition's initial assets $\Sigma_{i \in S} w^i$ that yields the ith player a utility of at least u_i (for $i \in S$). Let this allocation be represented by $\{x^i(S)\}$ with $u_i[x^i(S)] \geq u_i$ (for all $i \in S$) and $\Sigma_S x^i(S) = \Sigma_S w^i$.

We then define the commodity bundles $x^1, x^2, \ldots, x^n$ by

$$x^1 = \sum_{S \supset \{1\}} \delta_S x^1(S)$$

$$x^2 = \sum_{S \supset \{2\}} \delta_S x^2(S)$$

$$\vdots$$

$$x^n = \sum_{S \supset \{n\}} \delta_S x^n(S).$$

For each i, x^i is a convex combination of commodity bundles each of which provides the ith player with a utility at least u_i, and therefore the convexity of preferences implies that $u_i(x^i) \geq u_i$ for $i = 1, \ldots, n$. Therefore in order to show that $u \in V_N$, it is sufficient to demonstrate that $(x^1, x^2, \ldots, x^n)$ is an allocation of the total resources available to the coalition N or, in other words,

$$\sum_1^n x^i = \sum_1^n w^i.$$

But this is a simple consequence of the definition of $(x^1, \ldots, x^n)$, since

$$\sum_1^n x^i = \sum_{i=1}^n \left[\sum_{S \supset (i)} \delta_S x^i(S) \right]$$

$$= \sum_{S \in T} \delta_S \left[\sum_{i \in S} x^i(S) \right]$$

$$= \sum_{S \in T} \delta_S \left(\sum_{i \in S} w^i \right)$$

$$= \sum_{i=1}^n w^i \left(\sum_{S \supset \{i\}} \delta_S \right)$$

$$= \sum_{i=1}^n w^i.$$

Since the game is now seen to be balanced, theorem 8.3.6 will imply the existence of an allocation in the core if the technical conditions of 8.1.1 are satisfied. As the reader may verify with little difficulty, they are an immediate consequence of continuity of preferences. Assuming then that the major theorem is correct, we have demonstrated that an exchange economy with continuous and convex preferences has a nonempty core. It is interesting to note that this result has been demonstrated under weaker assumptions than those customarily used in an existence theorem for competitive equilibria. For example, no assumption guaranteeing that each individual's income at the equilibrium prices is positive is required. The argument may also be generalized quite easily to include production in the case in which each coalition has the same production possibility set—a closed, convex cone—available to it.

8.4. A PROOF OF THE MAIN THEOREM

In this section I shall demonstrate, by means of the computational techniques previously developed, that a balanced n-person game has a nonempty core. It is convenient to begin the analysis by considering the special case (fig. 8.4.1) in which each set V_S is—aside from the free disposal of utility—described by a finite number (designated by l) of utility vectors $u^{1,S}, u^{2,S}, \ldots, u^{l,S}$. Theorem 8.3.6 will first be demonstrated for games of this sort; the general case then follows by a trivial passage to the limit.

In order to motivate the proof it may be best to begin with an example of a three-person game in which each V_S (with S representing a two-

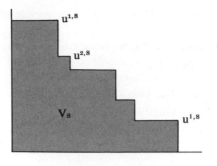

Figure 8.4.1

player coalition) contains two "corners." We represent the corners of the sets V_S by the columns of the following matrix:

$$X = \begin{array}{ccccccccc} u^{1,(1)} & u^{1,(2)} & u^{1,(3)} & u^{1,(12)} & u^{2,(12)} & u^{1,(13)} & u^{2,(13)} & u^{1,(23)} & u^{2,(23)} \\ \begin{bmatrix} 0 & 99 & 98 & 6 & 2 & 12 & 3 & 93 & 92 \\ 100 & 0 & 98 & 6 & 8 & 95 & 94 & 7 & 2 \\ 100 & 99 & 0 & 97 & 96 & 2 & 8 & 5 & 9 \end{bmatrix} \end{array}.$$

For example, the two corners in the set $V_{(13)}$ are (12, 2) and (3, 8). In general, if player i is not in the coalition S, then the entry in row i and column (j, S) will be an arbitrary but large number, differing from column to column.

We wish to consider for the columns of this matrix the concept of a primitive set developed in section 2.7 that involves lists of vectors which do not lie on the unit simplex. A set of three columns of this matrix form a primitive set if, after calculating the row-minima of these three columns, we verify that no column in the matrix has all of its entries strictly larger than these row-minima.

For example, consider the columns $u^{1,(12)}$, $u^{2,(12)}$, $u^{1,(13)}$ that yield the submatrix

$$\begin{bmatrix} 6 & \underline{2} & 12 \\ \underline{6} & 8 & 95 \\ 97 & 96 & \underline{2} \end{bmatrix}$$

whose row-minima are (2, 6, 2)'. For this to be a primitive set there must be no column all of whose entries are strictly larger than this vector. But there is such a column, $(3, 94, 8)'$, and this example does not lead to a primitive set.

Another way to describe this particular observation—which suggests the purpose to which primitive sets will be put—is that the vector of row-minima $(2, 6, 2)'$ is *blocked* by the coalition $(1, 3)$. This coalition has an achievable utility vector that guarantees its members a higher utility than that provided by the vector of row-minima.

As another example, consider the columns $u^{1,(12)}$, $u^{1,(23)}$, $u^{2,(23)}$ that yield

$$\begin{bmatrix} \underline{6} & 93 & 92 \\ 6 & 7 & \underline{2} \\ 97 & \underline{5} & 9 \end{bmatrix}$$

with row-minima $(6, 2, 5)'$. This triple of columns does form a primitive set since no column of X has all of its components strictly larger than the vector of row-minima. Again this observation may be given a game-theoretic interpretation: the vector of row-minima cannot be blocked by any proper coalition.

This property is quite general; a triple of columns will form a primitive set if and only if the vector of row-minima cannot be blocked by any proper coalition. A number of undominated utility vectors will therefore be obtained merely by examining the primitive sets of columns. It is this relationship between blocking and primitive sets that makes our class of algorithms applicable to theorem 8.3.6.

The vector $(6, 2, 5)'$ is unblocked by any proper coalition; if we knew in addition that this vector was contained in $V_{(1,2,3)}$, then any Pareto optimum point greater than or equal to $(6, 2, 5)'$ would be in the core. But, unfortunately, nothing permits us to verify that $(6, 2, 5) \in V_{(123)}$, and this particular example, while it provides us with an undominated utility vector, says nothing about that vector's feasibility.

The feasibility of a vector of row-minima must be obtained from the statement that the game is balanced. For example, consider the columns

$$\begin{array}{ccc} u^{1,(12)} & u^{2,(13)} & u^{1,(23)} \end{array}$$

$$\begin{bmatrix} 6 & \underline{3} & 93 \\ \underline{6} & 94 & 7 \\ 97 & 8 & \underline{5} \end{bmatrix}.$$

The vector of row-minima $(3, 6, 5)'$ cannot be blocked by any coalition and these three columns therefore form a primitive set. But in this case we can say something about the feasibility of $(3, 6, 5)$ because the three coalitions that generate the columns of this primitive set form a balanced collection $\{(1, 2), (1, 3), (2, 3)\}$. The vector $(3, 6, 5)$ is contained in $\tilde{V}_{(12)} \cap \tilde{V}_{(13)} \cap \tilde{V}_{(23)}$ and therefore, if the game is balanced, we can conclude that $(3, 6, 5) \in V_{(123)}$. Any Pareto optimum point in $V_{(123)}$ that is not less than $(3, 6, 5)$ will be in the core.

The particular balanced collection of the three two-player coalitions was not crucial to this argument; all that is required is a triple of columns forming a primitive set and generated by three coalitions that form a balanced collection. This can be put in a more useful way by introducing a matrix A of the same dimensions as X:

$$A = \begin{bmatrix} 1 & 0 & 0 & 1 & 1 & 1 & 1 & 0 & 0 \\ 0 & 1 & 0 & 1 & 1 & 0 & 0 & 1 & 1 \\ 0 & 0 & 1 & 0 & 0 & 1 & 1 & 1 & 1 \end{bmatrix}.$$

Each column of A will correspond to a column of X; it will contain a 1 in row i if player i is a member of the coalition generating that column of X and a 0 otherwise. The determination of a vector in the core is therefore reduced to finding three columns of X that form a primitive set and are such that the three associated columns of A form a feasible basis for the equations $A\delta = (1, 1, 1)'$. The reader need only glance at theorem 4.2.3 to see that we are in the presence of a general argument.

With these introductory remarks let us now consider an arbitrary balanced n-person game whose sets V_S are each generated by a finite number of corners $u^{1,S}, \ldots, u^{l_S,S}$ of non-negative vectors. We construct two matrices X and A with n rows and Σl_S columns, one column for each corner in each set V_S.

8.4.1. [DEFINITION] *The columns for both X and A are indexed by a pair (j, S) with $j = 1, \ldots, l_S$. The entry in column (j, S) and row i of the matrix A is given by 1 if $i \in S$ and 0 otherwise. For the matrix X this entry is given by $u_i^{j,S}$ (the ith component of the jth corner of V_S) if $i \in S$, and by an arbitrary large number $M_{j,S}$ if $i \notin S$. The only restrictions on these latter numbers is that they be different for different columns and that the $M_{j,S}$ for a single-player coalition S be larger than those in which S contains more than one player.*

With this definition we are now ready to apply the obvious generalization of theorem 4.2.3 to the list of vectors $x^{j,S}$ (the columns of X) and to the system of equations $A\delta = (1, \ldots, 1)'$. We must first verify that the required conditions are satisfied. The list of vectors is in standard form if we normalize by assuming that each player by himself can achieve a utility of zero. The vector b is non-negative, and finally the set $\{\delta \geq 0 | A\delta = (1, \ldots, 1)'\}$ is bounded.

The extension of theorem 4.2.3 involving the generalized primitive sets of section 2.7 may now be applied and we obtain a set of n columns of X which form a primitive set and whose associated columns of A form a feasible basis for $A\delta = (1, \ldots, 1)'$. Since no two columns of a feasible basis can be identical, these columns must refer to n distinct sets $S_1, \ldots, S_n$, which are therefore a balanced collection of coalitions.

For each of these sets one corner, say, $(u^{S_1}, u^{S_2}, \ldots, u^{S_n})$, has been selected to form the primitive set, and from the definition, the vector

$$u_1 = \min_{S_j \supset \{1\}} u_1^{S_j}$$

$$u_2 = \min_{S_j \supset \{2\}} u_2^{S_j}$$

$$\vdots$$

$$u_n = \min_{S_j \supset \{n\}} u_n^{S_j}$$

cannot be blocked by any proper coalition. But this vector is contained in $\tilde{V}_{S_j}$ for $j = 1, 2, \ldots, n$ because its projection into E^{S_j} is no larger than one of the corners of V_{S_j}. Since the game is balanced, we must have $u \in V_N$, and therefore any Pareto optimum vector in V_N that is not less than u will be in the core of the game.

This concludes the proof of our theorem for the case in which each V_S contains a finite number of corners. The general case is demonstrated by approximating each V_S by a game with a finite number of corners (as

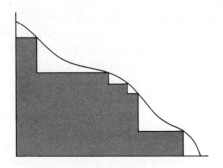

Figure 8.4.2

illustrated in the figure 8.4.2), obtaining a vector in the core of this game, and then passing to the limit.

8.5. OTHER EXAMPLES OF BALANCED GAMES*

EXAMPLE I. As our first example, let us consider a general n-person game with transferable utility, so that the sets $\tilde{V}_S$ are defined by

$$(8.5.1) \qquad \tilde{V}_S = \{u = (u_1, \ldots, u_n) \mid \sum_{i \in S} u_i \leq f_S\},$$

with f_S a specific number for each coalition S. It is interesting to note that for this class of examples the property that the game be balanced is not only sufficient for the existence of a vector in the core, but also necessary —a converse of the existence theorem, which is definitely not true in the general case in which the transferable utility assumption is not made.

To see this, let us assume that the game has a vector $\hat{u} = (\hat{u}_1, \ldots, \hat{u}_n)$ in the core, so that

$$\sum_1^n \hat{u}_i = f_N \quad \text{and}$$

$$\sum_{i \in S} \hat{u}_i \geq f_S$$

for every coalition S. Let us then show that this game is balanced. Take a balanced collection $T = \{S\}$, with weights δ_S, and let $u \in \bigcap_{S \in T} \tilde{V}_S$, or

$$\sum_{i \in S} u_i \leq f_S \leq \sum_{i \in S} \hat{u}_i \quad \text{for } S \in T.$$

In order to show that $u \in V_N$, we take the inequality

$$\sum_{i \in S} u_i \leq \sum_{i \in S} \hat{u}_i \qquad \text{for } S \in T,$$

multiply it by δ_S, and sum over all δ in T, obtaining

$$\sum_{S \in T} \delta_S \left(\sum_{i \in S} u_i \right) \leq \sum_{S \in T} \delta_S \left(\sum_{i \in S} \hat{u}_i \right).$$

But the left-hand side of this inequality is equal to

$$\sum_{i=1}^n u_i \left(\sum_{S \ni \{i\}} \delta_S \right) = \sum_{i=1}^n u_i,$$

and similarly for the right-hand side. We conclude that

$$\sum_{i=1}^{n} u_i \leq \sum_{i=1}^{n} \hat{u}_i = f_N,$$

so that $u \in V_N$ and the game is balanced. This demonstrates the converse of theorem 8.3.6 for the case of transferable utility.

Another simplification arising because of transferable utility is that theorem 8.3.6 can be demonstrated by means of the duality theorem for linear programming and does not require the use of fixed point theorems. Let us assume that the game is balanced and attempt to demonstrate the existence of a vector in the core.

Consider the linear programming problem of minimizing $u_1 + u_2 + \ldots + u_n$ subject to the constraints

$$\sum_{i \in S} u_i \geq f_S \qquad \text{for all coalitions } S.$$

The solution of this problem, which we denote by $\hat{u} = (\hat{u}_1, \ldots, \hat{u}_n)$, will be blocked by no coalition and will therefore be in the core if it is feasible for the coalition of all players, i.e., $\Sigma_1^n \hat{u}_i \leq f_N$. We use the property that the game is balanced to demonstrate that this latter inequality is correct.

The dual linear programming problem is the following: Find nonnegative weights δ_S, one for each coalition, that satisfy the equalities

$$\sum_{S \supset \{1\}} \delta_S = 1$$
$$\vdots$$
$$\sum_{S \supset \{n\}} \delta_S = 1$$

and that maximize $\Sigma_S f_S \delta_S$. Let an optimal solution for this problem be $\{\hat{\delta}_S\}$; the duality theorem tells us that

$$\sum_{S} \hat{\delta}_S f_S = \sum_{i} \hat{u}_i$$

and that

$$\sum_{i \in S} \hat{u}_i = f_S \qquad \text{for each } S,$$

with $\hat{\delta}_S > 0$.

In order to demonstrate that $\Sigma_i \hat{u}_i \leq f_N$, define the balanced collection T to consist of those coalitions S with $\hat{\delta}_S > 0$. Since $\Sigma_{i \in S} \hat{u}_i = f_S$ for all such S, we see that $\hat{u} \in \bigcap_{S \in T} \tilde{V}_S$. But the game is balanced, and this implies $\hat{u} \in V_N$ or $\Sigma_1^n \hat{u}_i \leq f_N$. $\hat{u}$ is therefore in the core and this concludes the proof of theorem 8.3.6 for the case of transferable utility.

EXAMPLE II. As our next example, let us consider a game in normal form in which the player's strategy spaces are given by $X^1, X^2, \ldots, X^n$ and with utility functions

$$u_1(x^1, \ldots, x^n),$$
$$\vdots$$
$$u_n(x^1, \ldots, x^n)$$

defined for all joint selections of strategies. I have indicated earlier one procedure for passing from the normal form to a characteristic form by defining a utility vector as achievable for a coalition S if the players in S have a joint selection of strategies guaranteeing their members this utility level regardless of the strategic choices made by the complementary coalition. With this definition of the sets $\tilde{V}_S$, a selection of strategies $\hat{x}^1, \ldots, \hat{x}^n$ (yielding utilities $\hat{u}_1, \ldots, \hat{u}_n$) will be in the core if no coalition S can guarantee higher utility levels by an alternative selection of strategies for all choices of the remaining players.

The imperfections of this method of solution—in particular its exceptionally conservative treatment of the threats of the complementary coalition—have been previously noted, but it is nevertheless of interest that the existence of such a solution can be demonstrated under very weak conditions.

8.5.2. [THEOREM] (Scarf 1971) *Let each player's strategy space X^i be a closed, bounded, convex subset of a finite dimensional Euclidean space, and let each utility function $u_i(x)$ be quasi-concave (i.e., $u[\alpha x + (1 - \alpha)x'] \geq \min[u(x), u(x')]$, for all $0 \leq \alpha \leq 1$) and continuous. Then the game is balanced and has a nonempty core.*

Let us remark, first of all, that the regularity conditions (that V_S is closed, etc.) are easily verified. The proof that the game is balanced, however, involves a few slightly subtle points and it may be best to introduce the argument by examining a game with four players and with the specific balanced collection $\{(1, 2), (1, 3), (1, 4), (2, 3, 4)\}$.

Let u be a vector contained in $\tilde{V}_{(12)} \cap \tilde{V}_{(13)} \cap \tilde{V}_{(14)} \cap \tilde{V}_{(234)}$. We therefore wish to demonstrate that u is contained in $V_{(1234)}$. The statement that u is in each of these four sets can be summarized by a row in the following matrix:

$$
\begin{array}{c}
 \quad (1) \qquad\quad (2) \qquad\quad (3) \qquad\quad (4) \\
\begin{array}{c}
(12) \\
(13) \\
(14) \\
(234)
\end{array}
\left[
\begin{array}{cccc}
x^1(12) & x^2(12) & y^3(12) & y^4(12) \\
x^1(13) & y^2(13) & x^3(13) & y^4(13) \\
x^1(14) & y^2(14) & y^3(14) & x^4(14) \\
y^1(234) & x^2(234) & x^3(234) & x^4(234)
\end{array}
\right].
\end{array}
$$

Each row refers to a specific coalition S and displays a set of strategies—denoted by $x^i(S)$ for $i \in S$—that guarantee the players in S the utility vector u for any choice of strategies $y^i(S)$ for the players i who are not in S. For example, the strategies $x^1(12)$ and $x^2(12)$ of the first row have the property that

$$u_1[x^1(12), x^2(12), y^3(12), y^4(12)] \geq u_1 \qquad \text{and}$$

$$u_2[x^1(12), x^2(12), y^3(12), y^4(12)] \geq u_2$$

for *any* choice of $y^3(12) \in X^3$ and $y^4(12) \in X^4$, and similarly for the remaining three rows of the matrix.

In order to argue that $u \in V_{(1234)}$, the specific strategies $x^i(S)$ for $i \in S$ must be combined in some way to produce four strategies $\hat{x}^1, \hat{x}^2, \hat{x}^3, \hat{x}^4$ that provide each of the four players with their component of the utility vector u. We do this by defining

$$\hat{x}^1 = \frac{x^1(12) + x^1(13) + x^1(14)}{3},$$

$$\hat{x}^2 = \frac{x^2(12) + 2x^2(234)}{3},$$

$$\hat{x}^3 = \frac{x^3(13) + 2x^3(234)}{3},$$

$$\hat{x}^4 = \frac{x^4(14) + 2x^4(234)}{3}.$$

By virtue of the convexity assumption on the strategy spaces, each $\hat{x}^i \in X^i$, and we must therefore verify that

$$u_i(\hat{x}^1, \hat{x}^2, \hat{x}^3, \hat{x}^4) \geq u_i \qquad \text{for } i = 1, \ldots, 4.$$

As we shall see, the argument that demonstrates this inequality depends upon the player selected. Take, for example, $i = 1$. We know that the three quadruples of strategies

$$[x^1(12), x^2(12), y^3(12), y^4(12)],$$

$$[x^1(13), y^2(13), x^3(13), y^4(13)],$$

$$[x^1(14), y^2(14), y^3(14), x^4(14)]$$

will each yield the first player a utility no less than u_1 for any choice of the y strategies. If we use the quasi-concavity assumption about player 1's utility function, any convex combination of these three quadruples will do the same; in particular the utility of

$$\frac{x^1(12) + x^1(13) + x^1(14)}{3},$$

$$\frac{x^2(12) + y^2(13) + y^2(14)}{3},$$

$$\frac{y^3(12) + x^3(13) + y^3(14)}{3},$$

$$\frac{y^4(12) + y^4(13) + x^4(14)}{3}$$

is at least u_1. But this choice of strategies can be made identical with $\hat{x}^1, \hat{x}^2, \hat{x}^3, \hat{x}^4$ if we select

$$y^2(13) = y^2(14) = x^2(234),$$

$$y^3(12) = y^3(14) = x^3(234),$$

$$y^4(12) = y^4(13) = x^4(234),$$

and this demonstrates that $u_1(\hat{x}^1, \hat{x}^2, \hat{x}^3, \hat{x}^4) \geq u_1$.

Quite a different argument must be used to verify the corresponding inequality for the second player. For this player we know only that the first and fourth rows of the matrix can be combined to yield the correct utility level. Let us take 1/3 of the first plus 2/3 of the fourth, obtaining

$$\frac{x^1(12) + 2y^1(234)}{3},$$

$$\frac{x^2(12) + 2x^2(234)}{3},$$

$$\frac{y^3(12) + 2x^3(234)}{3},$$

$$\frac{y^4(12) + 2x^4(234)}{3}.$$

For this joint strategy vector to be equal to $\hat{x}^1, \ldots, \hat{x}^4$, we must select

$$y^1(234) = \frac{x^1(13) + x^1(14)}{2},$$

$$y^3(12) = x^3(13),$$

$$y^4(12) = x^4(14),$$

a selection that is consistent with the convexity assumption on the strategy spaces, and we deduce therefore that $u_2(\hat{x}^1, \hat{x}^2, \hat{x}^3, \hat{x}^4) \geq u_2$. Similar arguments applied to the remaining two players permit us to deduce that $u \in V_{(1,2,3,4)}$. This concludes the discussion for the specific balanced collection $\{(1, 2), (1, 3), (1, 4), (2, 3, 4)\}$.

Let us now see how the argument can be extended to cover the general case of n players and an arbitrary balanced collection $T = \{S\}$. Let u be contained in $\bigcap_{S \in T} \tilde{V}_S$. Then for each $S \in T$, there is a collection of strategies $\{x^i(S)\}$ for $i \in S$ that guarantee the players in S their components of u, regardless of the choices of the complementary collection.

This family of strategies will be used to define the joint strategy choice $(\hat{x}^1, \hat{x}^2, \ldots, \hat{x}^n)$ in the following fashion:

(8.5.3)

$$\hat{x}^1 = \sum_{S \supset \{1\}} \delta_S x^1(S)$$

$$\vdots$$

$$\hat{x}^n = \sum_{S \supset \{n\}} \delta_S x^n(S).$$

The assumption of convex strategy spaces and the properties of the balancing weights imply that $\hat{x}^1 \in X^1, \ldots, \hat{x}^n \in X^n$; in order to show that $u \in V_N$, it is then sufficient to demonstrate that

$$u_1(\hat{x}^1, \ldots, \hat{x}^n) \geq u_1$$

$$\vdots$$

$$u_n(\hat{x}^1, \ldots, \hat{x}^n) \geq u_n.$$

I shall demonstrate only the first of these inequalities because the remaining ones would follow by renaming the players. Let us then try to represent $(\hat{x}^1, \hat{x}^2, \ldots, \hat{x}^n)$ as a convex combination of a number of joint strategy choices each of which yields the first player a utility of at least u_1. The stategy choices with this property are those $y^1(S), y^2(S), \ldots, y^n(S)$ with $S \supset \{1\}$, $y^i(S) = x^i(S)$ for $i \in S$, and the remaining $y^i(S)$ (for $i \notin S$) arbitrary, for these are precisely the strategies that imply $u \in \tilde{V}_S$.

If we can demonstrate that $(\hat{x}^1, \ldots, \hat{x}^n)$ is a convex combination of these joint strategy choices—with any particular designation of $y^i(S)$ for $i \notin S$ —then the quasi-concavity of u_1 is sufficient to show that $u_1(\hat{x}^1, \ldots, \hat{x}^n) \geq u_1$. To do this we define

$$(8.5.4) \qquad y^i(S) = y^i = \frac{\sum'_{G \in T} \delta_G x^i(G)}{\sum'_{G \in T} \delta_G},$$

where in both the numerator and denominator the summation is over those sets G in the balanced collection that contain player i, but *not* player 1.

Let us verify that $(\hat{x}^1, \ldots, \hat{x}^n)$ is a convex combination of those joint strategy choices by showing that for each i

$$\hat{x}^i = \sum_{S \supset \{1\}} \delta_S y^i(S).$$

We have

$$\sum_{S \supset \{1\}} \delta_S y^i(S) = \sum_{S \supset \{1,i\}} \delta_S x^i(S) + \sum_{\substack{S \supset \{1\} \\ S \not\supset \{i\}}} \delta_S y^i$$

$$= \sum_{S \supset \{1,i\}} \delta_S x^i(S) + y^i \sum_{\substack{S \supset \{1\} \\ S \not\supset \{i\}}} \delta_S$$

$$= \sum_{S \supset \{1,i\}} \delta_S x^i(S) + \sum_{\substack{G \supset \{i\} \\ G \not\supset \{1\}}} \delta_G x^i(G) \cdot c$$

where

$$c = \sum_{\substack{S \supset \{1\} \\ S \not\supset \{i\}}} \delta_S / \sum_{\substack{G \supset \{i\} \\ G \not\supset \{1\}}} \delta_G.$$

If $c = 1$, this expression will be equal to

$$\hat{x}^i = \sum_{S \supset \{i\}} \delta_S x^i(S).$$

This is immediate, however; we merely subtract $\Sigma_{S \supset \{1,i\}} \delta_S$ from both sides of the equality

$$\sum_{S \supset \{1\}} \delta_S = \sum_{S \supset \{i\}} \delta_S.$$

This concludes our demonstration of theorem 8.5.2.

In the previous section it was shown that an exchange economy in which each consumer has a continuous, quasi-concave utility function for his consumption will yield a balanced game and will therefore have a non-empty core. The same conclusion can be obtained from our present example if the exchange economy is represented as a game in normal form: we take as the set of possible strategies for the ith player the collection of all redistributions of his initial assets among the n players,

$$w^i = x^{i1} + x^{i2} + \ldots + x^{in}.$$

In other words, the strategies are cast in the rather unusual form of an arbitrary donation of player i's assets (keeping the vector x^{ii} for himself) without any reference to an explicit quid pro quo, a treatment that can be successful only if a cooperative solution, such as the core, is adopted.

A joint selection of strategies can then be summarized by a matrix

$$X = \begin{bmatrix} x^{11} & x^{12} & \ldots & x^{1n} \\ x^{21} & x^{22} & \ldots & x^{2n} \\ \vdots & \vdots & & \vdots \\ x^{n1} & x^{n2} & \ldots & x^{nn} \end{bmatrix},$$

whose column sums represent the commodity bundles actually obtained by each consumer. To complete the definition of the game in normal form requires a utility function for each consumer—as a function of the matrix X, representing a joint selection of strategies—and this may be taken for player j as his conventional utility for the sum of the entries in column j. Of course if this conventional utility function is quasi-concave, then the derived utility function for the normal form is also quasi-concave in the joint strategies, and theorem 8.5.2 is applicable. We conclude that there exists a reallocation of the totality of assets whose utility cannot be uniformly improved upon by an alternative redistribution of the assets of any coalition—if the complementary coalition is then permitted to redistribute its own assets in an arbitrary fashion. But if all goods are positively valued, the complementary coalition has a unique worst threat:

refusing to trade with the members of the blocking coalition. The core implied by theorem 8.5.2 is therefore identical with the customary one and we obtain an alternative existence proof.

The same method can be applied equally well to the more general case in which each consumer's utility depends not only on his own consumption, but also on the consumption of the remaining players as well, at least under the assumption that this utility be a quasi-concave function of these n consumption bundles taken jointly. In this case there is no unique worst threat of the complementary coalition, since the utilities of the members of a blocking coalition can be significantly modified by the strategic choices of those players outside of the coalition. But nevertheless there will exist an allocation of society's resources so that no coalition has an alternative redistribution that improves each player's utility *independently* of the actions of the complementary coalition.

EXAMPLE III. As our final example, we shall consider a model of an economy in which the production possibility set available to each coalition may exhibit increasing returns to scale. The particular example will involve only two commodities: a generalized output x, which is used for consumption, and a second commodity, labor, which is supplied as an input to production by each individual at some level no larger than the maximum he possesses. The ith individual is assumed to have a utility function $u_i(x^i, l^i)$ where x^i is the amount consumed and l^i is the quantity of labor supplied by him, with $0 \leq l^i \leq L^i$, his maximum available labor. The function u_i will be taken as continuous, monotonically increasing in the first variable, and decreasing in the second, so that preferred sets appear as in figure 8.5.1. No convexity assumption on preferences will be required.

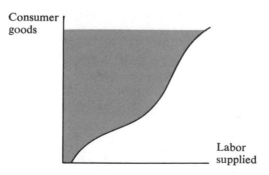

Figure 8.5.1

The common production function available to each coalition for transforming labor inputs into consumer goods will be denoted by $x = f(l)$ and will have nondecreasing returns to scale, i.e.,

$$f(l)/l \le f(l')/l' \qquad \text{for } l \le l'.$$

$\tilde{V}_S$, the set of utility vectors available to a coalition, is then given by

$$\left\{ u = (u_1, \ldots, u_n) | u_i \le u_i(x^i, l^i), \text{ for } i \in S, \text{ with } \sum_S x^i \le f\left(\sum_S l^i \right) \right\}.$$

The technical conditions involved in the definition of a game in characteristic form will be satisfied if the production function is continuous, and we take this to be the case.

8.5.5. [THEOREM] *This game is balanced.*

The theorem is rather remarkable in that no convexity assumptions are required on either the utility functions or the common production function. It also illustrates the capability of a game-theoretic approach in dealing with a problem that is of considerable economic interest and cannot be analyzed readily in terms of conventional competitive assumptions. On the other hand, the extension of theorem 8.5.5. to include distinct types of labor skills and, more importantly, a disaggregated description of production is by no means clear; no suitable generalizations are known. The game-theoretic treatment of increasing returns to scale is a complex and difficult topic which I shall not treat in this monograph, other than to give a proof of theorem 8.5.5.

Let there be n players, and let $T = \{S_1, S_2, \ldots, S_m\}$ be a balanced collection of coalitions with balancing weights $\delta_{S_1}, \ldots, \delta_{S_m}$. Let $u = (u_1, \ldots, u_n) \in \cap \tilde{V}_{S_k}$; in order to verify that the game is balanced we need to show that $u \in V_N$. For each coalition $S \in T$, we have therefore a set of commodity bundles $\{x^i(S), l^i(S)\}$ for $i \in S$, satisfying

$$u_i\{x^i(S), l^i(S)\} \ge u_i \qquad (\text{for } i \in S); \quad \text{and}$$

$$\sum_{i \in S} x^i(S) \le f\left[\sum_{i \in S} l^i(S) \right]$$

We shall denote by $a(S)$ the average productivity

$$a(S) = f\left[\sum_{i \in S} l^i(S) \right] \bigg/ \sum_{i \in S} l^i(S)$$

associated with the coalition S.

Let us assume that the sets in the balanced collection T have been arranged in a specific order $S_1, S_2, \ldots, S_m$. Consider the following sequence of partial sums of the balancing weights:

$$\delta_{S_1}, \delta_{S_1} + \delta_{S_2}, \ldots, \delta_{S_1} + \delta_{S_2} + \ldots + \delta_{S_m}.$$

Aside from the trivial case in which the balanced collection is a partition, the last term in the sequence will be strictly larger than unity. We can then define an integer k by means of the inequalities

$$\delta_{S_1} + \ldots + \delta_{S_k} \leq 1 < \delta_{S_1} + \ldots + \delta_{S_{k+1}}.$$

There is no loss in generality in assuming somewhat more, that the integer k actually satisfies

(8.5.6) $$\delta_{S_1} + \ldots + \delta_{S_k} = 1.$$

If this were not the case, we could form a new balanced collection identical with T, except that the set S_{k+1} appears twice. Its original weight $\delta_{S_{k+1}}$ could then be distributed over the two sets in such a way as to imply an equality of the form 8.5.6. We then partition the coalitions in T into the following two classes:

(8.5.7)
$$A = \{S_1, \ldots, S_k\}, \quad \text{and}$$
$$B = \{S_{k+1}, \ldots, S_m\}.$$

Let us assume that the game is not balanced, in particular that the vector u is not in V_N. We shall demonstrate that this gives rise to a contradiction by means of the following result.

8.5.8. [LEMMA] *Let k be the integer defined by 8.5.6. If u is not in V_N, then there exist weights*

$$\alpha_i \geq 0, \quad \sum_1^k \alpha_i = 1, \text{ and}$$

$$\beta_i \geq 0, \quad \sum_{k+1}^m \beta_i = 1,$$

so that

$$\sum_1^k \alpha_i a(S_i) < \sum_{k+1}^m \beta_i a(S_i).$$

Assuming the validity of this lemma, we obtain a contradiction by considering a specific ordering with $a(S_1) \geq a(S_2) \geq \ldots \geq a(S_m)$. Clearly, the final inequality in 8.5.8 cannot hold for this ordering.

The basic idea in proving lemma 8.5.8 is that a number of linear inequalities follow from the assumption that u is not in V_N. If these inequalities are averaged in a suitable fashion, we shall obtain the inequality of the lemma.

A typical inequality is obtained in the following way: Let G be an arbitrary coalition in T, and let $\{i_1, i_2, \ldots, i_j\}$ be the set of players *not* in G. Suppose that

$$(x^{i_1}, l^{i_1})$$
$$\vdots$$
$$(x^{l_j}, l^{l_j})$$

are arbitrary commodity bundles that satisfy

(8.5.9)
$$u_{i_1}(x^{i_1}, l^{i_1}) \geq u_{i_1}$$
$$\vdots$$
$$u_{i_j}(x^{i_j}, l^{i_j}) \geq u_{i_j}.$$

Then the allocation that assigns the commodity bundles $(x^{i_1}, l^{i_1}), \ldots,$ (x^{i_j}, l^{i_j}) to the players not in G and $[x^i(G), l^i(G)]$ to the players in G will provide a utility of at least $(u_1, u_2, \ldots, u_n)$. Since u is not in V_N, this allocation must be infeasible and we obtain the inequality

$$x^{i_1} + \ldots + x^{i_j} + \sum_{i \in G} x^i(G) > f\left[l^{i_1} + \ldots + l^{i_j} + \sum_{i \in G} l^i(G) \right].$$

Because

$$\sum_{i \in G} x^i(G) \leq f\left[\sum_{i \in G} l^i(G) \right],$$

it follows that

$$x^{i_1} + \ldots + x^{i_j} > f\left[l^{i_1} + \ldots + l^{i_j} + \sum_{i \in G} l^i(G) \right] - f\left[\sum_{i \in G} l^i(G) \right].$$

Since the production function has nondecreasing returns to scale, we may finally conclude that

(8.5.10) $$x^{i_1} + \ldots + x^{i_j} > a(G)(l^{i_1} + \ldots + l^{i_j}).$$

This important family of inequalities holds for any coalition $G \in T$ and for any way of assigning commodity bundles with the appropriate utility levels for the players not in G. We shall restrict our attention to coalitions

G that are contained in $A = \{S_1, \ldots, S_k\}$; to each such coalition the commodity bundles assigned to a player i who is not in G will be selected from among the set of $[x^i(S), l^i(S)]$ with S a coalition in $B = \{S_{k+1}, \ldots, S_m\}$ which contains player i.

The easiest way to view the resulting averaging is to construct a specific probabilistic model that first selects a coalition G in A at random and then for each player i not in G selects a commodity bundle $[x^i(S), l^i(S)]$ according to some distribution. Each such random choice produces a particular inequality of the form 8.5.10. The expectation over both sides of this inequality will yield lemma 8.5.8 if the probabilistic model is correctly designed.

8.5.11. [RULE] *Let G be selected at random from $A = \{S_1, \ldots, S_k\}$ with probability δ_G (from 8.5.6, $\delta_{S_1} + \ldots + \delta_{S_k} = 1$). Then for each i not in G, select S at random from those sets in $B = \{S_{k+1}, \ldots, S_m\}$ that contain i, with conditional probability*

$$\frac{\delta_S}{\displaystyle\sum_{\substack{R \in B \\ R \supset \{i\}}} \delta_R}.$$

Given G, the choice of S is made independently for each i.

This rule defines the probabilistic model that generates the now-random inequalities 8.5.10. Let i be a specific player and S a specific coalition from B that contains player i. The probability that the term $x^i(S)$ appears on the left-hand side of 8.5.10 is

$$\sum_{\substack{G \in A \\ G \not\supset \{i\}}} \delta_G \left(\frac{\delta_S}{\displaystyle\sum_{\substack{R \in B \\ R \supset \{i\}}} \delta_R} \right).$$

But this expression is actually equal to δ_S since

$$\sum_{\substack{G \in A \\ G \not\supset \{i\}}} \delta_G = \sum_{\substack{R \in B \\ R \supset \{i\}}} \delta_R.$$

To see this we merely observe that

$$\sum_{\substack{G \in A \\ G \not\supset \{i\}}} \delta_G = 1 - \sum_{\substack{G \in A \\ G \supset \{i\}}} \delta_G \qquad \left(\text{since } \sum_{G \in A} \delta_G = 1 \right)$$

$$= \sum_{\substack{G \in B \\ G \supset \{i\}}} \delta_G \qquad \left(\text{since } \sum_{\substack{G \in T \\ G \supset \{i\}}} \delta_G = 1 \right).$$

In other words, the probability that the term $x^i(S)$ appears on the left of 8.5.10 is δ_S.

Taking the expectation of the left-hand side of 8.5.10, we therefore have

$$\sum_{S \in B} \delta_S \left[\sum_{i \in S} x^i(S) \right].$$

But, by definition,

$$\sum_{i \in S} x^i(S) \le f \left[\sum_{i \in S} l^i(S) \right] = a(S) \sum_{i \in S} l^i(S).$$

Therefore the expectation of the left-hand side of 8.5.10 is less than or equal to

$$\sum_{S \in B} \delta_S a(S) \left[\sum_{i \in S} l^i(S) \right],$$

a non-negative combination of the average productivities $a(S)$ for S in B, with the sum of the weights given by

(8.5.12) $$\sum_{S \in B} \delta_S \left[\sum_{i \in S} l^i(S) \right].$$

When the expectation operator is applied to the right-hand side of 8.5.10, we obtain a non-negative combination of the average productivities $a(G)$ but this time for G in A. The probability that a term $l^i(S)$ (for S in B and containing i) appears as part of the contribution to the sum of the weights on the right-hand side is, as before, δ_S. The sum is therefore given by

$$\sum_{S \in B} \delta_S \left[\sum_{i \in S} l^i(S) \right].$$

Since this is identical with 8.5.12, we can normalize the two expectations and obtain lemma 8.5.8. This demonstrates that the game is balanced.

Appendix 1

A FORTRAN Program for the Replacement Step
of Section 6.3

The most useful variant of our computational procedures works with the regular grid of vectors on the simplex and the cyclic lexicographic rule for breaking ties. This grid has the virtues of being uniformly distributed throughout the simplex and of requiring a minimum of computer storage in order to recognize primitive sets and to carry out the replacement operation. The following computer program is a FORTRAN code for this replacement step and may be used as a part of a number of different programs depending on the specific application in mind. As we shall see, slack vectors are treated somewhat differently from section 6.3.

Let the grid consist of those vectors $(m_1/D, m_2/D, \ldots, m_n/D)$, with m_i representing non-negative integers summing to D. The following variables are used in the program:

$$ID = D$$
$$N = n$$
$$M(I, J) = \text{the matrix of size } n \times n \text{ whose columns represent the}$$
$$\text{numerators of the vectors in a primitive set}$$
$$IO(J) = I(j), \text{ the permutation describing the primitive set}$$
$$JOUT = \text{the number of the column of } M \text{ representing the}$$
$$\text{vector to be removed from the primitive set}$$
$$SUBROUTINE = \text{the program that determines, according to the problem}$$
$$\text{being done, the vector to be removed from the primitive}$$
$$\text{set}$$

THE FORTRAN PROGRAM

DIMENSION M(40, 40), IO(40)

C   AFTER THE FIRST ITERATION ENTER THE PROGRAM AT INSTRUCTION 16

1   READ ID, N

     JOUT = 1

```
      DO 10 J = 1, N
      DO 5 I = 1, N
 5    M(I, J) = 0
10    M(J, J) = −1
      DO 15 J = 1, N
      M(1, J) = M(1, J) + ID + 1
15    IO(J) = J
C     INPUT OVER
16    CALL SUBROUTINE
C     SUBROUTINE PROVIDES JOUT AND TERMINATES THE PROGRAM WHEN THE
      REQUIRED ANSWER IS FOUND
      JP = JOUT + 1
      IF (JOUT. EQ. N) JP = 1
      L00 = IO (JOUT)
      L10 = L00 − 1
      IF (L00. EQ. 1) L10 = N
      L01 = IO(JP)
      L11 = L01 − 1
      IF (L01. EQ. 1) L11 = N
      M(L00, JOUT) = M(L00, JOUT) + 1
      M(L11, JOUT) = M(L11, JOUT) + 1
      M(L01, JOUT) = M(L01, JOUT) − 1
      M(L10, JOUT) = M(L10, JOUT) − 1
      IO(JOUT) = L01
      IO(JP) = L00
      GO TO 16
      END
```

The two major differences between this program and the replacement step of section 6.3 are, first, that the initial primitive set is given by the matrix

$$(A.1.1) \qquad M = \begin{bmatrix} D & D+1 & \ldots & D+1 \\ 0 & -1 & \ldots & 0 \\ \vdots & \vdots & & \vdots \\ 0 & 0 & \ldots & -1 \end{bmatrix}$$

and, secondly, that the replacement step

(A.1.2)
$$m'_{ij} = m_{ij} + 1 \quad \text{for } i = I(j) \quad \text{and} \quad I(j+1) - 1,$$
$$m'_{ij} = m_{ij} - 1 \quad \text{for } i = I(j) - 1 \quad \text{and} \quad I(j+1)$$

is carried out on every iteration including those involving the replacement of a slack vector. Both of these features arise from a desire to keep the matrix M of constant size throughout the computation rather than having the number of columns expand and contract with the number of slack vectors in the primitive set.

Let us consider this version of the replacement step oriented toward obtaining a solution to the problem described in theorem 4.2.3. That is, each vector of the form $(m_1/D, \ldots, m_n/D)$ with m_i representing non-negative integers summing to D will be associated with a specific column in a matrix

$$A = \begin{bmatrix} 1 & \cdots & 0 & a_{1,n+1} & \cdots & a_{1,k} \\ \vdots & & \vdots & \vdots & & \vdots \\ 0 & \cdots & 1 & a_{n,n+1} & \cdots & a_{n,k} \end{bmatrix}$$

according to some rule. The vector $b = (b_1, \ldots, b_n)'$ is non-negative, as before. Because of the modification in our treatment of slack vectors, it is necessary to be explicit about the image of a column in a primitive set that contains one or more entries of -1. As we shall see, the entries never fall below -1 in the course of the algorithm.

A.1.3. [RULE] *Let $(m_1, m_2, \ldots, m_n)'$ be a column in a matrix with integer entries greater than or equal to -1 and satisfy the properties of theorem 6.2.1. Assume that some of the entries in this column are equal to -1, and let i be the smallest subscript for which this is true. The column is then associated with the ith slack vector of A.*

Under this rule, columns 2, 3, $\ldots$, n of the initial matrix A.1.1 are associated with the slack vectors 2, 3, $\ldots$, n of A. The first column of the initial matrix M, i.e., $(D, 0, \ldots, 0)'$, will be associated with, say, column j^* of A. A pivot step is carried out, resulting in the elimination of one of the first n columns of A. The column of M corresponding to this column of A is replaced according to rule A.1.2 and we proceed.

The initial matrix M has the property that each entry lies between -1 and $D + 1$. I shall demonstrate that this property is retained throughout the algorithm and that every desired replacement step will result in a matrix of this form, other than the replacement that removes the first column from the initial matrix A.1.1. The number of possible matrices that can occur is therefore bounded, and in conjunction with Lemke's argument, this requires the algorithm to terminate with an answer of the desired sort.

Consider a case in which the replacement step A.1.2 first produces an entry of -2 in the matrix M, say, in row i and column j. This requires the matrix to have a row of the form

$$(-1 \quad -1 \quad \ldots \quad -1 \quad \quad 0 \quad -1 \quad \ldots \quad -1)$$

$$j$$

immediately prior to the removal of column j. All of the remaining columns must therefore be associated with slack columns of A and, in fact, with the distinct columns $2, 3, \ldots, n$, since no column of M is associated with the first slack column of A prior to termination. Rows $2, 3, \ldots, n$ of M must therefore contain at least one entry of -1 and must be composed of -1s and 0s. But column j can have no entries of -1 because it is not associated with a slack column of A. The matrix M must, therefore, have the form

$$\begin{bmatrix} & & & D & & & \\ & & & 0 & & & \\ & & & \vdots & & & \\ -1 & \ldots & -1 & 0 & -1 & \ldots & -1 \\ & & & \vdots & & & \\ & & & 0 & & & \end{bmatrix}.$$

But then no column can have two entries of -1 for this would imply an entry in the first row greater than $D + 1$, contradicting the property that no two entries in any row differ by more than unity. As a consequence the matrix will be

$$\begin{bmatrix} D+1 & \ldots & D+1 & D & D+1 & \ldots & D+1 \\ 0 & \ldots & 0 & 0 & 0 & \ldots & 0 \\ \vdots & & \vdots & \vdots & \vdots & & \vdots \\ -1 & \ldots & -1 & 0 & -1 & \ldots & -1 \\ \vdots & & \vdots & \vdots & \vdots & & \vdots \\ 0 & \ldots & 0 & 0 & 0 & \ldots & 0 \end{bmatrix},$$

which is not of the form described by 6.2.1.

A similar argument verifies that no entry will ever become larger than $D + 1$ unless we are at the original matrix and attempt to remove the one column not associated with a slack vector. To see this we argue that immediately prior to a replacement step at which an entry becomes $D + 2$ there must be a row of M, say, the ith, with the following aspect:

$$(D + 1 \quad \ldots \quad D + 1 \quad D \quad D + 1 \quad \ldots \quad D + 1)$$

$$j$$

Since the column sums equal D, every column other than the jth must have a negative entry; $n - 1$ columns are therefore associated with slack vectors and these must be columns $2, 3, \ldots, n$ of A. This requires i to be the first row and every other row to be composed of 0s and $- 1$s:

$$\begin{bmatrix} D + 1 & \ldots & D + 1 & D & D + 1 & \ldots & D + 1 \\ -1 & & & 0 & & & \\ & & & \vdots & & & \\ & & & 0 & -1 & & \end{bmatrix}$$

But no column can have more than a single negative entry, since otherwise the column sums will be less than D. The matrix M must therefore be our original matrix A.1.1 (aside from a permutation of the columns), and we are attempting to remove the nonslack column—the sole replacement step that cannot be carried out. This concludes the argument for termination of the algorithm.

In some applications it may be convenient to work with strictly positive, nonslack vectors. This may be accomplished by adding 1 to each entry of the initial matrix M and by defining those vectors with a coordinate of 0 to be slack vectors.

The variant of the algorithm described in this appendix has its origins in Hansen's thesis (1968). As we see, it can be described with reference neither to primitive sets and the lexicographic rule for the resolution of degeneracy nor to the geometry of simplicial subdivisions. But aside from its treatment of slack vectors, it is identical with the algorithm of chapter 6.

Appendix 2

An Estimate of the Number of Iterations Required by the Algorithm

The numerical techniques of this volume have been successful for problems of modest size largely because the number of iterations required in practice is far smaller—by orders of magnitude—than any upper bound that might reasonably be deduced from the number of vectors in the grid. The number of iterations seems to display a fairly regular relationship, for any specific class of problems, to the parameters n and D that describe the grid. In the present section we shall apply the algorithm to a class of problems that could be solved in a simpler fashion in order to provide some evidence for the form of this relationship.

Let C be a non-negative square matrix of size n whose column sums are all unity. The mapping $x' = Cx$ carries the unit simplex into itself in a continuous fashion and therefore has a fixed point $\hat{x} = C\hat{x}$. The algorithm for approximating such a fixed point was applied to several numerical examples with n ranging from 3 to 15. For each value of n, four examples were tried with the entries of C selected at random. In all of these cases the column sums of matrices representing primitive sets were taken to be 100. Nonslack vectors were required to be strictly positive. The results are given in table A.2.1.

TABLE A.2.1. NUMBER OF ITERATIONS REQUIRED FOR THE ALGORITHM TO TERMINATE

	Example number					
n	1	2	3	4	Range	Average
3	131	93	163	191	93–191	144.5
6	588	560	552	570	552–588	567.5
9	1,289	1,235	1,247	1,201	1,201–1,289	1,243.–
12	2,180	2,075	2,198	2,111	2,075–2,198	2,141.–
15	3,315	3,137	3,475	3,273	3,137–3,475	3,300.–

238

A reasonable hypothesis is that within a class of problems the number of iterations is roughly equal to cn^2, with c a constant of proportionality. For example, let us select c so that the formula predicts 1,243 iterations for a problem of size 9—the average of the four iterations in the above table. We then have table A.2.2 which seems to support the hypothesis.

TABLE A.2.2.   FORMULA FOR THE NUMBER OF ITERATIONS

n	Range of number of iterations of 4 examples	Average number of iterations of 4 examples	Calculated number of iterations according to formula
3	93– 191	144.5	127
6	552– 588	567.5	553
9	1,201–1,289	1,243.–	1,243
12	2,075–2,198	2,141.–	2,209
15	3,137–3,475	3,300.–	3,452

Observe that apart from the case with $n = 12$, the calculated number of iterations according to the formula lies within the observed range of the number of iterations for all n.

As far as the grid size is concerned, there is substantial evidence that very strongly supports the estimate that the number of iterations is proportional to D, for any specific problem.

Table A.2.3 gives the average number of iterations per minute for an IBM 1130, on which all the above examples were run. It also gives the estimated number of iterations per minute on an IBM 360–50, which is about 17 times faster than the IBM 1130. The numbers in the table obviously apply only to this class of problems. In some applications with the same value of n the algorithm will work faster and in some slower.

TABLE A.2.3.   NUMBER OF ITERATIONS PER MINUTE FOR DIFFERENT VALUES OF n

n	Number of iterations per minute	
	IBM 1130	IBM 360–50 (estimated)
3	900	15,300
6	380	6,460
9	207	3,519
12	128	2,166
15	86	1,466

The examples considered are characterized by the fact that at nearly every iteration the vector $y^j = Cx^j$ has to be calculated. The time involved in this calculation increases with the square of n. This is the real time-consuming element at each iteration when n is sufficiently large. As a consequence, we expect the average time of each iteration to increase with the square of n when n is sufficiently large. The time for the algorithm to terminate will consequently increase with n to the fourth power. If we had run examples with $n = 30$ keeping $D = 100$, we would have expected the algorithm to take 16 times as much time as in the case of $n = 15$.

References

Arrow, K. J. 1951. *Social Choice and Individual Values.* New York: Wiley.

Arrow, K. J., H. D. Block, and L. Hurwicz. 1959. On the stability of the competitive equilibrium, II. *Econometrica* 27:82–109.

Arrow, K. J., and G. Debreu. 1954. Existence of an equilibrium for a competitive economy. *Econometrica* 22:265–90.

Arrow, K. J., and L. Hurwicz. 1958. On the stability of the competitive equilibrium, I. *Econometrica* 26:522–52.

Aumann, R. J. 1961. The core of a cooperative game without side payments. *Transactions of the American Mathematical Society* 98:539–52.

Barone, E. 1908. Il Ministerio della Produzione nello stato colletivista. *Giornale degli Economisti e Rivista di Statistica.* [English translation in *Collectivist Economic Planning,* ed. F. A. Hayek. London, 1935.]

Bondareva, O. 1962. The core of an n person game. *Vestnik Leningrad University* 17:141–42.

Brouwer, L. E. J. 1910. Über eineindeutige, stetige Transformationen von Flächen in Sich. *Mathematische Annalen* 67:176–80.

Burger, E. 1963. *Introduction to the Theory of Games,* trans. John E. Freund. Englewood Cliffs, N.J.: Prentice-Hall.

Cohen, D. I. A. 1967. On the Sperner lemma. *Journal of Combinatorial Theory* 2:585–87.

Cottle, R. W., and G. B. Dantzig. 1968. Complementary pivot theory of mathematical programming. *Linear Algebra and Its Applications,* vol. 1, pp. 103–25.

Dantzig, G. B. 1951. Maximization of a linear function of variables subject to linear inequalities. In *Activity Analysis of Production and Allocation,* ed. T. C. Koopmans, pp. 339–47. New York: Wiley.

———. 1963. *Linear Programming and Extensions.* Princeton, N.J.: Princeton University Press.

Debreu, G. 1959. *Theory of Value.* New York: Wiley.

Debreu, G., and H. Scarf. 1963. A limit theorem on the core of an economy. *International Economic Review* 4:235–46.

Eaves, B. C. 1970. An odd theorem. *Proceedings of the American Mathematical Society* 26:509–13.

———. 1971a. Computing Kakutani fixed points. *SIAM Journal of Applied Mathematics* 21:236–44.

————. 1971b. On the basic theorem of complementarity. *Mathematical Programming* 1:68–75.

————. 1972. Homotopies for computation of fixed points. *Mathematical Programming* 3:1–22.

Edgeworth, F. Y. 1881. *Mathematical Psychics*. London: Kegan Paul.

Freidenfelds, J. 1971. *Fixed-point algorithms and almost-complementary sets.* Technical Report No. 71–17, Operations Research House, Stanford University.

Gale, D. 1955. The law of supply and demand. *Mathematica Scandinavia* 3:155–69.

Habetler, G. J., and A. L. Price. 1971. Existence theory for generalized nonlinear complementarity problems. *Journal of Optimization Theory and Applications* 7:223–39.

Hansen, T. 1968. On the approximation of a competitive equilibrium. Ph.D. thesis, Yale University.

————. 1969. *A fixed point algorithm for approximating the optimal solution of a concave programming problem.* Cowles Foundation Discussion Paper No. 277.

Hansen, T., and T. C. Koopmans. 1972. Definition and computation of a capital stock invariant under optimization. *Journal of Economic Theory* 5:487–523.

Hansen, T., and H. Scarf. 1969. On the applications of a recent combinatorial algorithm. Cowles Foundation Discussion Paper No. 272.

Hayek, F. A. 1940. Socialist calculation: the competitive solution. *Economica* 7:125–49.

Hurwicz, W., and H. Wallman. 1941. *Dimension Theory*. Princeton, N.J.: Princeton University Press.

Kakutani, S. 1941. A generalization of Brouwer's fixed point theorem. *Duke Mathematical Journal* 8:457–58.

Kannai, Y. 1970. On closed coverings of simplices. *SIAM Journal of Applied Mathematics* 19:459–61.

Kantorovich, L. V. 1939. *Mathematical methods in the organization and planning of production.* Publication House of the Leningrad State University. [English translation in *Management Science* 6:366–422, 1960.]

Karamardian, S. 1969. The nonlinear complementarity problem with applications, parts I and II. *Journal of Optimization Theory and Applications* 4:87–98, 167–81.

————. 1971. The Complementarity Problem. *Mathematical Programming* 2:107–29.

Karlin, S. 1959. *Mathematical Methods and Theory in Games, Programming, and Economics*. Reading, Mass.: Addison-Wesley.

Koopmans, T. C. 1971. A model of a continuing state with scarce capital. In *Contribution to the von Neumann Growth Model*, ed. G. Bruckman and W. Weber, Supplementum 1, Zeitschrift für Nationalökonomie. New York: Springer-Verlag.

Kuhn, H. W. 1956. On a theorem of Wald. In *Linear Inequalities and Related Systems*, ed. H. W. Kuhn and A. W. Tucker, pp. 265–73. Princeton, N.J.: Princeton University Press.

————. 1960. Some combinatorial lemmas in topology. *IBM Journal of Research and Development* 4:518–24.

————. 1961. An algorithm for equilibrium points in bimatrix games. *Proceedings of the National Academy of Sciences, U.S.A.* 47: 1657–62.

————. 1968. Simplicial approximation of fixed points. *Proceedings of the National Academy of Sciences, U.S.A.* 61:1238–42.

Lange, O. 1936, 1937. On the economic theory of socialism. *Review of Economic Studies* 4:53–71, 123–42. Reprinted in O. Lange and F. M. Taylor, *On the Economic Theory of Socialism*, ed. B. E. Lippincott. Minneapolis: University of Minnesota Press, 1938.

————. 1967. The computer and the market. In *Socialism, Capitalism, and Economic Growth*, ed. C. H. Feinstein, pp. 158–61. Cambridge, Mass.: Cambridge University Press.

Lemke, C. E. 1965. Bimatrix equilibrium points and mathematical programming. *Management Science* 11:681–89.

————. 1970. Recent results on complementary problems. In *Nonlinear Programming*, ed. J. B. Rosen, O. L. Mangasarian, and K. Ritter, pp. 349–84. New York: Academic Press.

Lemke, C. E., and J. T. Howson. 1964. Equilibrium points of bi-matrix games. *SIAM Journal of Applied Mathematics* 12:413–23.

Mangasarian, O. L. 1964. Equilibrium points of bimatrix games. *SIAM Journal of Applied Mathematics* 12:778–80.

Mantel, R. R. 1968. Toward a constructive proof of the existence of equilibrium in a competitive economy. *Yale Economic Essays* 8:155–200.

McKenzie, L. W. 1954. On equilibrium in Graham's model of world trade and other competitive systems. *Econometrica* 22:147–61.

————. 1959. On the existence of general equilibrium for a competitive market. *Econometrica* 27:54–71.

Merrill, O. H. 1971. *Applications and extensions of an algorithm that computes fixed points of certain non-empty convex upper semi-continuous point to set mappings.* Technical Report No. 71–7, Dept. of Industrial Engineering, University of Michigan.

Miller, M., and J. Spencer. 1971. *The static economics effects of the U.K. joining the E.E.C. and their welfare significance: an attempt at quantification in a general equilibrium framework.* Preliminary Report, London School of Economics and Political Science, June 1971.

Mises, L. von. 1920. Die Wirtschaftsrechnung in sozialistischen Gemeinwesen. *Archiv für Socialwissenschaften* 47. [English translation in *Collectivist Economic Planning*, ed. F. A. Hayek. London, 1935.]

Nash, J. F. 1950. Equilibrium points in n-person games. *Proceedings of the National Academy of Sciences, U.S.A.* 36:48–49.

Nikaido, H. 1956. On the classical multilateral exchange problem. *Metroeconomica* 8:135–45.

Robbins, L. C. 1934. *The Great Depression.* London: Macmillan.

Robinson, S. M. 1972. Extension of Newton's method to nonlinear functions with values in a cone. *Numerische Mathematik* 19:341–47.

Scarf, H. 1960. Some examples of global instability of the competitive equilibrium. *International Economic Review* 1:157–72.

———. 1962. An analysis of markets with a large number of participants. In *Recent Advances in Game Theory*, Princeton University Conference Report.

———. 1967a. The core of an n person game. *Econometrica* 37:50–69.

———. 1967b. The approximation of fixed points of a continuous mapping. *SIAM Journal of Applied Mathematics* 15:1328–43.

———. 1967c. On the computation of equilibrium prices. In *Ten Essays in Honor of Irving Fisher*, ed. Fellner et al., pp. 207–30. New York: Wiley.

———. 1971. On the existence of a cooperative solution for a general class of n-person games. *Journal of Economic Theory* 3:169–81.

Shapley, L. S. 1965. *On balanced sets and cores*. RAND Corporation Memorandum, RM-4601-PR. June 1965.

———. 1972. *On balanced games without side payments*. RAND Corporation, P-4910, September 1972.

Shoven, J. B., and J. Whalley. 1972. A general equilibrium calculation of the effects of differential taxation of income from capital in the U.S. *Journal of Public Economics* 1:281–321.

Sonnenschein, H. 1973. Do Walras' identity and continuity characterize the class of community excess demand functions? *Journal of Economic Theory*. (In press.)

Sutherland, W. R. S. 1967. On Optimal Development Programs When Future Utility Is Discounted. Ph.D. thesis, Brown University.

———. 1970. On optimal development in a multi-sectorial economy: the discounted case. *Review of Economic Studies* 37:585–89.

Uzawa, H. 1962. Walras' existence theorem and Brouwer's fixed point theorem. *Economic Studies Quarterly* 13, no. 1.

Von Neumann, J. 1928. Zur Theorie der Gesellschaftsspiele. *Mathematische Annalen* 100:295–320.

———. 1937. Über ein Ökonomisches Gleichungssystem und eine Verallgemeinerung des Brouwerschen Fixpunktsatzes. *Ergebnisse eines Mathematischen Kolloquiums* 8:73–83. [Translated as "A model of general economic equilibrium," *Review of Economic Studies* 13:1–9, 1945.]

Von Neumann, J., and O. Morgenstern. 1947. *Theory of Games and Economic Behavior*. Princeton, N.J.: Princeton University Press.

Wagner, M. H. 1971. Constructive fixed point theory and duality in nonlinear programming. Technical Report No. 67, Operations Research Center, Massachusetts Institute of Technology.

Wald, A. 1935. Über die eindeutige positive Lösbarkeit der neuen Produktionsgleichungen. *Ergebnisse eines Mathematischen Kolloquiums* 6:12–20.

———. 1936. Über einige Gleichungssysteme der Mathematischen Ökonomie. *Zeitschrift für Nationalökonomie*, no. 7. [Translated as "On some systems of equations of mathematical economics," *Econometrica* 19:368–403.]

Walras, L. 1874. *Eléments d'économie politique pure*. Lausanne: Corbaz. [Translated as *Elements of Pure Economics*, trans. W. Jaffe. London: Allen and Unwin, 1954.]
Wolfe, P. 1959. The simplex method for quadratic programming. *Econometrica* 7:382–98.

Index

Approximation: degree of, for Kakutani fixed point, 89–93; for general equilibrium model with production, 107–08

Arrow, K. J., 6, 12, 204

Association: rule of, for fixed point of Kakutani mapping, 86; for general equilibrium model with production, 103–04; for nonlinear programming problem, 131; for computation of invariant optimal capital stock, 140

Aumann, R. J., 206

Barone, E., 2, 9

Barycentric subdivision of the simplex, 195–99

Block, H. D., 12

Bondareva, O., 209

Brouwer, L. E. J., 5, 12, 28

Brouwer's theorem, 13, 23, 28–31, 67, 74, 170; description of, 5–6; and existence of an equilibrium for an exchange economy, 12; demonstration of, using algorithm, 51–53

Burger, E., 12

Capital stock: optimal invariant, 136–43

Coalitions: in game theory, 201–06; balanced collections of, 209–10

Cohen, D. I. A., 191

Competitive equilibrium: proof of existence using alternative to Kakutani's theorem, 119–23

Computational experience: of fixed point algorithms, 16–17, 60–61, 163, 168–69; relationship between dimensionality and computation time, 238–40

Computer, electronic: importance of, for computational techniques, 10

Convexity: the importance of techniques of, 3

Convex programming, 69–71

Core of an n-person game: relationship to competitive equilibria, 14–15, 207–08; nonemptiness of, 14–15, 211, 214–19, 221–27; notion of blocking, 206; definition of, 207

Cottle, R. W., 14

Cycling: argument excluding, 45–48

Dantzig, G. B., 7, 14

Debreu, G., 6, 14, 119

Decomposition method of computing equilibrium, 162–69

Degeneracy: procedures for resolving, 61–62, 144–69

Eaves, B. C., 15, 50, 119, 121, 130, 188, 191

Edgeworth, F. Y., 206

Endowment: of resources, 98–99

Freidenfelds, J., 188

Gale, D., 6

Game theory: n-person, 200–31; normal form of, 200; characteristic form of, 201–06; balanced, 211; nonemptiness of core of n-person balanced game, 211, 214–19; game derived from n-person exchange economy, 213–14; examples of balanced games, 219–32

General equilibrium (neoclassical) model, 1–2; existence of an equilibrium, 2–6,

Cowles Foundation Monographs

1. Charles F. Roos, DYNAMIC ECONOMICS (out of print)
2. Charles F. Roos, NRA ECONOMIC PLANNING (out of print)
3. Alfred Cowles and Associates, COMMON-STOCK INDEXES (2d edition)
4. Dickson H. Leavens, SILVER MONEY (out of print)
5. Gerhard Tintner, THE VARIATE DIFFERENCE METHOD (out of print)
6. Harold T. Davis, THE ANALYSIS OF ECONOMIC TIME SERIES (out of print)
7. Jacob L. Mosak, GENERAL-EQUILIBRIUM THEORY IN INTERNATIONAL TRADE (out of print)
8. Oscar Lange, PRICE FLEXIBILITY AND EMPLOYMENT
9. George Katona, PRICE CONTROL AND BUSINESS (out of print)
10. Tjalling C. Koopmans, ed., STATISTICAL INFERENCE IN DYNAMIC ECONOMIC MODELS (out of print)
11. Lawrence R. Klein, ECONOMIC FLUCTUATIONS IN THE UNITED STATES, 1921–1941 (out of print)
12. Kenneth J. Arrow, SOCIAL CHOICE AND INDIVIDUAL VALUES (2d edition)
13. Tjalling C. Koopmans, ed., ACTIVITY ANALYSIS OF PRODUCTION AND ALLOCATION
14. William C. Hood and Tjalling C. Koopmans, ed., STUDIES IN ECONOMETRIC METHOD
15. Clifford Hildreth and F. G. Jarrett, A STATISTICAL STUDY OF LIVESTOCK PRODUCTION AND MARKETING
16. Harry M. Markowitz, PORTFOLIO SELECTION: Efficient Diversification of Investments
17. Gerard Debreu, THEORY OF VALUE: An Axiomatic Analysis of Economic Equilibrium
18. Alan S. Manne and Harry M. Markowitz, ed., STUDIES IN PROCESS ANALYSIS: Economy-Wide Production Capabilities (out of print)
19. Donald D. Hester and James Tobin, ed., RISK AVERSION AND PORTFOLIO CHOICE
20. Donald D. Hester and James Tobin, ed., STUDIES OF PORTFOLIO BEHAVIOR
21. Donald D. Hester and James Tobin, ed., FINANCIAL MARKETS AND ECONOMIC ACTIVITY
22. Jacob Marschak and Roy Radner, ECONOMIC THEORY OF TEAMS
23. Thomas J. Rothenberg, EFFICIENT ESTIMATION WITH A PRIORI INFORMATION
24. Herbert Scarf, THE COMPUTATION OF ECONOMIC EQUILIBRIA

Orders for Monograph 8 should be sent to Principia Press of Trinity University, 715 Stadium Drive, San Antonio, Texas.

Orders for Monograph 3 should be sent to the Cowles Foundation, Box 2125 Yale Station, New Haven, Conn. 06520.

Orders for Monographs 12, 13, 14, 16, 17, 21, 22, 23, and 24 should be sent to Yale University Press, 92A Yale Station, New Haven, Conn. 06530.

Orders for Monographs 15, 19, and 20 should be sent to John Wiley & Sons, Inc., 605 Third Avenue, New York, N.Y. 10016.